BREAKTHROUGH
GERMAN 2

A NEW, FULLY REVISED VERSION OF
BREAKTHROUGH FURTHER GERMAN

Ruth Rach
Producer, German department, BBC World Service

Ruth has taught German at Bath and Sussex Universities and has
been involved in adult education both as a teacher and researcher.
She has written several language courses.

Brian Hill
General Editor
Professor of Modern Languages
Language Centre, University of Brighton

MACMILLAN

First published 1985 by Pan Books Ltd
First Macmillan edition published 1988
Reprinted eight times
Second edition 1998
Published by
MACMILLAN PRESS LTD
Houndmills, Basingstoke, Hampshire RG21 6XS
and London
Companies and representatives throughout the world

ISBN 0–333–71914–X book
ISBN 0–333–71915–8 book and cassette pack
ISBN 0–333–71916–6 cassettes

A catalogue record for this book is available from the British Library.

This book is printed on paper suitable for recycling and made from fully managed and sustained forest sources.

Designed by D&J Hunter
Audio producer: Gerald Ramshaw, Max II
Actors: Hans Ulrich Pietsch, Gertrude Thoma, Johannes Dell

10	9	8	7	6	5	4	3	2	1
07	06	05	04	03	02	01	00	99	98

Printed in Hong Kong

Acknowledgements

The author and publishers would like to thank the following for permission to use copyright material: Lorsbacher Tal for their advertisement on p. 1; J. Allan Cash Ltd for the picture on p. 18; Deutsche Bahn for timetables and other material on pp. 22, 23, 24 & 25; Zeitbild-Verlag GmbH for their picture on p. 32; Postauto St. Moritz for its advertisement on p. 33; Kur-und Verkehrsverein Brig am Simplon for the picture on p. 52; Verkehrsverein Heidelberg for the logo on p. 67; the CDU and Bündnis 90 Die Grünen for their logos on p. 72; Süddeutsche Zeitung, Der Tagesspiegel Berlin, Die Welt for their logos on p. 97; Der Spiegel for its cover on p. 98; TV Hören und Sehen for its cover on p. 102 and article on p. 106; Therme Loipersdorf for their picture on p. 119; Teekanne GmbH for its packaging on p. 123; Bregenzer Festspiele for its entrance ticket on p. 130; German Wine Information Service for its pictures on pp. 135 & 143; Brigitte Young Miss for its article on p. 154; Brigitte for its article on p. 159 and for the ideas for the pictures on pp. 81 & 95; Herr Dr Werner Wurster for his visiting card on p. 168.

Radio programmes by courtesy of Südwestfunk, Baden-Baden.

Every effort has been made to trace all copyright holders, but if any have been inadvertently overlooked the publishers will be pleased to make the necessary arrangements at the first opportunity.

Contents

MAKING THE MOST OF THIS COURSE

Welcome to Breakthrough German 2

Please do take the time to read through this introduction. You'll be able to get more out of the course if you understand how it has been structured and what is expected of you.

Breakthrough German 2 is designed to take you on from *Breakthrough*, or indeed any similar beginner's course. We have consulted with hundreds of language learners on what they need at this level and the course has been built on their advice.

There are twelve units, each based on a theme which reinforces and extends your knowledge of real German. The emphasis is on the language used to understand and communicate effectively in a range of common situations. Each unit has the same basic structure.

1 The introductory page

This sets the scene, tells you what you will learn, reminds you of some key points from the previous unit and gives you a few tips on how to learn and what to watch out for.

2 Conversations

In each unit there are three Conversations in which the new vocabulary and structures are introduced. They have been specially recorded on location in Germany and cover different aspects of the unit theme. Please DO NOT expect to understand them immediately. By their nature, each one is introducing new vocabulary and structures. Try playing the Conversation through once or twice (reading the transcript at the same time if it helps). Then go through the Conversation using your PAUSE button and consulting the linked notes which explain things you may not yet have come across. Don't be afraid to make your own notes in the book or to underline things which are important to you. Finally, listen to the Conversation once or twice straight through without looking at the book before you move on to the Practice section.

3 Practice

Each Conversation has a number of exercises attached to it. These pick up the main points from the Conversations and give you practice in reading, listening, speaking and, to a lesser extent, writing. Instructions on how to do each exercise are given in the book with answers, where appropriate, listed at the end of each unit. You will probably need to go through these exercises several times, particularly the speaking practice, before you feel you have mastered them. It's wise to spend as much time as you need here so that you really do learn the main words and structures.

4 Key words and phrases

To help you pull together the most important points, each unit has a Key Words and Phrases page which follows the Conversation and Practice sections. Read these through, checking back to the notes linked to the Conversations if you need to refresh your memory. Then work through the list, first covering up the German translation to see if you can remember the matching phrase in English, then covering up the English to see if you can remember the German.

5 Grammar

This is not a grammar course. The Conversations have been selected on the basis of the topic and the vocabulary they introduce. However, it is often valuable, and indeed interesting, to see how the language works. This can increase your confidence in generating language of your own. Each unit explains a few important aspects of grammar which should help you develop a firmer foundation. Interspersed are exercises to practise the points which have been introduced. If you can't get on with grammar, look at this section more for reference rather than feeling you need to have mastered everything before moving on.

6 And finally...

Each unit ends with two or three activities including an exercise designed to encourage working with a partner. You can of course also work on them alone. The aim is to reinforce key points that have cropped up during the unit.

7 At the end

At the end of the book are a grammar summary, a vocabulary list and a grammar index.

A few final words

Be patient with yourself . . . above all don't get discouraged. Everybody comes across sticky patches when they feel they are not getting anywhere. Try looking back to some earlier Conversations to see just how much you have learned.

If you can, practise regularly. Thirty to forty minutes a day is usually better than a block of four hours once a week.

It helps to speak out loud in German as much as possible. This may seem strange at first but actually using the words, with a friend or to yourself, is a good way of practising and remembering.

There is a lot of material to take on board. Have confidence in us. Real language is quite complex and the course has been designed to build up your knowledge slowly, selecting what is important at each stage.

Viel Glück!

Brian Hill
Breakthrough Series Editor

A note on German spelling reform

For many years the German-speaking countries have debated a revision of the spelling of some German words. This involves particularly the use of the ß and whether words should be written as one long word or as separate entities. A series of revisions has been agreed and these should come into effect from 1 August 1998 with the process of change completed by 1 August 2005. At the time of going to press, however, there is considerable argument in the German-speaking world about whether indeed these changes should be imposed and the issue is being challenged in courts across Germany. Consequently this course does not use the revised spellings. Reprints of the course will use the revised spellings just as soon as the issue has been clarified.

1 FOOD AND OTHER PREFERENCES

**WHAT YOU
WILL LEARN**

► describing your favourite food and drink
► ordering food and drink in a restaurant
► discussing your shopping habits
► you will also learn how to compare things and how to talk about events in the past

Apfelwein der ist gesund

drum trinke ihn zu jeder Stund

Lorsbacher Tal

Eigene Kelterei

60594 Frankfurt-Sachsenhausen

Große Rittergasse 49-51

Tel.: 069 / 61 64 59

'Apple wine is healthy, so drink it all the time'

**BEFORE YOU
BEGIN**

● You may not have heard German for a while so it's worth listening to the Conversations several times just in order to get used to the sounds and rhythms of German again and refresh your memory. Many words will sound vaguely familiar yet you might have forgotten their meaning. Don't hesitate to use the vocabulary at the back of the book or even a dictionary to look them up – you might be surprised at how quickly the words come back to you!

● Once you have worked your way through the first Conversation, underline the phrases that you feel will be most useful to you and learn them by heart. Generally speaking it's a good idea to focus on acquiring what you think you will need most – to start with anyway. Then go on to the exercises. Don't get bogged down if you find an exercise too difficult (or too tedious) – just skip it for the time being and do another one that you find more enjoyable. If you like, you can always come back to it later. If you're learning with a friend, it will be very helpful to role-play some of the exercises. If you're alone, try and imagine how you would respond in certain Conversations and situations ...

A survey

LISTEN FOR...

Was essen Sie am liebsten? What's your favourite food?

Was trinken Sie am liebsten? What's your favourite drink?

Biba	Was essen Sie am liebsten?
Ingrid	Mmm – Schokoladeneis mit Schlagsahne.
Biba	Und was trinken Sie am liebsten?
Ingrid	Ah –'n guten Wein, 'n herben Frankenwein.

Biba	Was essen Sie am liebsten?
Silke	Eingelegte Heringe und Gemüse.
Biba	Und was trinken Sie am liebsten?
Silke	Ostfriesentee, das ist schwarzer Tee mit Sahne und Kandiszucker.

Biba	Was ißt du am liebsten?
Henning	Rehrücken mit Knödeln und Schwarzwälder Kirschtorte.
Biba	Und was trinkst du am liebsten?
Henning	Coca Cola.

Hopfen u. Malz

Gott erhalts!

Was essen Sie am liebsten? What's your favourite food? (lit. What do you eat with most pleasure?) **Ich esse am liebsten Torte** I like eating gateau best of all. Similarly: **Was trinken Sie am liebsten?** What's your favourite drink? **Ich trinke am liebsten Weißwein**. My favourite drink is white wine. More on this in Grammar, this unit.

das Schokoladeneis   chocolate ice cream; similarly **Vanilleeis** vanilla ice cream, **Himbeereis** raspberry ice cream, **Erdbeereis** strawberry ice cream.

die Schlagsahne   whipped cream

'n guten Wein   short for **einen guten Wein**; in colloquial German, **einen** can get shortened to **'n** or **'nen**, **eine** to **'ne** and **ein** to **'n**.

herb   dry

der Frankenwein   Franconian wine (from an area around Nuremberg)

eingelegte Heringe   pickled herrings; **der Hering** herring; **einlegen** to pickle

das Gemüse   vegetables; **das Gemüse** is always singular in German: **Wo ist das Gemüse?** Where are the vegetables? Similarly **das Obst** fruit.

der Ostfriesentee   literally East Frisian tea; this tea is served by pouring it over rock candy and then adding cream.

der Rehrücken   saddle of venison

der Knödel   dumpling

die Schwarzwälder Kirschtorte   Black Forest gateau; **die Kirsche** cherry

PRACTICE

1
Unusual foods. All the words below for food and drink consist of two or more words joined together. Uncouple them and make different, more conventional, combinations. Some 'ends' will go to the beginning and vice versa. You should come up with at least seven new palatable combinations. Don't forget to change the articles (words for 'the') as necessary.

> **der Schokoladenwein, der Frankenschlag, der Zuckerrücken, das Kandisreh, die Teetorte, der Kirschwälder, die Schwarzfriesensahne, das Osteis, der Weißtee**

das Schokoladeneis

Answers p. 16

2
Funny orders. These orders have got mixed up. Sort them out and write out more appetising ones. Various combinations are possible, depending on your own taste.
- **a** Ich möchte gerne Rehrücken mit Schlagsahne.
- **b** Und ich möchte Schokoladeneis mit Gemüse.
- **c** Ich möchte eingelegte Heringe mit Kandiszucker.
- **d** Ich möchte Ostfriesentee mit Knödeln.
- **e** Und ich möchte Cola mit Sahne!

Answers p. 16

3
Complaints. Five customers don't like their orders! Here are the words they will need to complain. See if you can guess what they mean and complete the complaints. Listen to the most likely answers on the recording.

> **matschig, bitter, hart, sauer, salzig**

4 Food survey. A group of people are asked about their favourite foods and drinks. Listen to the recording and fill in the grid – in English.

Spaghetti, Gemüse,
Kirschtorte, Wein,
Bier, Steak, Hamburger,
Knödel, Kaffee, Schlagsahne,
Cola, Salat

Answers p. 16

Name	favourite food	favourite drink
Hanna		
Erich		
Petra		
Sam		

5 Your turn to speak. Tell Gertrude about your favourite food and drink – and ask her about her own preferences. Hans will prompt you by telling you in English what to say. You then press the Pause button to give yourself time to think, say your answer in German, and then press Play to listen to the correct version on the recording. You may need to do this exercise several times to get the hang of it. Here are some useful phrases:

Was essen Sie am liebsten ? ... Ich esse/trinke am liebsten ...

In the „*Weißer Bock*", a pub in Heidelberg

Gabi	Guten Tag.
Ruth	Guten Tag. Ich möchte gerne was zu essen, bitte.
Gabi	Ja, hier ist die Tageskarte.
Ruth	Können Sie mir etwas empfehlen?
Gabi	Wir haben hier Fisch, er ist aber nicht frisch, er ist gefroren.
Ruth	Ach nee, das mag ich nicht so gern.
Gabi	Vielleicht das Jägerschnitzel?
Ruth	Hm – ist das sehr scharf?
Gabi	Nein, das ist nicht scharf.
Ruth	Und ist das mit Knoblauch?
Gabi	Ein wenig, ja.
Ruth	Ach nein – lieber nicht.
Gabi	Vielleicht das Rumpsteak mit Zwiebeln?

LISTEN FOR...

Tageskarte   menu
Können Sie mir etwas empfehlen?   Can you recommend something?

Ruth	Ja, hier steht „englisch" – was heißt das denn?
Gabi	Das ist blutig.
Ruth	Das mag ich nicht so gern. Aber vielleicht können Sie in der Küche sagen, ich möchte das gut durch?
Gabi	Ja. ... Wir haben dazu grüne Bohnen, die sind frisch.
Ruth	Gut, und ich möchte auch ganz gern 'nen Salat dazu noch, ja.
Gabi	Möchten Sie etwas trinken?
Ruth	Ja, gerne. Ich möchte gerne ein kleines Bier.
Gabi	Danke.

ich möchte gerne was zu essen   I'd like something to eat; **was** is short for **etwas** something. **Gerne** is often shortened to **gern**.

die Tageskarte   today's menu; **die (Speise)karte** menu

Können Sie mir etwas empfehlen?   Can you recommend (me) something? Possible answers: **Ich kann Ihnen den Fisch/das Steak empfehlen** I can recommend (you) the fish/steak. More on **können** (to be able to) in Grammar, Unit 2.

der Fisch   fish; **er ist aber nicht frisch** but it's not fresh; **er** means 'it' here and refers back to the masculine **Fisch**.

gefroren   frozen

nee   colloquial for **nein**

das mag ich nicht so gern   I don't like that so much. Note the word order: Ruth emphasises **das** (here: that) by putting it first. The verb comes second, as usual, and **ich** is third. Usual word order: **ich mag das nicht so gern**. More on **gern** in Grammar, this unit; more on **mögen** (to like) in Grammar, Unit 2.

das Jägerschnitzel   fried slice of veal or pork (**Schnitzel**) in mushroom sauce; **der Jäger** hunter

scharf   spicy, hot

der Knoblauch   garlic; **die Zwiebel** onion

ein wenig   a little

lieber nicht   (I'd) rather not

Was heißt das denn?   What does that mean (then)? **Heißen** can also mean 'to be called': **ich heiße Ruth** I'm called Ruth.

blutig   bloody; here: rare; similarly **das ist gut durch** that's well done (of meat)

grüne Bohnen   green beans; **die Bohne** bean

WIRTSHAUS AM SEE

A-6900 Bregenz
Vorarlberg
Austria

---

6 Phrase search. Find the German equivalents in Conversation 2.

a I'd like something to eat.

b Can you recommend something?

c I don't like that so much.

d I'd rather not.

e What does that mean?

f I'd like that well done.

g Is that very spicy?

Answers p. 16 **h** Is that with garlic?

7 Test your memory! Complete the statements about Conversation 2 in German. See whether you can write them in without looking at the text in your book!

a Ruth ist im „Weißen Bock" und möchte etwas _____

b Sie mag den Fisch nicht, weil er _____ ist.

c Das Jägerschnitzel mag sie auch nicht, weil es mit

_____ ist.

d Sie möchte das Rumpsteak _____

Answers p. 16 **e** Und sie möchte auch ein _____ Bier trinken.

8 Food groups. Look at all the food and drink items in Conversations 1 and 2 and list them next to the appropriate headings.
New words: **Nachtisch** dessert; **Getränk** drink

Fleisch	
Fisch	
Gemüse	
Nachtisch	
alkoholisches Getränk	
alkoholfreies Getränk	

Answers p. 16

9 The menu. Study the menu and listen to Gertrude reading it out on the recording. Then answer the questions below.

VOCABULARY

mit Pilzen	with mushrooms
die Nordsee-Scholle	North Sea plaice
gebraten	fried
die Kalbsleber	calf's liver
Kartoffeln	potatoes
die Pommes frites (pl.)	chips, French fries
der Reis	rice

Tageskarte

1 Großer Salatteller	DM 12,80
2 Omelette mit Pilzen und Salat	DM 14,90
3 Nordsee-Scholle, gebraten, mit Salat	DM 16,20
4 Kalbsleber mit Zwiebeln, Kartoffeln und Salat	DM 15,20
5 Jägerschnitzel mit Pommes frites	DM 19,70
6 Rumpsteak mit Zwiebeln, grünen Bohnen und Butterreis	DM 25,90

What would you order if you wanted:

a something hot but no fish and no meat   No. _____

b a fish dish   No. _____

c a cold, non-fattening dish   No. _____

d a meat dish without onions   No. _____

 Answers p. 16 **e** a meat dish with green beans   No. _____

10 More orders. On the recording, three people are ordering some food and drink. What are they having? Write down their orders.

Frau Kern: _____

_____

Herr Mommsen: _____

_____

Olivia: _____

Answers p. 16 _____

11 Your turn to speak and order some food for yourself and a friend from the menu in Exercise 9.

CONVERSATION 3

Where do you shop?

Ruth	Wo kaufen Sie normalerweise ein?
Biba	Lebensmittel kaufe ich

LISTEN FOR...

Wo kaufen Sie normalerweise ein?	Where do you normally shop?
Metzger	butcher
eine gute Auswahl	a good selection

normalerweise im Supermarkt, und das Fleisch kaufe ich frisch, beim Metzger um die Ecke.

Ruth   Und wo kaufen Sie das Gemüse?

Biba   Entweder auch im Supermarkt, oder am Samstag dann auf dem Markt. Dort gibt es eine gute Auswahl und auch mal was ganz Besonderes, wie Mangos oder Eissalat, oder irgendwelche Pilze. Heute zum Beispiel habe ich das hier gekauft ...

Ruth   Ja, was ist das denn? Das sieht ja ganz komisch aus ...

Biba   Ach, das sind so Pilze. Die hab' ich heute auch das erste Mal gesehen. Sie sollen aus China kommen.

Ruth   Halten die sich im Kühlschrank?

Biba   Nein, das glaube ich nicht. Pilze soll man gleich essen.

Wo kaufen Sie normalerweise ein?   Where do you normally shop? **Einkaufen** is a separable verb: it sometimes splits into two parts. More in Grammar, Unit 3.

Lebensmittel kaufe ich ...   Groceries I buy .... More on word order in Grammar, Unit 4.

im (**in + dem**) **Supermarkt**   in the supermarket; **der Supermarkt**   supermarket

das Fleisch   meat

beim (**bei + dem**) **Metzger**   at the butcher's; **beim Bäcker**   at the baker's

um die Ecke   around the corner

entweder ... oder   either ... or

am Samstag   on Saturday

auf dem Markt   in the market; **der Markt** market

dort gibt es eine gute Auswahl   there is a good choice there; **es gibt** there is/there are; **die Auswahl** choice, selection. More on word order in Grammar, Unit 4.

was (= **etwas**) **ganz Besonderes**   something really special

irgendwelche Pilze   mushrooms of some kind; **der Pilz** mushroom

der Eissalat   iceberg lettuce

zum Beispiel (abbreviated **z.B.**)   for example

heute habe ich ... gekauft   today I bought. **Ich habe gekauft** (lit. I have bought) is the perfect tense – more on this tense in Grammar, this unit. Another example of the perfect tense in this Conversation: **die hab' ich heute auch das erste Mal gesehen** I also saw them today for the first time. **ich habe ... gesehen** lit. I have seen.

das sieht ja komisch aus   that looks really strange; **komisch** strange, comical. **Aussehen** 'to look' is a separable verb (more on this in Grammar, Unit 3). **Ja** is a filler word here meaning 'really'.

sie sollen aus China kommen   they are supposed to come from China; more on **sollen** in Grammar, Unit 2.

Halten die sich im Kühlschrank?   Do they keep in the fridge? (**sich**) **halten** to keep; **der Kühlschrank** fridge

das glaube ich nicht I don't think so; **glauben** to think, believe

Pilze soll man gleich essen   mushrooms should be eaten straight away; **man** lit. one

---

12

Correct the statements about Conversation 3.

a Lebensmittel kauft Biba normalerweise auf dem Markt.

_____

b Fleisch kauft sie im Restaurant.

_____

c Auf dem Markt gibt es keine gute Auswahl.

_____

d Gestern hat Biba Pilze gekauft.

_____

e Die Pilze kommen aus Japan.

_____

f Die Pilze halten sich gut im Kühlschrank.

Answers p. 16

_____

13

Puzzle. The letters 1–10 will give you the word for a famous German 'institution', much appreciated in the summer.

a Auf dem Markt gibt es manchmal auch was ganz …
b Diese Pilze kommen aus …
c Das Fleisch kaufe ich gleich um die …
d Ich kaufe die Lebensmittel im …
e Der … hat frisches Fleisch.
f Auf dem Markt gibt es eine gute …
g Die Pilze halten sich nicht im …
h Am Samstag kaufe ich das Gemüse auf dem …
i Die Pilze muß man gleich …

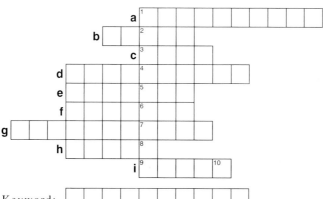

Answers p. 16   Keyword:

14 What did Katharina bring home? Here's Katharina's shopping list – turn to the recording where she will tell you what she brought home. But did she get everything on the list? Mark the missing items. She also bought some items not mentioned on the list. Write them down in German.

VOCABULARY	
der Apfel	apple
das Pfund	pound (500 grams)
die Flasche	bottle
die Kartoffel	potato

Einkaufsliste

1 Kilo Äpfel
1 Pfund Kirschen
Pilze
Butter
1 Pfund Bohnen
1 Kilo Kartoffeln
1 Kilo Zwiebeln
Knoblauch
1 Flasche Wein

Extra

_____
_____
_____
_____
_____
_____
_____

Answers p. 16

15 Shopping habits. Where do these people buy their food? Listen to the recording and take notes – in English.

Name	Items	Where?
Susanne		
Franco		
Anja		

Answers p. 16

16 Your turn to speak ... and talk about your own shopping habits. These phrases will come in useful:

im Supermarkt   **beim Metzger**   **auf dem Markt**

KEY WORDS
AND PHRASES

Was essen Sie am liebsten?	What's your favourite food?
Was ißt du am liebsten?	
Was trinken Sie am liebsten?	What's your favourite drink?
Was trinkst du am liebsten?	
Ich möchte gerne ...	I'd like ...
etwas zu essen	something to eat
etwas zu trinken	something to drink
ein kleines Bier	a small beer
Können Sie mir etwas empfehlen?	Can you recommend something?
Was heißt das?	What does that mean?
Ist das ...	Is that …
scharf?	hot?
mit Knoblauch?	with garlic?
frisch?	fresh?
gefroren?	frozen?
gut durch?	well done?
Das mag ich nicht.	I don't like that.
Ich kaufe ...	I buy ...
Lebensmittel ...	groceries ...
Gemüse ...	vegetables ...
Fleisch ...	meat ...
im Supermarkt	in the supermarket
beim Metzger	at the butcher's
auf dem Markt	at the market

Unit 1   Food and other preferences 11

Comparisons

No matter how long the adjectives or adverbs are, you add
- **-er** for the comparative
- **am ... -sten** for the superlative form

Linda ist klein	Linda is small	basic form	**klein**
Lena ist kleiner	Lena is smaller	comparative	**klein + er**
Hana ist am kleinsten	Hana is the smallest	superlative	**am klein + sten**

Minor variations
- In the comparative and superlative forms, an Umlaut is added where possible (i.e. on **a**, **o**, and **u**). You will also find minor changes in spelling to make pronunciation easier.

groß	**größer**	**am größten**	big	bigger	biggest
kurz	**kürzer**	**am kürzesten**	short	shorter	shortest

17 Translate into German, using the words supplied:

a The wine is cheaper.

b The room is the most expensive.

c The cake is sweeter.

d The house is the oldest.

e Anna is smaller.

das Haus	**das Zimmer**	**klein**
der Kuchen	**alt**	**süß**
der Wein	**billig**	**teuer**

Answers p. 16

Irregular comparisons
- gern – lieber – am liebsten

Was essen Sie gern?	What do you like to eat?	**gern**
Was essen Sie lieber?	What do you prefer to eat?	**lieber**
Was essen Sie am liebsten?	What do you most like to eat?	**am liebsten**

- gut – besser – am besten

Die Tabletten sind gut.	The tablets are good.	basic form	**gut**
Die Tinktur ist besser.	The tincture is better.	comparative	**besser**
Das Spray ist am besten.	The spray is best.	superlative	**am besten**

18 Translate into German. Some useful words are in the box.

a What's your (use **Sie**) favourite drink (i.e. what do you like best to drink)?

b Franconian wine is better.

c What do you (use **du**) prefer to hear – jazz or pop?

d The ice cream is best.

e I like learning Spanish best of all.

f I like fishing.

fischen
hören
lernen
Spanisch

Answers p. 16

The perfect tense

■ This is the most commonly used past tense in German. It is often used where English would use the simple past tense ('I bought'). It is formed by using the present tense of **haben** (or in a few instances **sein**, see Unit 3) and adding a verb form called the past participle.

ich	habe	gekauft	I have bought
du	hast	gekauft	you have bought
er/sie/es	hat	gekauft	he/she/it has bought
wir	haben	gekauft	we have bought
ihr	habt	gekauft	you have bought
sie/Sie	haben	gekauft	they/you have bought

In most verbs, the past participle is formed by

starting with the infinitive	**kauf-en**	(to buy)
taking the **-en** ending off the end	**kauf**	(this is called the stem)
adding **ge-** to the beginning	**ge-kauf**	
adding **-t** or **-et** to the end	**ge-kauf-t**	(bought)

19 Following the same pattern as with **kaufen**, write out all the perfect tense forms of **machen** (to make).

I have made _____

you have made _____

he/she/it has made _____

we have made _____

you have made _____

you/they have made _____

Answers p. 16

20 Translate into German. Here are the infinitives to help you – but they are not in the right order. Remember to turn all the infinitives into past participles.

a You (formal) have said _____

b We have asked _____

c Paul has cooked _____

d The man has smoked _____

e They have loved _____

f He has fished _____

g I have learnt _____

fragen
sagen
fischen
lieben
rauchen
lernen
kochen

Answers p. 16

21 Bilingual grid – fill in the gaps!

English	Deutsch
a We have danced.	_Wir haben getanzt._
b _I have ..._	Ich habe gefischt.
c I have heard.	
d _____	
	Sie haben gehört. (2 possibilities)
e She has said.	
f _____	Sie hat getanzt.
g They have fished.	

Answers p. 16

Strong verbs

There is, however, a group of verbs (so-called strong verbs) that do not follow the regular pattern. Generally speaking, strong verbs form their past participle by:

starting off with the infinitive	**trink-en**	(to drink)
changing the vowel in the stem	**trunk-en**	
adding **ge-** to the beginning	**ge-trunk-en**	(drunk)

Ich habe getrunken I have drunk
Wir haben getrunken We have drunk

■ As in English, strong verbs form their past participles in various unpredictable ways and are therefore best learnt by heart. Generally speaking, verbs which are strong in English are also strong in German.

sehen (to see) past participle **ge-seh-en** (seen)
Ich habe gesehen I have seen
essen (to eat) past participle **ge-gess-en** (eaten)
Er hat gegessen He has eaten

For a full list of strong verbs see pp. 200 – 1.

22 Translate into English:

a Meine Mutter hat zehn Knödel gegessen.
b Mein Bruder hat fünf Cola getrunken.
c Meine Frau hat einen guten Film gesehen.
d Ich habe einen Popsong gesungen.
e Sie hat Jessica geheißen.

Answers p. 16

AND FINALLY...

23 For and against. Anna and Mathias disagree about markets and supermarkets. Turn to the recording to hear what they said and read it below. Then find the German equivalents for the English phrases below:

Anna
Wochenmarkt!
Ich gehe normalerweise nicht gern einkaufen. Die Supermärkte sind mir zu kalt und unpersönlich, und Kaufhäuser sind viel zu laut. Am liebsten kaufe ich auf dem Wochenmarkt ein. Ich liebe die Atmosphäre: die Menschen sind freundlicher, oft treffe ich auch Freunde.

Mathias
Supermarkt!
Ich kaufe nicht gern ein. Jede Minute ist schon zu viel! Die Wochenmärkte sind am schlimmsten. Die vielen Menschen und die vielen Stände! Ich kaufe lieber im Supermarkt ein. Dort geht alles viel schneller, und ich kann alles auf einmal einkaufen.

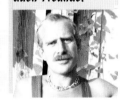

a The supermarkets are too impersonal.

b Department stores are too noisy.

c I love the atmosphere.

d The people are friendlier.

e I don't like shopping.

f I prefer to shop in the supermarket.

g There everything is (lit: goes) much quicker.

Answers p. 16

24 Who would say what?

	Mathias	Anna
a Ich mag nicht gern einkaufen.	☐	☐
b Ich gehe nicht gern zum Wochenmarkt.	☐	☐
c Ich gehe am liebsten in den Supermarkt.	☐	☐
d Ich finde die Supermärkte nicht sehr freundlich.	☐	☐
e Die Atmosphäre auf dem Wochenmarkt ist chaotisch.	☐	☐
f Die Atmosphäre auf dem Wochenmarkt ist viel freundlicher.	☐	☐
g Auf dem Wochenmarkt haben die Menschen mehr Zeit für mich.	☐	☐

Answers p. 16

25 Your turn to speak and talk about your own shopping preferences on the recording. Some of the sentences from Exercises 23 and 24 will come in very handy ...

26 If you can, pair up with a partner and role-play a discussion between Anna and Mathias, using all the arguments they have put forward – in German, of course. You could also interview each other about your own shopping preferences, using similar phrases to Anna and Mathias. Or imagine you and your friends are at the restaurant whose menu is printed in Exercise 9. Practise asking for different selections.

EXERCISE 1

der Weißwein, der Frankenwein, die Schlagsahne, der Kandiszucker, der Rehrücken, der Ostfriesentee, die Schwarzwälder Kirschtorte, der Schwarztee ...

EXERCISE 2

(a) Rehrücken mit Knödeln (or Gemüse)
(b) Schokoladeneis mit Schlagsahne
(c) eingelegte Heringe mit Gemüse
(d) Ostfriesentee mit Kandiszucker und Sahne
(e) Cola.

EXERCISE 4

Hanna: Spaghetti, Salat, Cola   **Erich:** Hamburger, Bier   **Petra:** Steak, Knödel, Kaffee   **Sam:** Gemüse, Kirschtorte, Schlagsahne, Wein

EXERCISE 6

(a) Ich möchte gerne was zu essen   (b) Können Sie mir etwas empfehlen?   (c) Das mag ich nicht so gern   (d) Lieber nicht   (e) Was heißt das?   (f) Ich möchte das gut durch   (g) Ist das sehr scharf?
(h) Ist das mit Knoblauch?

EXERCISE 7

(a) zu essen   (b) gefroren   (c) Knoblauch
(d) gut durch   (e) kleines

EXERCISE 8

Fleisch: Jägerschnitzel, Rumpsteak, Rehrücken; **Fisch:** eingelegte Heringe; **Gemüse:** Zwiebeln, Knoblauch, grüne Bohnen; **Nachtisch:** Schokoladeneis mit Schlagsahne, Schwarzwälder Kirschtorte; **alkoholisches Getränk:** Frankenwein, Bier; **alkoholfreies Getränk:** Ostfriesentee, Cola

EXERCISE 9

(a) 2   (b) 3   (c) 1   (d) 5   (e) 6.

EXERCISE 10

Frau Kern: großer Salatteller, kleines Bier
Herr Mommsen: Schnitzel mit Pommes frites, Gemüse und Salat, Glas Wein
Olivia: Schwarzwälder Kirschtorte, Schlagsahne, Tasse Kaffee.

EXERCISE 12

(a) Lebensmittel kauft Biba normalerweise im Supermarkt.   (b) Fleisch kauft sie beim Metzger um die Ecke.   (c) Auf dem Markt gibt es eine gute Auswahl.   (d) Heute hat Biba Pilze gekauft.
(e) Die Pilze kommen aus China.   (f) Die Pilze halten sich nicht gut im Kühlschrank.

EXERCISE 13

(a) BESONDERES   (b) CHINA   (c) ECKE
(d) SUPERMARKT   (e) METZGER   (f) AUSWAHL

(g) KÜHLSCHRANK   (h) MARKT   (i) ESSEN; Keyword BIERGARTEN

EXERCISE 14

Missing items: 1 Kilo Äpfel, Pilze, 1 Kilo Zwiebeln. Extra items bought: 1 grüner Salat, 1 Liter Milch, 1 Kilo Bananen, 6 Flaschen Bier.

EXERCISE 15

Susanne: alles im Supermarkt
Franco: Obst, Gemüse, Brot: Markt; Milch, Käse: Supermarkt   **Anja:** Fleisch, Wurst: Metzger; alles andere: Supermarkt.

EXERCISE 17

(a) Der Wein ist billiger.   (b) Das Zimmer ist am teuersten.   (c) Der Kuchen ist süßer.   (d) Das Haus ist am ältesten.   (e) Anna ist kleiner.

EXERCISE 18

(a) Was trinken Sie am liebsten?   (b) Frankenwein ist besser.   (c) Was hörst du lieber – Jazz oder Pop?   (d) Das Eis ist am besten.   (e) Ich lerne am liebsten Spanisch.   (f) Ich fische gern.

EXERCISE 19

ich habe gemacht, du hast gemacht, er/sie/es hat gemacht, wir haben gemacht, ihr habt gemacht, sie/Sie haben gemacht.

EXERCISE 20

(a) Sie haben gesagt.   (b) Wir haben gefragt.
(c) Paul hat gekocht.   (d) Der Mann hat geraucht.
(e) Sie haben geliebt.   (f) Er hat gefischt.
(g) Ich habe gelernt.

EXERCISE 21

(b) I have fished   (c) Ich habe gehört.   (d) They (or You) have heard.   (e) Sie hat gesagt.   (f) She has danced.   (g) Sie haben gefischt.

EXERCISE 22

Literal translations, with possible and sometimes preferable alternatives in brackets: (a) My mother has eaten (ate) ten dumplings.   (b) My brother has drunk (drank) five Cokes.   (c) My wife has seen (saw) a good film.   (d) I have sung (sang) a pop song.
(e) She has been (was) called Jessica.

EXERCISE 23

(a) Die Supermärkte sind zu unpersönlich.
(b) Kaufhäuser sind zu laut.   (c) Ich liebe die Atmosphäre.   (d) Die Menschen sind freundlicher.
(e) Ich kaufe nicht gern ein.   (f) Ich kaufe lieber im Supermarkt ein.   (g) Dort geht alles viel schneller.

EXERCISE 24

Mathias: (a), (b), (c), (e);   Anna: (a), (d), (f), (g)

2 GETTING ABOUT

WHAT YOU WILL LEARN

▶ asking how to get to somewhere
▶ buying a rail ticket
▶ enquiring about trains
▶ renting a car
▶ you will also learn how to ask questions and to talk about what you can, must or should not do

POINTS TO REMEMBER

● stating preferences: **am liebsten ...**
● saying you'd like something: **ich möchte ...**
● making comparisons: add **-er** for the comparative and **am -sten** for the superlative: **klein** (small) – **kleiner** (smaller) – **am kleinsten** (smallest)
● irregular comparisons: **gern – lieber – am liebsten**; **gut – besser – am besten**
● the perfect tense: **haben** plus **ge** + verb stem + **t**: **ich habe gekauft** I have bought.
● strong verbs follow a different pattern: **ich habe getrunken** I have drunk, **ich habe gegessen** I have eaten, **ich habe gesungen** I have sung.

BEFORE YOU BEGIN

There will be quite a few numbers in this unit, so do try and refresh your memory. You could set yourself a few home tests: how far can you count in German? Can you say the date? How about your birthday? If you need help, have a quick look at the numbers in the Grammar summary p. 199.

BAHN TOUR
Bader   Kulturreisen
REISEN MIT DER BAHN 1. KLASSE

3. bis 7. Juni
Donau-Nostalgie-Express
NACH
MIT KARTEN FÜR
Wien   *Madame Butterfly* in der Staatssoper

CONVERSATION 1

 ## How do I get there?

Biba	Wie komme ich am besten zum Heidelberger Schloß?
Gabi	Mit dem Bus kommen Sie am besten hin.
Biba	Und wo fährt der Bus ab?
Gabi	Hier. Die nächste Haltestelle ist hier über die Straße.
Biba	Und wann fährt der nächste Bus?
Gabi	Die fahren alle zehn Minuten ab.

LISTEN FOR...

Wie komme ich am besten? What's the best way?
die nächste the nearest

Wie komme ich am besten ...? What's the best way? (lit. How do I best come ...?)

zum (zu + dem) Heidelberger Schloß to the Heidelberg castle; similarly **Frankfurter Würstchen** sausages from Frankfurt; **Münchner Bier** beer from Munich

mit dem Bus with the bus, by bus; similarly **mit dem Auto** by car, **mit der Straßenbahn/U-Bahn/S-Bahn** by tram/underground/suburban train

hinkommen to get there; a separable verb (see Grammar, Unit 3).

abfahren to depart, go; another separable verb (see Grammar, Unit 3).

die nächste Haltestelle ist hier über die Straße the nearest bus stop is across the street here

der nächste Bus the next bus. **Nächste** means both 'next' and 'nearest'.

die (i.e. **die Busse**) **fahren alle zehn Minuten ab** they leave every ten minutes; **alle zwei Tage** every two days; **jede Stunde** every hour, **jede Woche** every week.

1 Anita wants to get to the city centre. She asks Klaus at the tourist information centre. Complete the conversation first, then compare your version with the recording.

Anita Wie komme ich _____ zum Stadtzentrum?

Klaus Am besten kommen Sie _____ der U-Bahn hin.

Anita Aha! Und _____ fährt die U-Bahn ab?

Klaus Die _____ Haltestelle ist am Marktplatz.

Anita Und wann fährt die _____ U-Bahn ab?

Klaus Die fahren _____ fünf Minuten ab.

2 Getting the gist! On the recording, more people are making enquiries. Where do they want to get to and how will they get there? Listen and take notes in German.

VOCABULARY	
Entschuldigung!	Excuse me!
Ist das weit?	Is that far?
Das weiß ich nicht.	I don't know.
zu Fuß	on foot
der Bahnhof	railway station
weit	far
zirka	about

Marienplatz
Theater
Bahnhof
Domstraße

Bus
U-Bahn
Taxi
zu Fuß

weit
alle 15 Minuten
zirka 10 Minuten

über die Straße
um die Ecke
am Marktplatz

Answers p. 32

wohin? (where to?)	womit? (what with?)	wo? (where to find it?)	wie oft? wie weit? (how often/how far?)
a			
b			
c			
d			

3 Your turn to speak: and now you make an enquiry. Turn to the recording where Hans will prompt you. You will find these words useful: **rechts** to the right, **links** to the left, **geradeaus** straight ahead, **die Post** post office, **der Hauptbahnhof** main railway station

---

CONVERSATION 2

At the station

Ruth	Ich möchte eine Karte nach Garmisch bitte.
Beamtin	Einfach oder hin und zurück?
Ruth	Einfach bitte.
Beamtin	Erster oder zweiter Klasse?
Ruth	Zweiter Klasse.
Beamtin	Möchten Sie einen InterCity-Zuschlag?
Ruth	Ja, bitte.
Beamtin	Vierundachtzig Mark bitte.
Ruth	Vierundachtzig Mark ... Hier sind hundert Mark.
Beamtin	Neunzig, einhundert ... Danke.

> ### LISTEN FOR...
>
> | | |
> |---|---|
> | **einfach** | single |
> | **hin und zurück** | return |
> | **InterCity-Zuschlag** | InterCity supplement |

ich möchte I'd like

eine Karte nach Garmisch a ticket to Garmisch; **die Karte** or **Fahrkarte** ticket; **nach** means 'to' with names of towns.

die Beamtin (f), **der Beamte** (m) official, here: ticket clerk

einfach single; **einfach** also means 'simple', 'easy'.

hin und zurück (lit. there and back) return

erster oder zweiter Klasse first or second class; **erster Klasse fahren** (to travel first class) is a fixed expression.

InterCity-Zuschlag InterCity supplement; if you travel on an InterCity train in Germany, you have to pay a supplement.

Ordinal numbers

- 4–19: add **-te** to the cardinal number, for example **vier + te** ▷ **vierte** fourth (4th), **fünf + te** ▷ **fünfte** (5th) ... **neunzehn + te** ▷ **neunzehnte** (19th)

- from 20 upward: add **-ste**, for example **zwanzig + ste** ▷ **zwanzigste** (20th) ... **hundert + ste** ▷ **hundertste** (100th)

- exceptions: 1st **erste**; 2nd **zweite**; 3rd **dritte**; 7th **siebte**

- Ordinal numbers are adjectives and follow the rules for adjective endings.

- For cardinal numbers see Grammar Summary p. 199

4 More tickets. On the recording, Anna is buying a ticket to Kassel. Listen and mark the right boxes below.

a What kind of ticket does she ask for?

single ☐   return ☐

b Which class does she want to travel in?

first ☐   second ☐

c What train does she want to travel on?

InterRegio ☐   InterCity ☐   Eurocity ☐

d How much is her ticket?

Answers p. 32

56 DM ☐   65 DM ☐   560 DM ☐

5 And now to Vienna. A student is buying a ticket to Vienna (**Wien**). What would she say at the ticket office ? Translate the English phrases into German ...

Guten Tag.   **a** Good day.

_____

Sie wünschen?   **b** A ticket to Vienna please.

_____

Einfach?   **c** No, return, please.

_____

Und möchten Sie einen InterCity-Zuschlag?   **d** No, thank you.

_____

Fahren Sie erster oder zweiter Klasse?   **e** Second class, please.

Answers p. 32

_____

6 Extending vocabulary. Study the extract from the information sheet on the ICE Nymphenburg 896 from Munich to Bremen. Not all the words will be familiar, but luckily the Deutsche Bahn has provided an English translation. Find the German equivalents for the English words listed below.

Herzlich willkommen im InterCityExpress!
Dieses Faltblatt informiert Sie über Fahrplan, Anschlüsse und wo Sie die Serviceleistungen dieses Zuges finden:
* Die Bildschirme für das *ICE*-Videoprogramm im ersten und letzten Wagen des Zuges.
* 3 Rundfunk- und 3 BordProgramme (Klassik / Pop / Märchen) können Sie an allen Plätzen über Kopfhörer empfangen, Kopfhörer sind beim Servicepersonal käuflich. Programmübersicht in der Zeitschrift „INTERCITY", die an Ihrem Platz ausliegt.
* Konferenzraum, *ICE*-Chef-Abteil, behindertengerechte Toilette und Wickeltisch, Rollstuhl-stellplätze im Service-Wagen in der 2. Wagenklasse.
* Große oder kleine, warme und kalte Speisen und Getränke halten wir im BordRestaurant/ BordTreff zwischen der 1. und 2. Wagenklasse für Sie bereit. **Geöffnet: München – Bremen.**
* Wertkartentelefone im Service-Wagen und im ersten Wagen der 1. Kl. hinter der Lokomotive. Wertkarten käuflich erhältlich beim *ICE*-Team. **Betriebsbereit: München – Bremen.**
* BordInformationssystem in allen Einstiegräumen und mit Eingabe-Terminal im Service-Wagen.
* Mietwagen können Sie an den mit 🚗 gekennzeichneten Bahnhöfen bestellen.
Für weitere Informationen steht Ihnen das Team dieses Zuges gerne zur Verfügung.
Wir wünschen Ihnen eine angenehme Reise!

Welcome on board of the InterCityExpress!
This leaflet contains information about the time schedule, the connecting trains and where to find the various services offered on board of this train:
* There are video screens in the first and the last coach where you can watch our *ICE*-video program.
* From all seats you can listen to 3 radio programs and 3 *ICE*-programs (classical music, pop music, Fairy-tales) via headphones which can be purchased from our *ICE*-team. For a program survey please refer to the INTERCITY-magazine at your seat.
* In the 2nd class service car you can find a conference room, the train manager's office, a toilet suitable for handicapped persons, a baby's changing table and space for wheelchairs.
* Hot and cold meals, snacks and drinks can be obtained in the restaurant-car which you find between the 1st and the 2nd class. The restaurant is **open during the whole journey from München to Bremen.**
* There is a card-phone in the service-car and another one in the first coach of the 1st class behind the power car. The telephone cards can be purchased from our *ICE*-team. **Operational: from München to Bremen.**

a welcome _____

b video screens _____

c coach _____

d via headphones _____

e seat _____

f conference room _____

g open _____

Answers p. 32 **h** card phones _____

7 Your turn to travel – you want to go to Frankfurt by InterRegio, first class. You are buying a return ticket. Turn to the recording, where Hans will prompt you.

Connections – Ruth asks about train times

LISTEN FOR...

umsteigen to change
Ermäßigung reduction

Ruth	Ich möchte nach Garmisch fahren bitte.
Beamter	Möchten Sie heute fahren?
Ruth	Nein, ich möchte morgen vormittag fahren.
Beamter	Morgen vormittag fährt ein InterCity-Zug in Heidelberg ab um 9.41 Uhr. Dort müßten Sie in München umsteigen und wären in Garmisch-Partenkirchen um 15.20 Uhr.
Ruth	Ach ja, und haben Sie Ermäßigung für Kinder?
Beamter	Die Ermäßigung für Kinder ist von vier bis elf Jahren der halbe Fahrpreis.

der Zug train

9.41 Uhr Note that you say **neun Uhr einundvierzig** but write **9.41 Uhr**.

dort müßten Sie umsteigen you'd have to change there; the man at the desk could have said: **dort müssen Sie umsteigen** 'you have to change there' but chose the more polite **müßten**. More on this form in Grammar, Unit 12. **Umsteigen** (to change) is a separable verb.

und wären in Garmisch ... and would be in Garmisch. Again the man could have said: **und sind in Garmisch** but preferred to use the more polite **wären**.

die Ermäßigung reduction

Kinder children; **das Kind** child; **der/die Erwachsene** grown-up

der halbe Fahrpreis half-fare; **der volle Fahrpreis** full fare

REMEMBER ...

morgen vormittag	tomorrow morning
morgen nachmittag	tomorrow afternoon
morgen abend	tomorrow evening
heute vormittag	this morning
heute nachmittag	this afternoon
heute abend	this evening
gestern vormittag	yesterday morning
gestern nachmittag	yesterday afternoon
gestern abend	yesterday evening

HERE ARE SOME OTHER IMPORTANT WORDS FOR RAIL TRAVEL.

die Abfahrt departure   **die Ankunft** arrival   **das Gleis** platform

Zeichenerklärung / Key to Symbols

ICE	= InterCityExpress (besonderer Fahrpreis / special fare)
EC	= EuroCity
IC	= InterCity
IR	= InterRegio
RSB	= RegionalSchnellBahn / regional fast train
D	= Schnellzug / fast train
E	= Eilzug / semi-fast train
Ⓢ	= S-Bahn / urban train

CB	= CityBahn
RB	= RegionalBahn / regional train
ohne Buchstaben	= Nahverkehrszug / local train
☐	= Buslinie / bus service
†	= an Sonn- und allg. Feiertagen / on Sundays and public holidays only
✗	= an Werktagen / on weekdays
① – ⑦	= Montag – Sonntag / Monday to Sunday
☐	= Kurswagen / train with through coach

PRACTICE

8 Complete the text on Conversation 3 and then listen to the answers on the recording.

	Fahrpreis	
Gleis		**Zuschlag**
	Ermäßigung	**umsteigen**

a Es gibt keinen direkten Zug nach Garmisch. Man muß einmal _____

b Kinder bezahlen nicht den vollen Preis. Sie bekommen eine _____

c Der InterCity ist schneller, aber er kostet auch einen _____

d Erwachsene bezahlen den vollen _____

e Der Zug fährt auf _____ sieben ab.

9 **Reiseverbindungen** – travel connections. When you buy a ticket, you usually get a computer print-out with the fastest connection to your destination. Study the print-out below and the **Zeichenerklärung** on p. 23, then answer the following questions:

Reiseverbindungen

```
                                         Gültig am Sonntag, dem 22.05.
VON    Frankfurt(M)Flugh.
NACH   Ravensburg
ÜBER

BAHNHOF                      UHR   ZUG      BEMERKUNGEN

Frankfurt(M)Flugh.     ab 16:22 S
  Frankfurt Hbf (Tief)  an 16:33
  Frankfurt(Main)Hbf    ab 16:43 ICE   597  Zugrestaurant
                        an 19:05
  Ulm Hbf               ab 19:12 E    3559
Ravensburg              an 20:07
```

a When does the train leave the airport?
b What sort of train is it?
c When does the train leave the main station in Frankfurt?
d What type of train is it?
e Where do you need to change trains?

Answers p. 32   **f** When do you get into Ravensburg?

10 Your turn to speak and get some information at the railway station. You want to go to Cologne – **Köln**. Hans will prompt you on the recording.

Renting a car

Ruth	Guten Tag. Ich möchte gerne ein Auto mieten. Welche Typen haben Sie?
Herr Wallenwein	PKW, LKW, Wohnmobile ...
Ruth	Ich suche einen PKW. Vielleicht einen VW Golf. Was würde der denn kosten?
Herr Wallenwein	Der Tagespreis liegt bei 169 Mark inklusive Kilometergeld.
Ruth	Gut. Haben Sie auch einen Wochenpreis?
Herr Wallenwein	Wochenpauschalen gibt es, die sehr günstig sind zu 649 Mark.
Ruth	Aha. Haben Sie auch Automatik?
Herr Wallenwein	Automatik gibt es auch.
Ruth	Wie kann ich denn bezahlen?
Herr Wallenwein	Sie können mit Kreditkarte bezahlen. American Express oder Eurocard ist möglich.
Ruth	Ja gut, vielen Dank!
Herr Wallenwein	Danke schön.

LISTEN FOR...

mieten	to rent
Tagespreis	daily rate
Wochenpauschale	weekly rate

ein Auto mieten to rent a car; **das Auto** car; **die Autovermietung** car rental

Welche Typen haben Sie? Which makes do you have?

der PKW short for **Personenkraftwagen** car; **der LKW** = **Lastkraftwagen** lorry; **das Wohnmobil** motor caravan, camper van

ich suche I'm looking for

Was würde der (VW) denn kosten? How much would that one be? Ruth could have said: **Was kostet der denn?** (How much is that one?) but chose to use the more polite form **würde**. More in Grammar, Unit 12.

der Tagespreis liegt bei ... the daily rate comes to ...; (**liegen** lit. to lie)

das Kilometergeld mileage, i.e. rate per kilometre

der Wochenpreis or **die Wochenpauschale** weekly rate

sehr günstig very reasonable (lit. favourable)

die Automatik automatic transmission; **Automatik gibt es auch** there are also automatics

Wie kann ich bezahlen? How can I pay?

die Kreditkarte credit card; **bar** in cash.

möglich possible

11 Memory test. Listen to Conversation 4 again. Then mark the correct boxes.

a Ruth sucht ...

einen PKW ☐   einen LKW ☐   ein Wohnmobil ☐

b Der Tagespreis für einen VW Golf ist ...

96 DM ☐   169 DM ☐   369 DM ☐

c Die Wochenpauschale für einen PKW ist ...

günstig ☐   nicht günstig ☐

d Ruth ...

kann mit Kreditkarte bezahlen ☐
kann nicht mit Kreditkarte bezahlen ☐

Answers p. 32

12 On the recording, three customers are renting cars. What do they want? Take notes – in German. You will hear: **das geht in Ordnung** that's OK.

	Name	welches Auto?	mit Automatik?	für wie lange?	Preis?
a					
b					
c					

Answers p. 32

13 In the car rental firm. How would you say in German ...

a I want to rent a car.
b What types have you got?
c How much would a Rolls Royce be?
d Is there a weekly rate?
e Is it with automatic transmission?
f Can I pay by credit card?

Answers p. 32

14 Your turn to speak and rent a car.

KEY WORDS
AND PHRASES

Directions

Wie komme ich am besten ...	What's the best way ...
nach Basel?	to Basle?
zum Stadtzentrum?	to the town centre?
zum Hauptbahnhof?	to the main station?
mit dem Bus/Auto/Zug	by bus/car/train
mit der Straßenbahn/U-Bahn/S-Bahn	by tram/underground/suburban train
Wann fährt der nächste Zug nach ...?	When's the next train to ...?
Wo ist die nächste Haltestelle?	Where's the nearest stop?

At the railway station

Ich möchte ...	I'd like ...
eine Fahrkarte nach Garmisch	a ticket to Garmisch
einfach	single
hin und zurück	return
mit dem InterCity/InterRegio fahren	to travel on the InterCity/InterRegio
erster/zweiter Klasse	first/second class
die Abfahrt	departure
die Ankunft	arrival
auf Gleis sechs	on platform six
Gibt es Ermäßigung?	Is there a reduction?
der halbe/volle Fahrpreis	half/full fare
Muß ich ...	Do I have to ...
umsteigen?	change?
einsteigen?	get on?
aussteigen?	get off?

Car rental

Ich möchte gern ein Auto mieten	I'd like to rent a car
Was kostet ein Fiat/Ford ...?	How much is a Fiat/Ford ...?
Ist der mit Automatik?	Is it with automatic transmission?
der Tagespreis	daily rate
die Wochenpauschale	weekly rate
das Kilometergeld	mileage
sehr günstig	very reasonable
Kann ich mit Kreditkarte bezahlen?	Can I pay by credit card?

Questions

■ Simple questions are formed by switching subject and verb, so that the verb comes first.

| Sie | sind | krank. | (They are ill) | ▷ | Sind | sie | krank? | (Are they ill?) |
| Das Kind | ist | krank. | (The child is ill) | ▷ | Ist | das Kind | krank? | (Is the child ill?) |

15 Turn the statements into questions.

a Er fährt nach Berlin. _____ ?

b Du trinkst Wein. _____ ?

c Das Auto hat Automatik. _____ ?

d Der Mann bezahlt mit Kreditkarte. _____ ?

e Der PKW kostet 40 000 Mark. _____ ?

> **Answers p. 32**

■ Another way of forming a question is to start with a question word.

wo	where	wie	how
was	what	wann	when
wieviel	how much/many	wer	who
wohin	where to	woher	where from
warum	why	welche(r/s)	which
womit	what with		

| Was | ist das? | What is that? |
| Warum | hat er kein Geld? | Why does he have no money? |

Welche behaves like an adjective, changing its ending accordingly:
Welcher Mann ist das?   Which man is that?
Welche Frau ist das?   Which woman is that?

16 Translate the following questions into German:

a When is he coming? _____

b Where are you (informal) going (to)? _____

c Why are you (informal) here? _____

d Who pays for the ticket? _____

e Which car is the most expensive? _____

f Which train is the best? _____

g How far is it to the station? _____

h Where do you (formal) come from? _____

> **Answers p. 32**

Modal verbs

- Modal verbs are nearly always used with another verb which they qualify. One example is **können** (to be able to). In the present tense the modal verb takes its usual second position in the sentence and changes its endings. The second verb goes to the end and remains in the infinitive form.

Ich	kann	heute bar	**bezahlen.**	I can pay in cash today.
Mein Vater	muß	diese Woche schwer	**arbeiten.**	My father has to work hard this week.

Here is a list of modal verbs and their present tense forms:

- **können** (can, to be able to)

ich kann	I can	**wir können**	we can
du kannst	you can	**ihr könnt**	you can
er/sie/es kann	he/she/it can	**sie/Sie können**	they/you can

- **müssen** (must, to have to)

ich muß	I have to	**wir müssen**	we have to
du mußt	you have to	**ihr müßt**	you must
er/sie/es muß	he/she/it has to	**sie/Sie müssen**	they/you have to

Remember:
Du mußt Peter nicht besuchen.   You don't have to visit Peter.
Wir müssen jetzt nicht arbeiten.   We don't have to work now.

- **wollen** (to want)

ich will	I want to	**wir wollen**	we want to
du willst	you want to	**ihr wollt**	you want to
er/sie/es will	he/she/it wants to	**sie/Sie wollen**	they/you want to

Remember: **ich will** I want but: I will/shall **ich werde**

17 Complete the grid by writing in the missing English or German sentences:

a	Sie können hier nicht parken.		_____
b	_____		You (polite) must pay by credit card.
c	Wir wollen um zehn Uhr in Wien sein.		_____
d	_____		Cordula wants to take the taxi.
e	Hana muß nicht Deutsch lernen.		_____
f	Du kannst auch bar bezahlen.		_____
g	Ich will im Sommer nach China fahren.		_____

Answers p. 32

More modal verbs

- **dürfen** (may, to be allowed to)

ich darf	I am allowed	**wir dürfen**	we are allowed
du darfst	you are allowed	**ihr dürft**	you are allowed
er/sie/es darf	he/she/it is allowed	**sie/Sie dürfen**	they/you are allowed

Remember: **Du darfst nicht rauchen!**   You must not smoke!

- **sollen** (shall, to be to, to be supposed to)

ich soll	I am to	**wir sollen**	we are to
du sollst	you are to	**ihr sollt**	you are to
er/sie/es soll	he/she/it is to	**sie/Sie sollen**	they/you are to

Sie sollen sofort nach Hause telefonieren.   You are to ring home at once.

- **mögen** (to like)   **möchte** (would like)

ich mag	I like		**ich möchte**	I'd like
du magst	you like		**du möchtest**	you'd like
er/sie/es mag	he/she/it likes		**er/sie/es möchte**	he/she/it would like
wir mögen	we like		**wir möchten**	we'd like
ihr mögt	you like		**ihr möchtet**	you'd like
sie/Sie mögen	they/you like		**sie/Sie möchten**	they/you would like

Remember both forms are also used without other verbs:
Ich möchte einen Salat.   I'd like a salad.
Ich mag Rotwein.   I like red wine.

18   Translate into German:

a   We are allowed to park here. _____

b   The children are not allowed to sing. _____

c   May I smoke? _____

d   They're supposed to come from China. _____

e   I don't like eating fish. _____

Answers p. 32

19   **Mag** or **möchte?** Use up all the words to make up the sentences.

Er	möchte	Knoblauch	a I'd like a glass of wine.
Sie	möchte	die Karte	b She'd like a black tea.
Wir	mag	Schlagsahne	c Elke likes garlic.
Ich	mögen	einen schwarzen Tee	d We'd like the menu.
Elke	möchten	Frankenwein	e They like Frankenwein.
Sie	mag	ein Glas Wein	f He likes whipped cream.

Answers p. 32

AND FINALLY...

20 Your chance to speak – you are the customer at Frankfurt, enquiring about your connection to Ravensburg. Useful words and phrases:

Wie komme ich ...? Wann fährt ...? Muß ich ein/aus/umsteigen?

21 Choose a place on the map as your starting point. Then ask a partner for directions. Afterwards switch roles.
Useful direction words: **links**, **rechts**, **geradeaus**, **die erste/zweite/... Straße**, **nach zirka 5 Minuten**, **direkt vor/hinter Ihnen** (in front of/behind you)

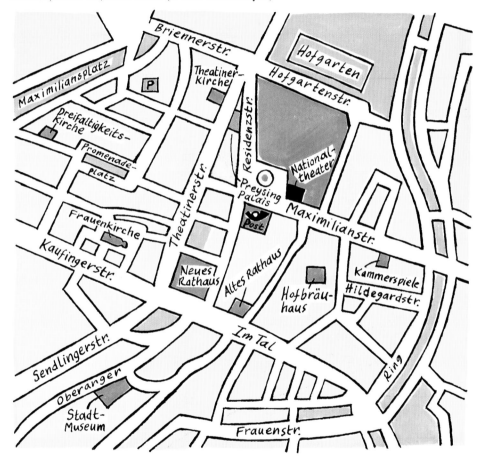

22 Write out the following words on different pieces of paper and put them into four separate piles:

a: Berlin, Dresden, Magdeburg, Freiburg
b: 1st class, 1st class, 2nd class, 2nd class
c: single, single, return, return
d: InterCity, ICE, InterRegio, suburban line

Then pair up with a German-speaking partner. One of you is the customer and picks one piece of paper from each pile. This gives the destination and other details about what sort of ticket to buy. The other partner plays the ticket clerk.

EXERCISE 2

(a) Theater – U-Bahn – hier am Marktplatz
(b) Bahnhof – Bus – hier um die Ecke – alle 15
Minuten (c) Domstraße – zu Fuß – zirka 10
Minuten (d) Marienplatz – Taxi – weit.

EXERCISE 4

(a) return (b) second (c) InterRegio
(d) 56 DM

EXERCISE 5

(a) Guten Tag (b) Eine Fahrkarte nach Wien bitte
(c) Nein, hin und zurück bitte (d) Nein danke
(e) Zweiter Klasse bitte.

EXERCISE 6

(a) (Herzlich) willkommen (b) Bildschirme
(c) Wagen (d) über Köpfhörer (e) Platz
(f) Konferenzraum (g) geöffnet
(h) Wertkartentelefone.

EXERCISE 9

(a) 16.22 (b) S-Bahn (Suburban train) (c) 16.43
(d) ICE (InterCityExpress) (e) in Ulm (f) 20.07.

EXERCISE 11

(a) einen PKW (b) 169 Mark (c) günstig
(d) kann mit Kreditkarte bezahlen.

EXERCISE 12

(a) Heidegger; VW Polo; eine Woche; 639 DM
(b) Urban; BMW 523i mit Automatik; einen Tag;
249 DM (c) Kohl; Jaguar, ohne Automatik; drei
Tage; 459 DM pro Tag.

EXERCISE 13

(a) Ich möchte ein Auto mieten (b) Welche Typen
haben Sie? (c) Was kostet ein Rolls Royce? or:

Was würde ein RR kosten? (d) Gibt es eine
Wochenpauschale? (e) Ist der mit Automatik?
(f) Kann ich mit Kreditkarte bezahlen?

EXERCISE 15

(a) Fährt er nach Berlin? (b) Trinkst du Wein?
(c) Hat das Auto Automatik? (d) Bezahlt der Mann
mit Kreditkarte? (e) Kostet der PKW 40 000 Mark?

EXERCISE 16

(a) Wann kommt er? (b) Wohin gehst du?
(c) Warum bist du hier? (d) Wer zahlt die Karte?
or: Wer bezahlt für die Karte? (e) Welches Auto ist
am teuersten? (f) Welcher Zug ist am besten?
(g) Wie weit ist es zum Bahnhof? (h) Woher
kommen Sie?

EXERCISE 17

(a) You cannot park here. (b) Sie müssen mit
Kreditkarte (be)zahlen. (c) We want to be in Vienna
at 10. (d) Cordula will das Taxi nehmen. (e) Hana
doesn't have to learn German. (f) You can also pay
cash. (g) I want to go to China in the summer.

EXERCISE 18

(a) Wir dürfen hier parken. (b) Die Kinder dürfen
nicht singen. (c) Darf ich rauchen? (d) Die (or:
Sie) sollen aus China kommen. (e) Ich mag keinen
Fisch essen.

EXERCISE 19

(b) Sie möchte einen schwarzen Tee. (c) Elke mag
Knoblauch. (d) Wir möchten die Karte. (e) Sie
mögen Frankenwein. (f) Er mag Schlagsahne.

3 HOLIDAYS

WHAT YOU WILL LEARN

▶ talking about holidays
▶ saying what you do at Christmas
▶ understanding the weather forecast
▶ you will also learn more about the past and future tenses

POINTS TO REMEMBER

● asking the way: **Wo ist die nächste Haltestelle? Wie komme ich am besten ...?**
● directions: **rechts, links, geradeaus, um die Ecke**
● buying a ticket: **einfach, hin und zurück, erster/zweiter Klasse, IC Zuschlag**
● at the station: **einsteigen, umsteigen, aussteigen, Abfahrt, Ankunft, Gleis**
● renting a car: **ein Auto mieten, Tagespreis, Wochenpauschale, Kilometergeld**
● means of payment: **bar, mit Kreditkarte**
● modal verbs: **können, müssen, wollen, dürfen, mögen, sollen**

BEFORE YOU BEGIN

Certain words and structures are similar in German and English and they will be easily assimilated. Other constructions and phrases are, however, idiomatic: there's no point in translating them literally – in fact, this will probably make matters more confusing than necessary. So it's best to learn these by heart. Announcements in German may sound rather daunting, because they are usually delivered at great speed, but if you concentrate on a few key words you will soon notice that they follow quite repetitive patterns. The weather forecast is another example. In these cases it's best to concentrate on the key elements, learn them by heart and deal with the rest later.

St. Moritz
Lugano
PALMEXPRESS

CONVERSATION 1

Summer holidays

Ruth	Wann machen Sie Sommerferien?
Heide	Naja, wir haben zwei Kinder – eins ist in der Schule, und das andere ist im Kindergarten, und das müssen wir beachten.
Ruth	Ja, fahren Sie dann überhaupt weg?
Heide	Ja, ja, das schon, aber wir fahren genau dann weg, wenn die Kinder Ferien haben, also, so im Juli oder August.
Ruth	Ja, und wohin fahren Sie denn da?
Heide	Wir fahren in den Bayrischen Wald. Wir machen Urlaub auf einem Bauernhof. Das ist nicht allzu teuer, die Leute sind freundlich zu den Kindern, die Luft ist gesund, das Essen ist gut, und wir können Ausflüge machen. Außerdem gibt's Ermäßigungen für die Kinder, und das brauchen wir.

LISTEN FOR...

Ferien or **Urlaub**   holiday

Wann machen Sie Sommerferien?   When do you go on your summer holiday?; **die Sommerferien** (pl.) summer holidays. Note that **die Ferien** (pl.) and **der Urlaub** both mean 'holidays' or 'vacation' but **Ferien** is always used in the plural. For example: **Meine Ferien sind im August** but **Mein Urlaub ist im August**.

die Schule   school

das andere   the other one (child)

im (**in** + **dem**) **Kindergarten**   in kindergarten; **der Kindergarten** kindergarten/nursery school

das müssen wir beachten   we have to take that into account. Note the word order – more in Grammar, Unit 4.

beachten   to take into account; **die Achtung** attention; **Achtung!!** Watch out!!

Fahren Sie dann überhaupt weg?   Do you go away at all? **Wegfahren** is a separable verb – see Grammar, this unit; **überhaupt** at all; **dann** is a filler word here, see also: **Wohin fahren Sie denn da?**   Where are you going then? **Da** is a filler here which carries no special meaning.

wir fahren in den Bayrischen Wald   we are going to the Bavarian Forest – a large forest region in the south-east of Bavaria. Note that there is no German equivalent to the English continuous tense.

der Bauernhof   farm

allzu teuer   all that expensive

die Leute (pl.)   the people

freundlich   friendly; **der Freund** (male) friend, **die Freundin** (female) friend

die Luft ist gesund   the air is healthy

wir können Ausflüge machen   we can go on excursions; **der Ausflug** trip

außerdem   besides

das brauchen wir   we need that; again note the word order (Grammar, Unit 4)

PRACTICE

1

How would you say in German ...

a   My daughter is at school.

VOCABULARY	
die Tochter	daughter
der Sohn	son

b   My son is at kindergarten.

c   We go away in July or August.

d   We go to the Bavarian Forest.

e   We have a holiday on a farm.

f   The people are friendly to the children.

Answers p. 48

2

More holidays. Listen to the recording, where lots of people are asked about their holidays. Tick all the words you hear mentioned from the lists below.

wohin?	wann?	Jahreszeit?	wie lange?
Frankreich	Januar	Frühling	3 Tage
Griechenland	Februar	Sommer	1 Woche
Indien	März	Herbst	2 Wochen
Irland	April	Winter	3 Wochen
Italien	Mai		1 Monat
Kanada	Juni		1 Jahr
Spanien	Juli		
	August		
	September		
	Oktober		
	November		
	Dezember		

Answers p. 48

3

Where? When? And how long? Your turn to speak about holiday plans. Turn to the recording, where Hans will prompt you. Keep the book open so that you can use the lists in Exercise 2.

4 Holiday advertisements. Study the advertisements – then listen to the recording. Write down (in English) what sort of holiday the man and the woman want to have. Then decide which holiday they would be happiest with.

VOCABULARY

der See	lake
der Strand	beach
die ruhige Lage	peaceful position
das Hallenschwimmbad	indoor pool
eigen	own
der Meerblick	sea view

A

Schweiz – Wallis

Exklusives großes **Chalet** mit eigenem **Hallenschwimmbad** und **Tennisplatz** in ruhiger Lage zum Tagespreis ab Fr. 330,- zu vermieten. Das Chalet liegt auf 1000 m Höhe in der Nähe von Anzère und Montana-Crans.

B

Österreich

Komfortable, große Ferienwohnungen am Wolfgangsee, eigener Badestrand.

C

Buchen Sie ein Ferienhaus im schweizerischen **Tessin** für 4–7 Personen direkt beim Vermieter.

D

Korfu + Griechenland

Ferienhäuser + Appartements in ruhiger Lage zu vermieten.

E

Georgis Appartements, griechische Insel Santorin. In autofreiem Dorf. Meerblick, preisgünstig. Sehr nette Leute.

F

Irland

Der Spezialist für Top-Ferienhäuser, Kabinenboote, Fähren, Flüge und viel mehr.

Answers p. 48

5 **Wandas Ferien.** Here are Wanda's holiday plans. Study her letter, then write the missing verbs in the text below.

Wir machen normalerweise im Sommer Ferien. Leider müssen wir dieses Jahr zu Hause bleiben, weil wir ein kleines Baby haben. Ich habe zur Zeit keinen Job, und wir haben einfach nicht genug Geld, um wegzufahren. Aber wir können auch hier viel unternehmen: Ausflüge machen, im Wald spazierengehen, schwimmen und Freunde besuchen. Außerdem kommen meine Eltern zu Besuch. Vielleicht wollen sie babysitten, und dann können wir – mein Mann und ich – auch mal abends ausgehen ...

a Wanda _____ im Sommer Ferien.

b Dieses Jahr _____ Wanda zu Hause bleiben.

c Wanda _____ keinen Job und kein Geld.

d Wanda _____ aber auch zu Hause viel unternehmen.

e Vielleicht _____ Wandas Mutter babysitten.

f Dann _____ Wanda mit ihrem Mann ausgehen.

Answers p. 48

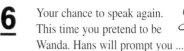

6 Your chance to speak again. This time you pretend to be Wanda. Hans will prompt you ...

CONVERSATION 2

Christmas

Silke

Eigentlich ist Weihnachten ein Familienfest. Da sitzt die ganze Familie zusammen, unterm Weihnachtsbaum. Die Mutter hat was Gutes gekocht, die Kerzen brennen, die Kinder singen Lieder, es ist eigentlich sehr gemütlich. Vor allen Dingen: Geschenke zu bekommen ist eine spannende Sache.

Irgendwie hat sich aber die Bedeutung von dem Fest für mich geändert. Ich sitze heute am liebsten in der Wohngemeinschaft, wir kochen was sehr Schönes, zünden Kerzen an, unterhalten uns und machen uns einen sehr schönen gemütlichen Abend.

LISTEN FOR...

Weihnachten	Christmas
gemütlich	cosy
Geschenke	presents

eigentlich ist Weihnachten ... basically Christmas is … More on this type of word order in Grammar, Unit 4.

das Familienfest family occasion; **das Fest** party, celebration

da sitzt die ganze Familie zusammen (there) the whole family sits together

unterm (= **unter dem**) **Weihnachtsbaum** under the Christmas tree; and if the tree isn't quite so big: **vor dem Weihnachtsbaum** in front of the tree

was (= **etwas**) **Gutes** something good; **etwas Kleines** something small, **etwas Schlechtes** something bad

kochen to cook; **der Koch** the cook

die Kerze candle

brennen to burn

das Lied song; plural **Lieder**

gemütlich cosy

vor allen Dingen above all (things)

Geschenke zu bekommen to get presents; **das Geschenk** present; remember **bekommen** means 'to get' and not 'to become'!

eine spannende Sache exciting (lit. an exciting affair). In Germany presents are usually handed out on Christmas Eve: **der Heilige Abend**.

irgendwie hat sich die Bedeutung von dem Fest für mich geändert somehow the meaning of the festival has changed for me; **sich ändern** to change. This is quite a complicated construction which you needn't master yet.

die Wohngemeinschaft group of people living communally, sharing a house or apartment as students perhaps or young working people.

wir zünden Kerzen an we light candles; **anzünden** (separable verb – see Grammar, this unit) to light; (**wir**) **unterhalten uns** (we) chat, from the verb **sich unterhalten** (see Grammar, Unit 6).

wir machen uns einen schönen Abend we have (lit. make ourselves) a nice evening

7 Verb check! See whether you can fill in the gaps without looking at Conversation 2.

a Weihnachten _____ ein Familienfest.

b Die Familie _____ vor dem Weihnachtsbaum.

c Die Kinder _____ Lieder.

d Die Kerzen _____

e Wir _____ Kerzen an.

Answers p. 48 f Wir _____ uns einen schönen Abend.

8 What people do at Christmas. Listen to the recording, where Petra and Hannes are talking about their Christmas. Then decide which statements are true (**richtig**) and false (**falsch**).

VOCABULARY

der Skikurs the skiing course; skiing lessons

a Petra fährt Weihnachten weg.

b Hannes will nach Indien fahren.

c Hannes fährt Weihnachten nach Österreich.

d Er hat dort Freunde.

e Hannes kann Ski fahren.

f Petra kann auch Ski fahren.

g Petra macht im Januar Urlaub.

h Sie fährt im Januar in die Schweiz.

Answers p. 48 i Hannes will einen Skikurs machen.

9 Season's greetings. In Germany, many local papers carry Christmas and New Year's messages from firms and restaurants to thank their customers. Here are two examples ...

Restaurant-Pizzeria Weststadt
Schmalegger Straße 18, Telefon 93507

Frohe Weihnachten
und ein gutes neues Jahr

Unsere Öffnungszeiten über die Feiertage:
**Heiligabend + 1. Weihnachtsfeiertag geschlossen.
2. Weihnachtsfeiertag und Mittwoch geöffnet.**

Für einen netten Silvesterabend empfehlen wir uns mit unserem Fondue.

Frohe Feiertage, herzlichen Dank für Ihre Treue und alles Gute für das neue Jahr
Ihr

RESTAURANT ZUR POST

*Familie Garamella und Mitarbeiter Weingarten, Postplatz 8
Telefon (0751) 52575*

Look at the advertisements and write down: We wish you a happy Christmas and a good new year !

Wir wünschen Ihnen _____

10 Time was ... This is what Ingrid, Silke's friend, has to say about Christmas. Read the passage and answer the questions below. Alternatively, you could listen to the recording and fill in the questionnaire without studying the text below.

VOCABULARY	
war	was (more on this tense in Grammar, Unit 5)
sich freuen auf	to look forward to
die Kirche	church
kommerzialisiert	commercialised
Geld ausgeben	(sep. verb) to spend money
zum Schluß	at the end
niemand	nobody

Früher war Weihnachten viel schöner. Ich habe mich immer wochenlang auf den 24. Dezember gefreut. Am Heiligen Abend sind wir zuerst in die Kirche gegangen, dann haben wir etwas gegessen, nichts Besonderes, meistens nur eine kalte Platte mit Butterbroten. Dann haben wir die Weihnachtskerzen angezündet und Lieder gesungen. Und ganz zum Schluß erst haben wir die Geschenke bekommen – es hat keine großen Geschenke gegeben, auch nicht viele – vielleicht zwei oder drei pro Person. Aber alles war sehr romantisch und gemütlich. Heute ist alles so laut, so kommerzialisiert. Jeder kauft zuviel, gibt zuviel Geld aus, und niemand kann sich richtig über das Fest freuen.

VOCABULARY	
romantisch	romantic
langweilig	boring
mehr	more
glücklich	happy

Weihnachten – fünf Fragen

a Wie war Weihnachten früher?

   romantischer ☐   langweiliger ☐

b Wieviel Geschenke haben die Leute früher bekommen?

   weniger ☐   mehr ☐

c Wieviel Geld geben die Leute heute aus?   weniger ☐   mehr ☐

d Sind die Leute heute glücklicher über das Fest?   ja ☐   nein ☐

e Was hat man früher gegessen?   etwas Einfaches ☐   viel zu viel ☐

Answers p. 48

11 Your turn to speak about your Christmas. Hans will prompt you on the recording.

CONVERSATION 3

The weather

Reisewetterbericht gültig bis Donnerstag.
Norddeutschland: Morgen heiter bis wolkig und kein
Regen, am Mittwoch regnet's dann aber und ist
ziemlich windig. Ab Donnerstag wieder freundlicher, 17
bis 21 Grad.
Süddeutschland: Heiter bis wolkig und trocken, später
überwiegend veränderlich, bewölkt und etwas Regen. Höchsttemperaturen 17 bis 21 Grad.

der Wetterbericht weather report
gültig valid
heiter bright, fine
wolkig or **bewölkt** cloudy; **die Wolke** cloud
der Regen rain; **etwas Regen** some rain
regnen to rain
ziemlich windig rather windy; **der Wind** wind

Grad degree (Centigrade here)
trocken dry
später later
überwiegend veränderlich mostly variable
Höchsttemperaturen maximum temperatures

REMINDER ...

Montag Monday
Dienstag Tuesday
Mittwoch Wednesday
Donnerstag Thursday
Freitag Friday
Samstag/Sonnabend Saturday
Sonntag Sunday

OTHER IMPORTANT WEATHER TERMS

die Sonne scheint the sun's shining
sonnig sunny
bedeckt overcast
der Nebel fog; **neblig** foggy
Niederschläge showers
der Schauer shower
das Gewitter thunderstorm
der Schnee snow
es schneit it's snowing
das Eis ice; **das Glatteis** black ice
der Frost frost
unter Null below zero (freezing)

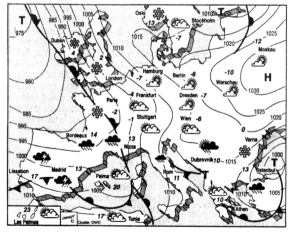

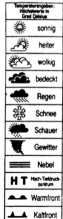

12 Listen to the weather report in Conversation 3 several times. Try not to look at the transcript in the book. Mark the chart under the appropriate symbols and fill in the temperatures.

	Sonne	Regen	Wolken	Wind	Temperaturen
Norddeutschland morgen: Mittwoch: Donnerstag:		✗	✓	✓	17-21
Süddeutschland zuerst: später:	✓	✓			21

Answers p. 48

13 More weather. Listen to the recording and complete the transcript. You will probably need to listen several times.

Der _____ fürs

_____ . Süddeutschland:

Am _____ sonnig und

_____ ; schwacher

_____ aus Nordost.

_____ 21 bis 24

_____ . Am

_____ zunehmende

Bewölkung und _____ .

Tageshöchsttemperaturen

_____ bis _____ Grad.

_____ : Am Samstag _____ bis wolkig, später

windig und _____ . Höchsttemperaturen _____

Grad. Am Sonntag _____ und _____ .

Höchsttemperaturen _____ .

Answers p. 48

14

A skiing holiday. Anne and Elke are away on a skiing holiday over Christmas. Read the postcard Anne has written to her friend Margot and answer the questions below – in English. Alternatively you could listen to the recording and try and answer the questions without looking at the postcard.

Liebe Margot!

Viele Grüße aus unserem Skiurlaub. Es ist gut, daß wir Skigymnastik gemacht haben: wir sind sehr fit. Elke macht ihren ersten Skikurs und fährt noch auf dem Idiotenhügel, ich mache schon längere Touren. Es gibt viel Schnee, und das Wetter ist wunderbar: viel Sonne und blauer Himmel. Weihnachten ohne Familie ist sehr schön. Am Heiligen Abend waren wir im Chalet und haben uns einen gemütlichen Abend gemacht. Leider hat es keine Geschenke gegeben. Am interessantesten ist immer der Après-Ski ...

Bis bald
Deine Anne

VOCABULARY

die Skigymnastik	exercises to prepare you for skiing
der Idiotenhügel	(colloquial) ski slope for beginners
blauer Himmel	blue sky

a Are the girls fit? _____

b Are they both past beginner's level? _____

c Are they missing Christmas with their families? _____

d What did they do on Christmas Eve? _____

Answers p. 48

e Were there any presents? _____

15

Your turn to speak. On the recording, Johannes will interview you about your skiing holiday ...

     Unit 3 Holidays

KEY WORDS
AND PHRASES

Die Ferien, der Urlaub

Holidays, vacation

Wir machen Urlaub	We go on holiday
auf einem Bauernhof	on a farm
Wir machen einen Ausflug	We go on a trip
Die Luft ist gesund	The air is healthy
(das) Weihnachten	Christmas
der Heilige Abend	Christmas Eve
der Weihnachtsbaum	Christmas tree
das Geschenk	present
das Weihnachtslied	Christmas song
das Fest	party, celebration
das Familienfest	family occasion
Wir machen uns einen gemütlichen Abend	We have a cosy evening
Wir unterhalten uns	We talk
Wir zünden Kerzen an	We light candles
Frohe Weihnachten!	Happy Christmas!
Ein gutes neues Jahr!	A happy new year!
Viel Glück!	The best of luck!

Das Wetter

The weather

der Wetterbericht	weather report
die Temperatur	temperature
über/unter Null	above/below zero (freezing)
Grad	degree
trocken	dry
sonnig	sunny
heiter	fine
bewölkt	cloudy
die Sonne	sun
der Regen	rain
Niederschläge	showers
der Nebel	fog
der Wind	wind
der Schnee	snow
das Glatteis	black ice

GRAMMAR AND EXERCISES

The future

■ If there is a clear reference to a time in the future, you can use the present tense:

Ich fahre Weihnachten nach Österreich. I am going to Austria at Christmas.
Anina kommt in zwei Jahren zurück. Anina is coming back in two years' time.

■ If there is no clear time reference, you need to use the future tense. It is formed by using the verb **werden** + infinitive of the main verb.

ich	werde	kommen	I shall come
du	wirst	kommen	you will come
er/sie/es	wird	kommen	he/she/it will come
wir	werden	kommen	we shall come
ihr	werdet	kommen	you will come
sie/Sie	werden	kommen	they/you will come

16 Fill in the correct forms of **werden**.

a Wir _____ alle zum Essen gehen.

b Ich _____ ein Konzert besuchen.

c Er _____ die ganze Nacht tanzen.

d Und Sie? Was _____ Sie machen?

e Maria und Walter _____ nach Italien fahren.

A note of caution: do not confuse **ich werde** with **ich will**:

Ich will kommen I want to come
Ich werde kommen I shall come
Meine Eltern wollen sich ein Haus kaufen. My parents want to buy a house.
Meine Eltern werden sich ein Haus kaufen. My parents will buy a house.

Answers p. 48

17 How many sentences can you make up from the grid? When you've finished, translate the English sentences, using up all the words.

subject	main verb	when?	what or where?	infinitive
Wir	wird		keine Zeit	
Wir	geht	am Sonntag	zum Mittagessen	haben
Sie	werden	im Winter	in den Kindergarten	fliegen
Sie	gehen	Weihnachten	in die Oper	
Er	kommen		nach Australien	

a We are going to the opera at Christmas. _____
b He will fly to Australia. _____
c She will go to kindergarten in the winter. _____
d They will have no time. _____
e We'll come to lunch on Sunday. _____

Answers p. 48

44   Unit 3   Holidays

The perfect tense (2)

■ In Grammar, Unit 1 you learnt that the perfect tense is usually formed by using **haben** + the past participle of the main verb. There is, however, a smallish number of verbs that form the perfect tense with **sein** (to be) rather than **haben**. These are usually (but not always) verbs expressing change or movement.

ich	bin	gereist	I have travelled
du	bist	gereist	you have travelled
er/sie/es	ist	gereist	he/she/it has travelled
wir	sind	gereist	we have travelled
ihr	seid	gereist	you have travelled
sie/Sie	sind	gereist	they/you have travelled

■ Here are some more common verbs that form their perfect tense with **sein**:

gehen	(to go)	Wir sind nach Hause gegangen.
fahren	(to drive, travel)	Er ist viel zu schnell gefahren.
kommen	(to come)	Sie sind nach Berlin gekommen.
bleiben	(to stay)	Wie lange bist du in London geblieben?
laufen	(to walk)	Ich bin fünf Stunden gelaufen.

18 Complete the sentences using the appropriate perfect forms of the verbs in brackets.

a (to stay)   Wir _____ viel zu lange in der Bar _____

b (to come)   Wann _____ du gestern nach Hause _____ ?

c (to travel) Ich _____ wochenlang durch Alaska _____

d (to go)   Sie _____ alleine ins Kino _____

e (to walk)   _____ du zur Arbeit _____ ?

> Answers p. 48

■ Possibly the most important verb that forms its perfect tense with **sein** is **sein** itself. **Sein** is a strong verb with an irregular past participle: **gewesen**.

ich	bin	gewesen	I have been
du	bist	gewesen	you have been
er/sie/es	ist	gewesen	he/she/it has been
wir	sind	gewesen	we have been
ihr	seid	gewesen	you have been
sie/Sie	sind	gewesen	they/you have been

19 Translate into German. Use the perfect tense throughout and remember to place the past participle at the end of the sentence!

a She walked very quickly. _____

b I went to the cinema. _____

c We were at home. _____

d He travelled to Berlin. _____

e We have been in London. _____

f Were you (informal) happy? (2 possibilities!) _____

g He has come with Agnes. _____

> Answers p. 48

Separable verbs

- Verbs such as **anzünden** (to light) or **einsteigen** (to get in) are separable: this means that the prefix splits off from the main verb and goes right to the end of the sentence or phrase. Common prefixes that separate are **an-, ein-, aus-, weg-, auf-**.

Ich steige ein.	I get on.
Ich steige in den Zug ein.	I get on the train.
Wir zünden Kerzen an.	We light candles.

In questions, too, the prefix goes to the end:

Steigen Sie ein?	Are you getting on?
Wann zünden Sie die Kerzen an?	When do you light the candles?

In the perfect tense, the prefix is tagged onto the past participle of the main verb:
einsteigen (to get on) ▷ **ein + gestiegen** ▷ **eingestiegen**

Ich bin in den Zug eingestiegen.	I have got on the train.
Wir haben Kerzen angezündet.	We have lit candles.

20 Rewrite the sentences below in the present tense.

a Wir sind in Hamburg umgestiegen. _____

b Hast du die Kerzen angezündet? _____

c Wann ist deine Mutter abgefahren? _____

d Er ist am Dienstag weggefahren. _____

e Wie bist du am besten hingekommen? _____

Answers p. 48

- Not all verbs that have a prefix are separable. The most common prefixes that do not separate are **be-, ge-, ent-, zer-, er-, ver-**:
  beginnen (to begin) ▷ **ich beginne**
  These verbs with inseparable prefixes have no **ge** in the past participle ▷ **begonnen**

vergessen (to forget)	**Ich vergesse das Wort.**	**Ich habe das Wort vergessen.**
empfehlen (to recommend)	**Er empfiehlt den Fisch.**	**Er hat den Fisch empfohlen.**
verstehen (to understand)	**Ich verstehe nichts.**	**Sie hat nichts verstanden.**

21 What are the main verbs in the following sentences?
Write down their infinitive forms.

a Rita ist in Ulm ausgestiegen. _*aussteigen*_

b Wir steigen in Frankfurt um. _____

c Wir haben alles verstanden. _____

d Der Film hat viel zu spät begonnen. _____

e Wann kommst du in München an? _____

f Meine Mutter ist nicht gut hingekommen. _____

g Wer hat dir den Fisch empfohlen? _____

Answers p. 48

22 Holidays. Study the travel advertisements and match them up with the customers below.

Ich will wieder einmal so richtig kreativ sein.....

Bernd

Wir möchten auch Urlaub machen — aber wir haben nicht so viel Geld...

... und ich will den ganzen Tag in der Sonne liegen und schwimmen.

Familie Hundertwasser

Angelika

a

AUF ZYPERN BADETE SCHON APHRODITE

Zypern – diesen Urlaub werden Sie nie vergessen

b

Ägypten

10 Tage klassische Rundreise ab 2499,–
Informationen über Land und Kultur

c

TOSCANA – VILLA MIT SWIMMING-POOL

SCHREIBEN – TANZ– MUSIK – ein Urlaub für Individualisten!
2 Wochen ab DM 1999,–

d

Zurück zur Natur
Kommen Sie auf unseren Hof in Oberbayern! Kinder und Tiere sind bei uns willkommen!

e

KANADA!

Im Kanu durch das Yukon-Territorium, oder Trail-Wandern in British Columbia in den schönsten Nationalparks

Answers p. 48

23 Your turn to speak and choose your own holiday from the offers on this page. On the recording, Hans will prompt you as usual. You'll need the word **heiß**, hot.

24 In pairs, choose a holiday destination, time of year and duration from the list in Exercise 2. Your partner asks where you are going, when and for how long. Then switch roles.

EXERCISE 1

(a) Meine Tochter ist in der Schule.   (b) Mein Sohn ist im Kindergarten.   (c) Wir fahren im Juli oder August weg.   (d) Wir fahren in den Bayrischen Wald.   (e) Wir machen Ferien/Urlaub auf einem Bauernhof.   (f) Die Leute sind freundlich zu den Kindern.

EXERCISE 2

These are the ones you should *not* have ticked:
Frankreich, Griechenland, April, Mai, Juni, Juli, August, November, Sommer, 1 Woche

EXERCISE 4

MAN: flat, lake, beach, swimming B;
WOMAN: family, house, Southern Europe D.

EXERCISE 5

(a) macht   (b) muß   (c) hat   (d) kann   (e) will   (f) kann.

EXERCISE 7

(a) ist   (b) sitzt   (c) singen   (d) brennen   (e) zünden   (g) machen

EXERCISE 8

richtig: **b**, **c**, **d**, **e**, **g**, **h**

EXERCISE 9

Frohe Weihnachten (or: ein frohes Weihnachtsfest) und ein gutes neues Jahr!

EXERCISE 10

(a) romantischer   (b) weniger   (c) mehr   (d) nein   (e) etwas Einfaches.

EXERCISE 12

	Sonne	Regen	Wolken	Wind	Temperaturen
Norddeutschland					
morgen	✔		✔		17–21°
Mittwoch		✔		✔	
Donnerstag	✔				
Süddeutschland					
zuerst	✔		✔		17–21°
später		✔	✔		

EXERCISE 13

Der Wetterbericht fürs Wochenende.
Süddeutschland: Am Samstag sonnig und trocken; schwacher Wind aus Nordost.
Tageshöchsttemperaturen 21 bis 24 Grad. Am Sonntag zunehmende Bewölkung und Gewitter.
Tageshöchsttemperaturen 23 bis 25 Grad.
Norddeutschland: Am Samstag heiter bis wolkig, später windig und etwas Regen.
Höchsttemperaturen 18 bis 21 Grad. Am Sonntag bedeckt und Regen. Höchsttemperaturen 15 bis 17 Grad.

EXERCISE 14

(a) yes   (b) no, Elke is a beginner, but Anne already goes on longer runs   (c) no   (d) they were in a chalet and had a cosy evening   (e) no

EXERCISE 16

(a) werden   (b) werde   (c) wird   (d) werden   (e) werden.

EXERCISE 17

(a) Wir gehen Weihnachten in die Oper.   (b) Er wird nach Australien fliegen.   (c) Sie geht im Winter in den Kindergarten.   (d) Sie werden keine Zeit haben.   (e) Wir kommen am Sonntag zum Mittagessen.

EXERCISE 18

(a) Wir sind viel zu lange in der Bar geblieben.
(b) Wann bist du gestern nach Hause gekommen?
(c) Ich bin wochenlang durch Alaska gereist/gefahren.   (d) Sie ist alleine ins Kino gegangen.   (e) Bist du zur Arbeit gelaufen?

EXERCISE 19

(a) Sie ist sehr schnell gelaufen.   (b) Ich bin ins Kino gegangen.   (c) Wir sind zu Hause gewesen.
(d) Er ist nach Berlin gereist/gefahren.   (e) Wir sind in London gewesen.   (f) Bist du glücklich gewesen? or: Seid ihr glücklich gewesen?   (g) Er ist mit Agnes gekommen.

EXERCISE 20

(a) Wir steigen in Hamburg um.
(b) Zündest du die Kerzen an?   (c) Wann fährt deine Mutter ab?   (d) Er fährt am Dienstag weg.   (e) Wie kommst du am besten hin?

EXERCISE 21

(a) aussteigen   (b) umsteigen   (c) verstehen   (d) beginnen   (e) ankommen   (f) hinkommen   (g) empfehlen.

EXERCISE 22

Bernd: **c**; Familie Hundertwasser: **d**; Angelika: **a**

4 LEISURE ACTIVITIES

WHAT YOU WILL LEARN

▶ talking about your weekend
▶ describing your hobbies and interests
▶ you will also find out about the basic structures of German sentences

POINTS TO REMEMBER

● holiday and Christmas words: **wir machen Ferien/Urlaub/einen Ausflug; Weihnachten, der Heilige Abend, das Geschenk, der Weihnachtsbaum, das Familienfest**

● best wishes: **Frohe Weihnachten! Viel Glück! Ein gutes neues Jahr!**

● when talking about the future you can use the present tense as long as there's a clear time reference. If not, use **werden** + main verb: **ich werde gehen** (I'll go), **du wirst, er/sie/es wird, wir werden, ihr werdet, sie/Sie werden** ...

● some verbs form the perfect tense with **sein** rather than **haben** – they're mostly verbs of motion: **ich bin gegangen** (I have gone), **ich bin gekommen** (I have come) ...

● weather terms: **die Sonne** sun, **der Regen** rain, **die Wolke** cloud, **bedeckt** overcast, **der Nebel** fog, **der Schnee** snow, **Temperaturen unter Null** temperatures below zero.

BEFORE YOU BEGIN

Sometimes people find it hard to understand spoken German because of the word order: they claim that the most important bits usually come at the end of the sentence, by which time they have forgotten the beginning. This may be true for very long sentences. However, quite often the words at the end can be guessed from the context, especially if they are verbs. For example: **Wollen Sie in ein Restaurant gehen?** Here, **gehen** is so guessable that it could, in fact, be left out altogether. The main words, carrying the crucial information, are **wollen** and **Restaurant**. Pay special attention to the sentence structures in this unit and ask yourself which are the crucial words that carry the meaning.

Unit 4 Leisure activities

Easter in Zell

Ruth

Wir wollen gerne Ostern nach Zell am See – so 'ne Art verlängertes Wochenende. Was kann man da denn alles machen?

Frau Jonas

Also, als erstes würde ich Ihnen empfehlen, daß Sie rechtzeitig buchen – das ist nämlich sehr stark gebucht. Und Sie können dort also, wenn's Wetter schön ist, am See irgendwas unternehmen: Bootfahren, Surfen. Sie können auch wandern. Sehr viele Spazierwege gibt's dort ... könnte natürlich auch sein, daß es noch Schnee gibt, und dann können Sie Ski fahren.

Ruth

Und was machen wir, wenn's regnet?

Frau Jonas

Wenn's regnet, gibt's also sehr viele Möglichkeiten. Sie können ins Schwimmbad. Sie können in die Sauna, es gibt Kegelbahnen, es gibt Tanzveranstaltungen. Das ist überhaupt kein Problem.

LISTEN FOR...	
Ostern Easter	
Wochenende weekend	
buchen to book	

das Ostern   Easter

nach Zell am See   to Zell (resort in Austria); remember to use **nach** (to) for a named place and **zum/zur** for a building, street or area: **ich gehe nach Berlin** (I'm going to Berlin) but: **ich gehe zur Bank** (I'm going to the bank)

so 'ne (= eine) Art verlängertes Wochenende a kind of long weekend; **die Art** kind

als erstes würde ich Ihnen empfehlen ... firstly I would recommend (to you). Frau Jonas is using the more polite form **würde**. She could also have said: **als erstes empfehle ich Ihnen** firstly I recommend (to you). More on **würde** in Grammar, Unit 12.

... daß Sie rechtzeitig buchen   ... that you book well ahead; **rechtzeitig** in time. Certain words such as **daß** send the verb to the end of the phrase. See also Grammar, this unit.

das ist nämlich sehr stark gebucht   it gets (lit. is) very heavily booked; **nämlich** is a filler word here and carries little extra meaning.

Sie können dort also ... am See irgendetwas unternehmen   you can do something by the lake. **Also** is another filler word here with no extra meaning.

das Bootfahren   boating

wenn's (= wenn das) Wetter schön ist ...   if the weather is nice ... More on word order in Grammar, this unit.

sehr viele Spazierwege gibt's (= gibt es) dort there are many walks there. Note the word order. The normal word order would be: **es gibt dort sehr viele Spazierwege**. But Frau Jonas wants to emphasise **sehr viele Spazierwege** and therefore places it at the beginning of the sentence and follows it immediately by the verb. **einen Spaziergang machen** to go for a walk

könnte natürlich sein ...   (it) could of course be ...

die Möglichkeit   possibility

Sie können ins Schwimmbad (gehen)   you can go to the swimming pool. Note that the main verb **gehen** has been dropped as the meaning of the sentence is quite obvious without it.

die Kegelbahn   bowling alley

Tanzveranstaltungen   dances; **die Veranstaltung** event; **der Tanz** dance; **tanzen** to dance

das ist überhaupt kein Problem   that's no problem at all

1 **Ostern in Zell am See** – what is there to do? Listen to Conversation 1 again and complete the grid below.

bei Sonnenschein	bei Schnee	bei Regen
Bootfahren		

Answers p. 64

2 Three crucial questions. Listen to the recording and write down the German equivalents for the following questions:

a   What can one do there? ―――――――――――――――

b   Do we have to book early? ――――――――――――――――

Answers p. 64

c   What hotel can you recommend (to us)? ――――――――――――

3 More active people. On the recording, Herr Müller and Frau Schmidt are talking about their activities. Listen and take notes – in English.

FRAU SCHMIDT

where to?

planned activities?

HERR MÜLLER

where to?

planned activities?

Answers p. 64

4 Brig is a town in the Swiss Alps. What does it have to offer? Here's an extract from the official tourist brochure. Study it and answer the questions below, in German. Write complete sentences.

a In welcher Straße kann man gut einkaufen?

_____

b Gibt es in Brig auch eine Altstadt?

_____

c Und wo kann man Konzerte hören?

_____

d Wie bleibt man auch in Brig fit?

| Answers p. 64 |

_____

**Lebendiges Brig –
weltoffen und dynamisch**
Shopping in der belebten
Bahnhofstrasse, einer stattlichen Allee.
Seitwärts locken Kleinläden in
verträumte Altstadtteile. Folkloristische
Umzüge, Musikfeste, Cafés und Dancings
halten Sie bei guter Laune.
Beschaulicher: ein Konzert im Schloss,
das Museum, eine Kunstgalerie. Und mit
Schwimmen, Tennis oder Squash bleibt
man auch in Brig fit. Alles in allem:
Genau das richtige Umfeld für den
Kongressort Brig.

5 Your turn to speak. You are planning to spend a week at the Chiemsee, a popular lake in Bavaria.

At home

Horst

Am Samstagnachmittag da mach' ich erst mal das
Übliche: Auto waschen, im Garten arbeiten, und dann
mach' ich meine ganzen Hobbys – „Do it yourself", wissen
Sie. Ich hab' schon einen Tisch gebaut, und eine Bank,
und jetzt mach' ich gerade ein Bücherregal. Gegen Abend leg' ich mich dann in die Badewanne.

Heide

Ich geh' meine Eltern besuchen, die wohnen nicht weit weg, gleich um die Ecke. Meistens nehm'
ich die zwei Kinder mit. Wir trinken Kaffee, essen Kuchen und reden miteinander. Oder ich leg'
mich einfach faul in die Sonne, in den Garten, lese ein Buch. Und einmal im Monat gehe ich zum
Kaffeekränzchen. Da gibt's immer was zu plaudern und zu lachen.

Horst

Am Sonntag machen wir uns meistens einen ruhigen Tag. Wir stehen spät auf, außer Claudia,
die steht um acht schon auf und geht um neun in die Kirche. Oft fahren wir ins Grüne, gehen im
Wald spazieren, kehren dann in einem Gasthof ein. Am Abend gibt's dann meistens Fernsehen.

LISTEN FOR...	
das Übliche	the usual
arbeiten	to work
das Kaffeekränzchen	coffee party

das Übliche the usual; **üblich** usual. **das ist
nicht üblich** that is not usual.

wissen Sie you know; **ich weiß** I know, **du
weißt** you know, **er weiß** he knows, **wir
wissen** we know ...

bauen to build, to make

der Tisch table; **die Bank** bench; **das
Bücherregal** bookshelf

gegen Abend towards evening

leg' (= lege) ich mich I lie (lit. put myself)

die Badewanne bathtub

faul lazy

wir reden miteinander we
talk to each other

einmal im Monat once a
month

das Kaffeekränzchen
the German
equivalent to an English
tea party: where you meet
friends for coffee, cakes
and a chat.

plaudern to chat

lachen to laugh

wir machen uns einen ruhigen Tag we take
it easy (lit. make ourselves a quiet day).

wir stehen spät auf we get up late;
aufstehen (sep.) to get up

wir fahren ins Grüne we go to the
countryside; **grün** green

spazierengehen or **einen Spaziergang
machen** to go for a walk

wir kehren in einem Gasthof ein we stop off
at an inn; **einkehren** (sep.) to stop off (at a
pub or inn).

das Fernsehen television; **der Fernseher** TV
set; **fernsehen** (sep.) to watch TV.

6 Spot the difference! Have a look at this account of Heide's Saturday. It's not quite right. Spot the mistakes and correct them!

Heide sees her parents, but they live quite far away. She always takes her two children with her. They all have coffee and cakes together and talk to each other. At other times Heide sunbathes on her balcony, swims in the pool and reads a book. Twice a month she meets her friends for coffee and cakes.

Answers p. 64

7 Here are some weekend activities. Match the words from the right-hand column with those in the left – one has been done for you.

das Auto _**waschen**_   legen

im Garten _____ bauen

einen Tisch _____ einkehren

sich in die Badewanne _____ spazierengehen

die Eltern _____ gehen

ein Buch _____ ~~waschen~~

zum Kaffeekränzchen _____ arbeiten

in einem Gasthof _____ besuchen

im Wald _____ lesen

Answers p. 64

8 Your turn to speak and practise some of the activities from Exercise 7 ...

9 Antonia hates Saturdays. Here's the reason why. First listen to her letter on the recording, then correct the statements below.

Ich hasse den Samstag. Am Samstagmorgen ist immer die große Hektik: in der Stadt sind Massen von Leuten, die Straßen sind voller Autos, in den Cafés findet man keinen Platz, und überall in den Geschäften sind lange Schlangen. Am Nachmittag fängt dann der große Haus- und Gartenputz an. Die Leute waschen die Autos, mähen den Rasen, schneiden die Hecken. Alles ist schrecklich langweilig! Und abends geht dann jeder ins Kino oder in die Kneipe, und dann findet man dort wieder keinen Platz.

Answers p. 64

True or false? Correct the false statements.

a Sie haßt das Wochenende, weil es langweilig ist.

b Sie haßt den Samstagmorgen, weil jeder einkaufen geht.

c Sie haßt den Samstagnachmittag, weil jeder ins Kino oder in die Kneipe geht.

d Sie haßt den Samstagabend, weil sie im Café keinen Platz findet.

Corrected statements:

_____

_____

_____

_____

10 Your turn to speak. Turn to the recording and pretend to be Antonia.

The sports fanatic

Horst Also, ich finde, du treibst entschieden zu viel Sport.

Mark Wie kommst du denn darauf?

Horst Ja, schau doch mal hin: am Sonntagmorgen bist du auf dem Fußballplatz, am Sonntagnachmittag bereits wieder auf dem Handballplatz. Und während der Woche machst du alles: Schwimmen, Reiten, Tennisspielen, Leichtathletik – alles.

Mark Das siehst du falsch. Zum Beispiel Fußball spiele ich schon seit meiner frühesten Jugend. Und die anderen Sportarten mach' ich zwar nicht jede Woche, aber ich treib' sie als Ausgleichsport.

Horst Ich finde, du könntest als Ausgleich einmal an einem Sonntagmorgen ein gutes Buch lesen. Das würde dir und deiner Familie bestimmt gut tun.

Mark Ich weiß nicht, ob das meiner Familie guttut, wenn ich ein Buch lese und irgendwo in der Ecke sitze.

LISTEN FOR...	
Fußball	football
Handball	handball
Reiten	riding
Leichtathlethik	athletics

du treibst entschieden zuviel Sport you definitely do too much sport. **Sport treiben** or **Sport machen** to do (a) sport.

Wie kommst du denn darauf? What makes you think that?

Schau doch mal hin! Just look at it! **hinschauen** (sep.) to look (at).

der Fußball football; **der Handball** handball; **reiten** to ride; **das Reiten** riding; **die Leichtathletik** athletics

das siehst du falsch you've got it wrong (lit. you see it wrong)

seit meiner frühesten Jugend since my earliest days; **die Jugend** youth, adolescence

zwar to be precise; also 'admittedly'

ich treib' sie als Ausgleichsport I do them as a balance; **der Ausgleich** balance

das würde dir guttun that would do you good

ich weiß nicht, ob das meiner Familie guttut, wenn ich ein Buch lese... I don't know whether it would do my family any good if I read a book... More on word order after phrases beginning with **ob** and **wenn** in Grammar, this unit.

irgendwo somewhere; **irgendwie** somehow; **irgendwer** somebody (anybody); **irgendwas** something (anything)

11

Sportfanatiker! Answer the questions by listening to Conversation 3 again but without looking at the text. Write complete sentences.

a Wann spielt Mark immer Fußball?

_____

b Wann spielt er Handball?

_____

c Wann geht er zum Schwimmen?

_____

d Seit wann spielt er Fußball?

_____

e Was sollte Mark als Ausgleich tun?

Answers p. 64

_____

12

Ich hasse das Wochenende ... I hate the weekend. Klaus is not very keen on weekends and poured out a litany of woe on the local radio station. The transcript of his outburst is below. Listen to the recording and fill in the gaps.

VOCABULARY

wackelig	wobbly
stinklangweilig	very boring (**stinken** to smell!)
trotz	despite

Ich _____ das Wochenende! Die Väter _____

Autos, _____ im Garten, oder _____ ihre

langweiligen Hobbys. Mein Vater hat schon drei Tische

_____ , und alle drei sind wackelig. Der Sonntag ist noch

schrecklicher. Morgens in die Kirche, dann die Grillparty im Garten –

natürlich Würstchen. Am Nachmittag _____ der

obligatorische Spaziergang: Guten Tag, Herr Hinz, guten Tag, Frau Kunz! ...

Einfach schrecklich!!! Und dann kommt das Beste:

_____ bei Tante Elsbeth. Stinklangweilig!

Abends _____ dann die ganze Familie vor dem Fernseher.

Meistens _____ einen schlechten Film oder eine Talkshow für

90-jährige. Ich bin froh, wenn ich im _____ bin. Wie schön ist

Answers p. 64
doch der _____ – trotz Schule...

13 Problems ... sum them up! Irene is worried about Toni. Here's her letter to an agony aunt and the reply she receives. Read the letters and answer the questions below, in English.

Liebe Frau Liane

ich habe ein Problem. Mein Freund Toni treibt immer mehr Sport. Er hat fast keine Zeit mehr für mich und ist jeden Abend irgendwo beim Training: Fitness, Gewichtheben, Jogging, Tennis. Er hat sich so verändert, ich kenne ihn fast nicht mehr. Früher war er schön rund und knuddelig, so wie ich, jetzt ist er dünn wie eine Bohnenstange! Was soll ich machen?

Irene

Liebe Irene,

vielleicht hat Toni das Problem, nicht Sie! Sie haben zwei Möglichkeiten: erstens treiben Sie auch mehr Sport, mit oder ohne Toni – vielleicht ist das gar nicht so schlecht für Ihre Figur und Ihre Gesundheit. Zweitens reden Sie mit Tony und finden heraus, warum er so viel Sport macht – vielleicht will er so dünn sein, oder vielleicht hat er eine neue, dünne Freundin? Wenn das der Fall ist, suchen Sie sich am besten einen neuen, runden, knuddeligen Freund...

Viel Glück!

Frau Liane

a Why is Irene worried about Toni?

b What did he look like before and what does he look like now?

c What is her first option, according to Frau Liane? Are there any extra advantages with it?

d What is her second option?

e What might be the reasons for his change?

Answers p. 64

14 Your turn to speak. Max asks you out but you are too busy to have fun. Turn to the recording where Hans will prompt you.

KEY WORDS
AND PHRASES

am Wochenende	during the weekend
ein verlängertes Wochenende	a long weekend
am Samstag/Sonntag	on Saturday/Sunday
am Samstagabend	on Saturday evening
am Samstagmorgen	on Saturday morning
Es gibt viele Möglichkeiten	There are many possibilities
Sie müssen rechtzeitig buchen	You must book in good time

Ich ...	I ...
mache meine Hobbys	pursue my hobbies
arbeite im Garten	work in the garden
gehe zum Kaffeekränzchen	go for coffee, cakes and a chat
lege mich faul in die Sonne	lie lazily in the sun
besuche meine Eltern	visit my parents

Wir ...	We ...
stehen spät auf	get up late
fahren ins Grüne	go to the country
gehen in die Sauna	go to the sauna
gehen ins Schwimmbad	go to the swimming pool
kehren in einem Gasthof ein	stop off at an inn
plaudern	chat
lachen	laugh
reden miteinander	talk to each other

Ich treibe (or mache) Sport	I go in for sports
die Sportarten	kinds of sports
der Fußball	football
der Handball	handball
das Schwimmen	swimming
das Reiten	riding
der Tennis	tennis
die Leichtathletik	athletics
das Surfen	surfing
das Skifahren	skiing

GRAMMAR AND EXERCISES

Cases

- As you know, all German nouns have a gender (masculine, feminine or neuter) which also affects the articles: the definite articles are **der**, **die**, **das**, the indefinite articles are **ein**, **eine**, **ein**.
- German also has four cases. Depending on the role that a noun has in the sentence, it can be in the *nominative*, *genitive*, *dative* or *accusative* case. Both the nouns and the articles change according to the case they are in.

In this unit and the next two you will be learning when the different cases are used. Here are the forms of nouns and articles in the four cases:

	Nominative	Accusative	Dative	Genitive
Masculine	**der Mann**	**den Mann**	**dem Mann**	**des Mannes**
Feminine	**die Frau**	**die Frau**	**der Frau**	**der Frau**
Neuter	**das Kind**	**das Kind**	**dem Kind**	**des Kindes**
Plural	**die Männer**	**die Männer**	**den Männern**	**der Männer**
(all genders)	**die Frauen**	**die Frauen**	**den Frauen**	**der Frauen**
	die Kinder	**die Kinder**	**den Kindern**	**der Kinder**

- The nominative case is always used for the subject of the sentence: '**der Mann**' in **der Mann baut den Tisch**, because he carries out the action expressed by the verb '**baut**'.
- The accusative case is used for direct objects: '**den Tisch**' in **der Mann baut den Tisch**, because it is the object of the action in the verb '**baut**' – it is what he builds.
- The dative case is used for indirect objects – more in Grammar, Unit 5. So far in this book you have it in certain phrases after prepositions such as: **in der Schule**, **auf dem Fußballplatz**, **mit dem Bus**.
- The genitive case is like 'of' in English: **der Hund des Königs** 'the king's dog' or 'the dog of the king'.

15 Complete the sentences using the correct definite articles.

a _____ Frau sitzt auf _____ Bank.

b _____ Mann liest _____ Buch.

c _____ Vater arbeitet in _____ Haus.

d Mark ist auf _____ Handballplatz.

e _____ Kind spielt in _____ Ecke.

f _____ Junge ist in _____ Schule.

g _____ Leute sind in _____ Stadt.

h _____ Mädchen sieht _____ Kleid in _____ Boutique.

i _____ Dame fährt mit _____ Zug.

> **Answers p. 64**

Word order

■ In simple sentences, the verb takes up second position.

1st position	2nd position	
Ich	fahre	nach London.
Mein Haus	ist	zu groß.
Er	geht	im Sommer nach Italien.

■ This rule also applies if the sentence begins with an expression of time or place, and then the subject must come in third place, immediately after the verb:

1st position	2nd position	3rd position	
Oft	fahren	wir	ins Grüne
In London	habe	ich	viele Freunde.

■ It's the same if a sentence begins with a question word.

1st position	2nd position	3rd position	
Wohin	gehst	du?	
Was	gibt	es	zum Essen?

■ In the perfect tense, **haben** or **sein** takes up the usual second position while the main verb goes right to the end of the sentence.

Wir	haben	zu viel	gegessen.
Maria und Walter	sind	schon oft nach Italien	gefahren.

16 Rearrange the jumbled sentences so that they make sense – sometimes there's more than one possibility.

a fliegen wann wir Mallorca nach?

b wohin zum fährst Skifahren du?

c Hunger hat wer?

d Schnee der wunderbar ist

e gestern spät Hause nach ich bin gekommen

f habe ich Sommer im Ferien vier Wochen

g meine Familie ich Weihnachten besucht habe

Answers p. 64

Word order in complex sentences

- In complex sentences (i.e. sentences consisting of more than one clause), matters are slightly more complicated. Study this example:

Ich weiß,	daß er keine Zeit	hat.	I know that he has no time.
Ich will nicht,	daß sie morgen	kommt.	I don't want her to come tomorrow.
Er lacht,	weil er glücklich	ist.	He laughs because he is happy.
Sie kommt,	wenn sie Zeit	hat.	She'll come if she has time.

The clauses starting with **daß**, **weil**, **wenn** are called subordinate clauses. They are separated from the main clause by a comma.

Here is the rule:
- In subordinate clauses starting with words like **daß** (that), **weil** (because), **wenn** (if, when), **ob** (whether), the verb is sent from the usual second position to the end of the clause.

17 Translate into German:

a He eats because he's hungry.

b She knows that it's late.

c I cannot come if I have no time.

d They say that they are happy.

e I know that they are at home.

f It could be that there is still snow there.

Answers p. 64

- Now study this sentence from Conversation 1:
Wenn es regnet, gibt es viele Möglichkeiten.
Frau Jonas could also have said: **Es gibt viele Möglichkeiten, wenn es regnet.**

Note the change of word order in the main sentence:
es gibt viele Möglichkeiten ▷ **gibt es viele Möglichkeiten.**

Here is the rule:
- If the complex sentence starts with the subordinate clause (here: **Wenn es regnet**), the verb in the main clause remains in second position in the sentence, following the subordinate clause, and the subject moves to follow it.

More examples
Wenn er Zeit hat, kommt er.
Weil sie glücklich ist, lacht sie.

18 No sports fanatic. Listen to the recording to find out what Uwe has to say about his attitude to sport. Then complete the sentences below.

This is the pattern you should follow

Jogging ▷ **Er mag Jogging nicht, weil es zu langweilig ist**

Some of these adjectives will be useful:

langweilig riskant passiv naß (wet) **chaotisch langsam** (slow) **teuer hektisch schnell**

a Tennis ▷

_____

b Yoga ▷

_____

c Schwimmen ▷

_____

d Reiten ▷

_____

e Skifahren ▷

_____

Answers p. 64

19 Your turn to speak about your weekend and explain why you're not too keen on some activities. Turn to the recording where Hans will prompt you, as usual.

20 Ask a partner to go to the cinema with you. For every time you ask them, they look at the diary below and explain why they can't come: **Am Dienstag nachmittag kann ich nicht kommen, weil ich arbeite.** Eventually, however, you should strike lucky and hit upon a gap in the diary ... Then swop roles. If you're learning on your own, you can still work out why you couldn't go at the various times …

	Montag	Dienstag	Mittwoch	Donnerstag
Vormittag	Arbeit	Arbeit	Arbeit	frei
Nachmittag	Arbeit	Arbeit	frei	Arbeit
Abend	frei	frei	Tennis	Arbeit
	Freitag	Samstag	Sonntag	
Vormittag	Arbeit	frei	Yoga	
Nachmittag	Arbeit	frei	Tennis	
Abend	Theater	frei	Konzert	

EXERCISE 1

Sonnenschein: Bootfahren, Surfen, Wandern, Spazieren; Schnee: Skifahren; Regen: Schwimmbad, Sauna, Kegelbahn, Tanzen

EXERCISE 2

(a) Was kann man da alles machen?   (b) Müssen wir früh buchen?   (c) Welches Hotel können Sie uns empfehlen?

EXERCISE 3

Frau Schmidt: lake in Austria; hiking, going for walks, if it snows: skiing. Herr Müller: luxury hotel in Majorca; lying in the sun, swimming; in the evening: dancing or bowling.

EXERCISE 4

(a) In der Bahnhofstraße kann man gut einkaufen
(b) Ja – es gibt eine Altstadt   (c) Im Schloss kann man Konzerte hören   (d) Man kann sich mit Schwimmen, Tennis und Squash fit halten

EXERCISE 6

Heide sees her parents – *they don't* live far away. *Most of the time* she takes her two children with her. They have coffee and cakes and talk to each other. At other times Heide sunbathes *in her garden* and reads a book. *Once* a month she meets her friends for coffee and cakes.

EXERCISE 7

Correct sequence of verbs: waschen, arbeiten, bauen, legen, besuchen, lesen, gehen, einkehren, spazierengehen.

EXERCISE 9

True: **a**, **b**. Corrected: **c** Sie haßt den Samstagabend, weil jeder ins Kino oder die Kneipe geht   (d) Sie haßt den Samstagmorgen, weil sie im Café keinen Platz findet.

EXERCISE 11

(a) Mark spielt am Sonntagmorgen Fußball.
(b) Er spielt am Sonntagnachmittag Handball.
(c) Er geht während der Woche zum Schwimmen.
(d) Er spielt seit seiner frühesten Jugend Fußball.
(e) Er sollte als Ausgleich ein gutes Buch lesen.

EXERCISE 12

The missing words: hasse, waschen, arbeiten, machen, gebaut, kommt, Kaffeekränzchen, sitzt, gibt's, Bett, Montag.

EXERCISE 13

(a) He does too much sport and doesn't spend enough time with her.   (b) He used to be round and cuddly, now he's as thin as a beanpole.   (c) She could do more sport herself – it might even benefit her figure.
(d) She should talk to Toni and find out why ...
(e) Perhaps he wants to be thin, but perhaps he has a new, thin, girlfriend

EXERCISE 15

(a) die; der   (b) der; das   (c) der; dem   (d) dem;
(e) das; der   (f) der; der   (g) die; der   (h) das; das; der   (i) die; dem.

EXERCISE 16

(a) Wann fliegen wir nach Mallorca?   (b) Wohin fährst du zum Skifahren?   (c) Wer hat Hunger?
(d) Der Schnee ist wunderbar.   (e) Ich bin gestern spät nach Hause gekommen. or: Gestern bin ich spät nach Hause gekommen.   (f) Ich habe im Sommer vier Wochen Ferien. or: Im Sommer habe ich vier Wochen Ferien.   (g) Ich habe meine Familie Weihnachten besucht. or: Weihnachten habe ich meine Familie besucht.

EXERCISE 17

(a) Er ißt, weil er Hunger hat.   (b) Sie weiß, daß es spät ist.   (c) Ich kann nicht kommen, wenn ich keine Zeit habe.   (d) Sie sagen, daß sie glücklich sind.   (e) Ich weiß, daß sie zu Hause sind.   (f) Es könnte sein, daß es dort noch Schnee gibt.

EXERCISE 18

Er mag ...   (a) Tennis nicht, weil es zu hektisch ist.
(b) Yoga nicht, weil es zu langsam ist.
(c) Schwimmen nicht, weil es zu naß ist.
(d) Reiten nicht, weil es zu teuer ist.   (e) Skifahren nicht, weil es zu riskant ist.

5 THE ART OF CONVERSATION

WHAT YOU WILL LEARN
- ▶ starting a conversation
- ▶ what to say at a dinner party
- ▶ talking about politics
- ▶ you will also learn about another tense

POINTS TO REMEMBER
- ● sports: **Sport treiben, Fußball, Handball, Schwimmen, Reiten, Tennis, Skifahren**
- ● a long weekend: **ein verlängertes Wochenende**, (**rechtzeitig**) **buchen, Samstagabend, Sonntagmorgen**
- ● word order: in simple sentences, the verb takes second position: **Ich fahre nach Ulm**; if there are two verbs, the second one goes to the end: **Ich bin nach Ulm gefahren**.
- ● clauses starting with **daß, weil, wenn, ob**: the verb is sent from its usual second position to the end of the clause.

BEFORE YOU BEGIN
Finding the right words to strike up and maintain a conversation is of course not merely a linguistic skill – in a real-life situation, plenty of native speakers can be lost for words, too, for a variety of reasons. But whatever the reason, it normally helps to have a stock list of 'conversation openers' handy, and a few more questions and phrases if you want to get into a discussion of sports or politics. As you go through this unit, compile your own list of useful conversation phrases and imagine in what situations they might actually come in handy.

In Heidelberg

Ruth	Sind Sie hier im Urlaub?
Student	Ja.
Ruth	Seit wann?
Student	Schon seit drei Tagen.
Ruth	Und wie gefällt es Ihnen?
Student	Mir gefällt es gut hier, weil das Wetter schön ist und die Leute dann freundlich sind.
Ruth	Reisen Sie alleine?
Student	Ja, ich bin mit dem Rucksack unterwegs.
Ruth	Und woher kommen Sie eigentlich?
Student	Ich komm' aus Nürnberg.
Ruth	Aus Nürnberg. Ist das 'ne interessante Stadt?
Student	Für die Touristen ist es interessant, ja, aber wenn man sein ganzes Leben schon in Nürnberg gewohnt hat, möchte man auch mal was anderes sehen.

> ## LISTEN FOR...
>
> **Wie gefällt es Ihnen?** How do you like it?

Wie gefällt es Ihnen? How do you like it? Answer: **Mir gefällt es gut**. **Wie gefällt Ihnen der Film?** How do you like the film? **Er gefällt mir.** I like it. **Er gefällt mir nicht.** I don't like it.

weil das Wetter schön ist und (weil) die Leute dann freundlich sind because the weather is nice and the people are friendly. Note the position of **ist** and **sind** at the end of the clause with **weil** (see Grammar, Unit 4).

ich bin mit dem Rucksack unterwegs I am travelling with my rucksack/backpack; **unterwegs** on the road.

wenn man sein ganzes Leben schon in Nürnberg gewohnt hat if one has spent all one's life in Nuremberg (note the end position of **hat** in the **wenn** clause – see Grammar, Unit 4). Main clause order would be: **Man hat sein ganzes Leben in Nürnberg gewohnt.**

1 Asking questions. If someone gave you these answers, what might your questions have been? Use the polite **Sie** form.

a _____?

Ja, ich komme aus Hamburg.

b _____?

Ja, ich bin hier im Urlaub.

c _____?

Seit zwei Wochen.

d _____?

Ja, mir gefällt es gut.

e _____?

Answers p. 80

Nein, ich reise mit meinem Freund.

VOCABULARY

der Geist	esprit
der Witz	here: wit
der Zauber	magic
das Jahrhundert	century
reich	rich
die Gasse	alleyway
die Umgebung	environment
das Neckartal	Neckar (a tributary of the Rhine) valley

2 Heavenly Heidelberg! Here's the transcript of a radio commercial about Heidelberg. Some words are missing – fill them in while you listen to the recording. When you've done that read the text and see how much you've understood.

_____ (a) um Heidelberg!

_____ (b) Stadt,

_____ (c) Herz!! Jeder

_____ (d) Heidelberger ist

Student. Deutschlands_____ (e)
Universität im idyllischen Neckarstädtchen (sie existiert seit 1386) hat Geist, Witz und ein großes Herz. Der Zauber von

_____ (f) Jahrhunderten ist für jeden Besucher

faszinierend: _____ (g) Fassaden,

_____ (h) Kneipen, _____ (i)

Gassen, _____ (j) Ruinen, historische Kuriositäten.
„Die Stadt mit ihrer Umgebung hat etwas Ideales", hat schon der

_____ (k) Goethe vor 200 Jahren gesagt –

_____ (l) von Touristen sagen das auch heute noch.
Besonders zu empfehlen: Wanderungen auf dem Philosophenweg, ein Ausflug auf der Weinstraße und Schiffstouren im Neckartal.

Answers p. 80

3 Your turn to speak – about Heidelberg. So keep your book open.

freundliches
♥
Heidelberg

Dinner talk

Biba	Darf ich Ihnen noch etwas von dieser Pastete anbieten?
Frau Schmitt	Oh nein danke, es tut mir leid, ich bin Vegetarierin.
Biba	Ach, aber dann nehmen Sie doch noch etwas von diesem Salat vielleicht?
Frau Schmitt	Ja, gern – danke!
Biba	Und Sie, Herr Frauenfeld, nehmen Sie noch von dieser Pastete?
Herr Frauenfeld	Oh ja, gerne.
Biba	Bitte sehr!
Herr Frauenfeld	Danke!
Herr Schmitt	Ist diese Pastete selbstgemacht?
Biba	Ja, das ist ein Rezept meiner Mutter.
Herr Schmitt	Mhm, schmeckt sehr fein.
Frau Schmitt	Da haben Sie aber ein wundervolles Gemälde an der Wand. Das gefällt mir ja sehr gut.
Biba	Ja, das hat mein Mann zum Geburtstag von seiner Firma bekommen.
Frau Schmitt	Ah ja. Ach, Sie hatten Geburtstag vor kurzem ...
Biba	Ja ...
Alle	Herzlichen Glückwunsch ... Herzlichen Glückwunsch ... Alles Gute!!

LISTEN FOR...

anbieten	to offer
selbstgemacht	home-made

Darf ich Ihnen noch etwas von dieser Pastete anbieten? May I offer you a bit more of this pâté? **anbieten** (sep.) to offer; **ich biete Ihnen eine Zigarette an** I offer you a cigarette; other useful words when socialising: **der Gastgeber** host, **die Gastgeberin** hostess.

die Pastete pâté

es tut mir leid I'm sorry

der Vegetarier/die Vegetarierin vegetarian

selbstgemacht home- (lit. self-) made

ein Rezept meiner Mutter a recipe of my mother's (here's an example of the genitive case); **das Rezept** recipe (also: prescription)

(das) schmeckt sehr fein that's quite delicious; more often you'll hear **Das schmeckt sehr gut!** That tastes very good. **Wie schmeckt's?** How does it taste? **Hat es geschmeckt?** Did you enjoy it? **Guten Appetit!** Enjoy your meal!

das Gemälde painting; **malen** to paint; **das Bild** picture

an der Wand on the wall; **die Wand** wall.

zum Geburtstag for (his) birthday; **der Geburtstag** birthday

von seiner Firma from his company; **die Firma** firm, company

vor kurzem a short while ago

Herzlichen Glückwunsch! Congratulations! **Alles Gute!** All the best!; **gratulieren** to congratulate

ALLES GUTE

Du bist wie eine Flasche Wein – mit jedem Jahr wirst du besser

ZUM GEBURTSTAG

4 True or false? Only five statements are true. Correct the false ones!

a Biba ist die Gastgeberin des Abends.
b Frau Schmitt ist Vegetarierin.
c Herr Schmitt kann die Pastete nicht essen, weil er Vegetarier ist.
d Herr Frauenfeld sagt, daß ihm die Pastete sehr fein schmeckt.
e Frau Schmitt gefällt das Gemälde an der Wand.
f Bibas Mann hat vor kurzem Geburtstag gehabt.
g Er hat das Gemälde von seiner Mutter bekommen.
h Das Rezept für die Pastete kommt von Bibas Mutter.

Corrected statements: _____

_____

Answers p. 80 _____

5 Puzzle. The numbered squares give you the name of a famous wine-growing region in Germany.

a produced at home

b is celebrated once a year

c has plenty of vitamins

d is mostly made of meat or fish

e will tell you how to cook a certain dish

f female who does not eat meat

a ⬜⬜⬜⬜⬜⬜⬜⬜⬜⬜ 1 ⬜
b ⬜ 2 ⬜⬜⬜⬜⬜⬜
c ⬜ 3 ⬜⬜⬜
d ⬜⬜ 4 ⬜⬜
e ⬜⬜ 5 ⬜⬜
f ⬜⬜⬜⬜⬜⬜⬜⬜⬜⬜ 6 ⬜

Answers p. 80 Keyword: ⬜⬜⬜⬜⬜⬜

6 More table talk. Listen to the recording and take notes – in English. Hans will be the host. What are Herr and Frau Platt having? What do they especially like?

VOCABULARY

der Schinken ham
ausgezeichnet excellent

	Frau Platt	Herr Platt
takes more		
has had enough		
especially likes		

Answers p. 80

7 Manners. Here are the dos and don'ts, according to one newspaper. Read the list, study the cartoons opposite and decide which specific point of the social codex has been violated. Then write down what the 'hero' should have done – in German!

Example

Point 3:
Er sollte beim Gähnen die Hand vor den Mund halten!

Answers p. 80

Gute Manieren

1 Männer sagen zuerst guten Tag, Jüngere grüßen Ältere!
2 Handschuhe und Hut bei der Begrüßung anbehalten!
3 Beim Gähnen bitte Hand vor den Mund halten!
4 Beim Zahlen mit Kreditkarten das Trinkgeld in bar geben!
5 Männer gehen hinter Frauen die Treppe hoch!

Schlechte Manieren

6 Bei der Begrüßung die Hand in der Hosentasche lassen!
7 Beim Telefonieren Kaugummi kauen!
8 Im Restaurant mit dem Handy telefonieren!
9 Mit dem Essen anfangen, wenn der Ober noch serviert!
10 Zu wenig körperliche Distanz halten!

VOCABULARY ·

die Handschuhe	gloves
das Handy	mobile phone
die Hosentasche	trouser pocket
der Hut	hat
der Kaugummi	chewing gum; **kauen** to chew
die Manieren	manners
der Ober	waiter
die Treppe	stairs
das Trinkgeld	tip
anbehalten	to keep on (clothes)
gähnen	to yawn
grüßen	to greet; **die Begrüßung** greeting, welcome
hinter	behind
körperlich	physical; **der Körper** body

8 Your turn to speak and make conversation at a dinner party. Turn to the recording, where Hans will prompt you.

CONVERSATION 3

Talking politics

Biba	Was sind die wichtigsten Parteien in der Bundesrepublik?
Ingrid	Da sind einmal die Christdemokraten, die CDU/CSU – eher rechtskonservative Parteien, die Liberalen – die FDP – klein, aber

LISTEN FOR...

Parteien	political parties
Bundesrepublik	Federal Republic
Koalitionspartner	coalition partner
Umweltschutz	protection of the environment

	wichtig als Koalitionspartner. Die Sozialdemokraten – die SPD – eine eher Mitte-Links-Partei; die Grünen, eine Umweltschutz-Partei.
Biba	Und wie oft wird in der Bundesrepublik gewählt?
Ingrid	Normalerweise alle vier Jahre, manchmal auch früher.
Biba	Welche Rolle hat eigentlich der Bundeskanzler?
Ingrid	Er steht an der Spitze der Regierung und bildet das Kabinett.
Biba	Und wie wichtig ist der Präsident?
Ingrid	Er ist relativ unwichtig und hat vor allem repräsentative Funktionen.

die wichtigsten Parteien the most important parties; **wichtig** important; **die Partei** party

die Bundesrepublik Federal Republic; **die Bundesregierung** Federal Government; **der Bundestag** Federal Parliament; **das Bundesland** Federal state

CDU Christian Democratic Union, **CSU** Christian Social Union. The **CSU** is the sister party of the **CDU** in Bavaria.

eher rechtskonservative Parteien parties on the rightwing, conservative side

die Liberalen the liberals; the **FDP** (Free Democratic Party) is a small but important party because of its role as a possible coalition partner with one or other of the two big parties.

SPD Social Democratic Party of Germany

die Grünen the Greens

der Umweltschutz protection of the environment

Wie oft wird gewählt? How often are elections? **wählen** to choose, to elect; **die Wahl** election, choice; **es wird gewählt** cannot be translated literally. Similarly: **es wird getanzt und gespielt** people dance and play; more on this construction in Grammar, Unit 7.

alle vier Jahre every four years

er steht an der Spitze der Regierung he heads the government (lit. he stands at the top of the government); **die Regierung** government.

(er) bildet das Kabinett (he) forms the cabinet.

relativ unwichtig relatively unimportant

vor allem above all, mainly

repräsentative Funktionen representational functions

PRACTICE

9

Pick the right words from the box and write them in the blanks.

die SPD **die Grünen**
  die CDU/CSU **der Bundespräsident**
    die FDP **der Bundeskanzler**

a _____ ist konservativ.
b _____ ist liberal.
c _____ ist Mitte links.
d _____ wollen eine bessere Umwelt.
e _____ ist der Chef der
Regierung.
f _____ hat repräsentative
Aufgaben.

Answers p. 80

10

Who's voting for whom? Listen to the recording and complete the
sentences below.

a Heide wählt die _____, weil sie
_____

b Helmut wählt die _____, weil er
_____

c Herta wählt die _____, weil sie
_____

d Sepp wählt die _____, weil er
_____

Answers p. 80

11 Here is a map of the Federal Republic with its 16 federal states. But not all the place names have been filled in. Listen to the conversation on the recording and fill in the names that are missing ... Here they are, but in a different order:

Stuttgart Schwarzwald Zugspitze Sachsen

Nordsee Düsseldorf Schleswig-Holstein

Bayern Ostsee

Answers p. 80

VOCABULARY	
der Berg	mountain
die Hauptstadt	capital
zwischen	between
das Meer	sea

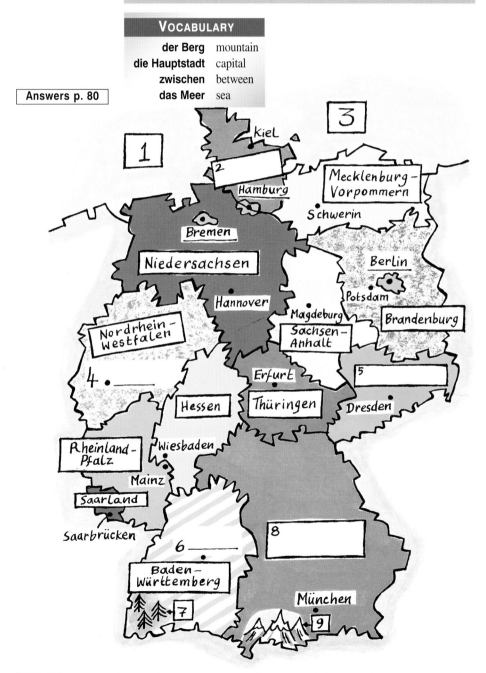

Starting a conversation

Wie gefällt es Ihnen?	How do you like it?
Mir gefällt es gut/nicht	I like it/don't like it.
Woher kommen Sie?	Where are you from?
Seit wann sind Sie schon unterwegs?	Since when have you been travelling?

Dinner party talk

Darf ich Ihnen ... anbieten?	May I offer you ...?
Das schmeckt gut.	That tastes good.
Das ist selbstgemacht.	That's home-made.
Ich bin Vegetarier(in).	I'm a vegetarian.
Herzlichen Glückwunsch!	Congratulations!
Alles Gute!	All the best!

Politics

die Partei	(political) party
Ich wähle die ...	I vote for the ...
CDU	Christian Democrats
SPD	Social Democrats
FDP	Liberal Democrats
Grünen	Greens
die Bundesrepublik	Federal Republic
die Bundesregierung	Federal Government
der Bundestag	Federal Parliament
der Bundeskanzler	Federal Chancellor
der Bundespräsident	Federal President
das Bundesland	Federal State
an der Spitze der Regierung	at the head of the government
bildet das Kabinett	forms the cabinet
repräsentative Funktionen	representational functions
der Umweltschutz	protection of the environment

INFORMATIONEN AUS DER POLITIK

Journal für Deutschland

http://www.bundesregierung.de
Infos der Bundesregierung im InterNet

The imperfect tense

Phrases such as 'I was', 'he drank', 'we sang' use the imperfect tense to tell you about something that happened in the past.

Generally, Germans seem to favour the perfect tense in spoken German (see Unit 2); but you will still come across the imperfect a great deal, especially in written German. The most important forms to remember are the imperfect forms of **sein** and **haben**, which are often used.

■ **sein**   to be

ich	war	I was
du	warst	you were
er/sie/es	war	he/she/it was
wir	waren	we were
ihr	wart	you were
sie/Sie	waren	they/you were

■ **haben**   to have

ich	hatte	I had
du	hattest	you had
er/sie/es	hatte	he/she/it had
wir	hatten	we had
ihr	hattet	you had
sie/Sie	hatten	they/you had

12 Translate into German.

a   I was ill. _____

b   He had a car. _____

c   We were in the cinema. _____

d   Were you (formal) in Berlin? _____

e   She had a problem. _____

f   Did you (formal) have a ticket? _____

Answers p. 80

■ Most other verbs – the so-called weak verbs – form their imperfect by adding **-te**, **-test**, **-tet** and **-ten** after the stem. For example, here are the imperfect forms of **tanzen** (to dance), stem **tanz**, and **fragen** (to ask), stem **frag**.

ich	tanzte	I danced
du	tanztest	you danced
er/sie/es	tanzte	he/she/it danced
wir	tanzten	we danced
ihr	tanztet	you danced
sie/Sie	tanzten	they/you danced

ich	fragte	I asked
du	fragtest	you asked
er/sie/es	fragte	he/she/it asked
wir	fragten	we asked
ihr	fragtet	you asked
sie/Sie	fragten	they/you asked

13   Translate into German:

a   I learned German.

___

b   You (informal singular) believed it.

___

c   He heard the dog.

___

d   We built the table.

___

> Answers p. 80

Adjective endings

- In sentences like: **Die Milch ist heiß** (The milk is hot) or **Das Ei ist kalt** (The egg is cold) the adjective never changes. It stays the same for masculine, feminine or neuter nouns, singular or plural. More examples: **Der Ring ist schöner** (The ring is more beautiful). **Das Kleid ist besser** (The dress is better).
- But if an adjective comes in front of the noun, there are certain changes, which depend on four things:

1   the gender of the noun (masculine? feminine? neuter?)
2   the article (is it definite: **der/die/das** or indefinite: **ein/eine/ein**?)
3   the case (nominative? accusative? genitive? dative?)
4   the number (singular? plural?)

These are the rules for adjectives following the definite article (**der/die/das**) for the three most important cases:

- *Nominative* case (the noun is the subject – see also Grammar, Unit 4) .

Der frische Fisch schmeckt gut.	The fresh fish tastes good.
Die kalte Milch ist gut.	The cold milk is good.
Das deutsche Bier ist wunderbar.	The German beer is wonderful.
Die schönen Mädchen sind hier.	The beautiful girls are here.

In the nominative singular, all adjective endings are **-e** and in the plural they are **-en**.

14   Translate into German.

a   The small glass is expensive.

___

b   The friendly people are from Ulm.

___

c   The long dresses are not cheap.

___

d   The big shop is around the corner.

___

> Answers p. 80

■ *Accusative* case (the noun is the object – see also Grammar, Unit 4)

Ich trinke den italienischen Wein.	I drink the Italian wine.
Er heiratet die französische Lehrerin.	He marries the French teacher.
Ich nehme das englische Bier.	I take the English beer.
Sie will die kalten Nudeln essen.	She wants to eat the cold noodles.

The adjective ending is **-en** for masculine singular and all genders plural; otherwise it's **-e**.

15 Translate into German:

a He buys the French wine.

b Martin wants the new table.

c I want to drink the cold beer.

d She visits the German family.

e The woman sings the beautiful songs.

Answers p. 80

■ *Dative case* (after some prepositions, and when the noun is the indirect object – it benefits or suffers from the action.) Sometimes it helps to rephrase a sentence in order to find the indirect object, which can often follow 'to' or 'for' in English. For example, 'She gives the sick baby a tablet' can be rephrased as 'She gives the tablet to the sick baby' – 'to the sick baby' is the dative case.

Ich gebe dem armen Mann etwas Geld.	I give some money to the poor man.
Wir bringen der alten Frau einen Kuchen.	We bring a cake to the old woman.
Sie gibt dem kleinen Kind Wasser.	She gives water to the small child.
Er schenkt den guten Studenten ein Buch.	He gives a book to the good students.

The adjective ending **-en** is the same for all genders, singular and plural.

16 Translate into German:

a We give the book to the little girl.

b She brings a bottle of wine to the old man.

c I give a present to the good woman.

d They give money to the little children.

Answers p. 80

17 **Herzlichen Glückwunsch!** On an SWF3 radio show, Frank Metzler delivers birthday greetings. Listen and take notes – in English – of the main points. You might well need to listen several times to get all the points down.

VOCABULARY	
die Oma	granny
der Enkel, das Enkelkind	grandchild
Grillbraten	grilled meats

a whose birthday ─────────

b living in ─────────

c age today ─────────

d number of grandchildren ─────────

celebrations:

e afternoon ─────────

f evening ─────────

Answers p. 80

18 And now you are the birthday star: Your turn to speak on the recording. Hans will prompt you, as usual.

19 A geography test, based on the map on page 74. Prepare five questions to ask a partner (or think through yourself). See who scores the most points. You might want to ask:

Was ist die (Bundes)Hauptstadt von ...?

Welches Land ist nördlich/östlich/südlich/westlich von ...? etc.

EXERCISE 1

(a) Kommen Sie aus Hamburg? (b) Sind Sie hier im Urlaub? (c) Seit wann (sind Sie hier im Urlaub)? (d) Gefällt es Ihnen? (e) Reisen Sie alleine?

EXERCISE 2

(a) rund (b) kleine (c) großes (d) fünfte (e) älteste (f) acht (g) reiche (h) gemütliche (i) alte (j) romantische (k) alte (l) Tausende

EXERCISE 4

Correct: (a), (b), (e), (f), (h). Incorrect: (c) Herr Schmitt kann die Pastete essen. (d) Herr Schmitt sagt, daß sie sehr fein schmeckt. (g) Er hat das Gemälde von seiner Firma bekommen.

EXERCISE 5

(a) selbstgemacht (b) Geburtstag (c) Salat (d) Pastete (e) Rezept (f) Vegetarierin; keyword: Hessen.

EXERCISE 6

Frau Platt: takes more sausage, has had enough salad, especially likes ham, but also loves sausage and salad. Herr Platt: has had enough ham and cheese, but will have some more chocolate cake, which he especially likes (and so does his wife).

EXERCISE 7

(a) Er sollte hinter der Frau die Treppe hochgehen. (b) Er sollte bei der Begrüßung die Hand nicht in der Hosentasche lassen. (c) Er sollte im Restaurant nicht mit dem Handy telefonieren. (d) Er sollte mehr körperliche Distanz halten.

EXERCISE 9

(a) die CDU/CSU (b) die FDP (c) die SPD (d) die Grünen (e) der Bundeskanzler (f) der Bundespräsident

EXERCISE 10

(a) Grünen, weil sie die Umwelt schützen wollen. (b) FDP, weil er die beiden großen Parteien nicht besonders mag. (c) CDU, weil sie eine gute Familienpolitik hat. (d) SPD, weil er ihre Sozialpolitik gut findet.

EXERCISE 11

1 Nordsee 2 Schleswig-Holstein 3 Ostsee 4 Düsseldorf 5 Sachsen 6 Stuttgart 7 Schwarzwald 8 Bayern 9 Zugspitze

EXERCISE 12

(a) Ich war krank. (b) Er hatte ein Auto. (c) Wir waren im Kino. (d) Waren Sie in Berlin? (e) Sie hatte ein Problem. (f) Hatten Sie eine Karte?

EXERCISE 13

(a) Ich lernte Deutsch. (b) Du glaubtest es. (c) Er hörte den Hund. (d) Wir bauten den Tisch.

EXERCISE 14

(a) Das kleine Glas ist teuer. (b) Die freundlichen Leute sind aus Ulm. (c) Die langen Kleider sind nicht billig. (d) Das große Geschäft ist um die Ecke.

EXERCISE 15

(a) Er kauft den französischen Wein. (b) Martin will den neuen Tisch. (c) Ich möchte (or: will) das kalte Bier trinken. (d) Sie besucht die deutsche Familie. (e) Die Frau singt die schönen Lieder (or: Songs).

EXERCISE 16

(a) Wir geben dem kleinen Mädchen das Buch. (b) Sie bringt dem alten Mann eine Flasche Wein. (c) Ich gebe der guten Frau ein Geschenk. (d) Sie geben den kleinen Kindern Geld.

EXERCISE 17

(a) Frau Kropf (b) Zell (c) 56 (d) 4 (e) coffee (f) nice supper with grilled meats and various salads. Transcript: M Jetzt sind wir bei unserem Geburtstagskind des Tages – das sollte sein: die liebe Frau Kropf – ist das richtig? – in Zell? K Ja, das ist richtig. M Frau Kropf, einen schönen guten Morgen erst mal. K Guten Morgen, Herr Metzler. M Wie alt werden Sie heute? 56? K 56! M Nee, ich find' das nett, so 'ne junge Oma. Wieviel Enkel haben Sie? K Vier. Vier Enkelkinder hab' ich. M Vier Enkelkinder schon! K Ja. M Und jetzt erzählen Sie mal 'n bißchen: Das muß doch 'n großes Fest werden. K Ja, am Nachmittag gibt es Kaffee, und am Abend gibt's dann 'n schönes Abendbrot mit Grillbraten und verschiedene Salate ... M Sehen Sie, das ist wichtig, nicht? K Ja. So, und am Nachmittag kommen dann meine Kinder mit Enkelkindern. M Das wird ein richtiges Familienfest werden? K Das wird 'n Familienfest, ja.

6 ROUTINES

WHAT YOU WILL LEARN

▶ talking about your daily life
▶ describing your work
▶ discussing a typical evening
▶ you will also read about four sources of irritation to the average German

POINTS TO REMEMBER

● conversation starters: (**Wie**) **gefällt Ihnen ...? Es gefällt mir gut!**
● table talk: **Darf ich Ihnen ... anbieten? Das schmeckt gut. Ich bin Vegetarier(in)**
● congratulations: **Herzlichen Glückwunsch! Alles Gute!**
● talking politics: **die Partei; ich wähle die** (**CDU, SPD, FDP, Grünen**); **die Bundesregierung, die Bundesrepublik, der Bundeskanzler, der Bundespräsident; der Umweltschutz**
● imperfect tense of **haben** (**ich hatte, du hattest, er/sie/es hatte, wir hatten, ihr hattet, sie/Sie hatten**) and **sein** (**ich war, du warst, er/sie/es war, wir waren, ihr wart, sie/Sie waren**)

BEFORE YOU BEGIN

By now you should be well acquainted with the 'aha' experience – when you come across a linguistic feature that used to puzzle you and is suddenly making sense. One example might be the word order in sentences starting with **wenn** or **weil**. Take a quick look back at a Conversation in one of the earlier units that you used to find tricky and see what happens now!

CONVERSATION 1

The house-husband

LISTEN FOR...

Hausmann	house-husband
Tagesablauf	daily routine
frühstücken	to have breakfast

Helmut

Ich bin Hausmann. Mein Tagesablauf sieht ungefähr so aus; wir frühstücken morgens gemeinsam. Meine Frau fährt dann zur Schule. Sie ist Lehrerin. Ich habe zwei Kinder, einen dreijährigen Sohn und eine zweijährige Tochter. Um neun Uhr bringe ich meinen Sohn zum Kindergarten, gehe dann mit meiner Tochter spazieren, beim schlechten Wetter in den Zoo, oder in Geschäfte, einkaufen, das ist ganz vom Wetter abhängig. (Ich) bereite mittags etwas zum Essen vor. Je nachdem, wann meine Frau zurückkommt, essen wir gemeinsam, oder ich esse mit meinen Kindern allein.

der Hausmann house-husband; **die Hausfrau** housewife

der Tagesablauf daily routine

ungefähr approximately

aussehen (sep.) to look like; **er sieht gut aus** he looks good.

frühstücken to have breakfast

gemeinsam together

sie ist Lehrerin she is a teacher. When you're saying what someone does for a living there is no definite article in the German; similarly: **mein Mann ist Bankier** (or **Banker**) my husband is a banker.

dreijährig three-year-old; **zweijährig** two-year-old

um neun Uhr bringe ich meinen Sohn zum Kindergarten at nine o'clock I take (lit. bring!) my son to the kindergarten

das ist vom Wetter abhängig that is dependent on the weather; **abhängen** to depend; **das Baby ist von der Mutter abhängig** the baby is dependent on the mother.

ich bereite etwas zum Essen vor I prepare something to eat; **vorbereiten** (sep.) to prepare; **ich bereite die Hochzeit vor** I prepare for the wedding.

je nachdem, wann meine Frau zurückkommt depending on when my wife returns. **Je nachdem** (depending on, that depends) is an idiom best learnt by heart. It can also stand on its own: **Kommst du morgen schwimmen? Das weiß ich noch nicht. Je nachdem.** Are you coming swimming tomorrow? I don't know yet. It depends.

As a teacher, Helmut's wife could well finish teaching at lunchtime depending on her timetable that day. Most German schools are morning only and teachers can leave as soon as they have finished.

1 Here's an abbreviated account of Helmut's day in English, but it's not quite accurate. Spot the five mistakes and correct them.

We have breakfast together and then my wife goes off
to school. At eight o'clock I take my four-year-old
son to kindergarten. Then I go for a walk with my
daughter. She is three years old. If the weather is
good we go to the zoo or we go shopping. At lunchtime,
we eat out, sometimes with my wife if she is back from
work in time, sometimes just me and the children.

Answers p. 96

2 Here's a receipt Helmut brought back from one of his shopping trips. Study it and answer the questions below.

```
        MODEHAUS SOMMER
88212 RAVENSBURG 0751/36900
        KIRCHSTRASSE 2-6

        ES BEDIENTE SIE
    809    FRAU REUTER

KINDER-JEANS            59.90
6910 2

TOTAL                   59.90

BAR                     60.00
RUECKGELD                0.10

VIELEN DANK FÜR IHREN EINKAUF
UMTAUSCH: NUR BEI VORLAGE VON
KASSENBON UND WARENETIKETTEN!
BON  DATUM  ZEIT  BED  KASS
8215 26.05.98 16:33 0011 0011
```

a What did he buy?

_____

b How much was it?

_____

c How did he pay: cash or cheque?

_____

d Who served him?

_____

e What's the name of the shop?

_____

Answers p. 96

3 Your turn to speak. Describe Helmut's day from his wife's point of view. Hans will prompt you, as usual.

4 Housewife. On the recording, Margit talks about her typical day. How does she say the following phrases in German?

VOCABULARY

putzen	to clean
während	during, while
weinen	to cry

a I'm a housewife.

_____

b My husband is a building worker.

_____

c At the moment he has no job.

_____

d So I work three times a week as a cleaner.

_____

e Normally I get up two or three times a night.

_____

f When I come back I do the housework.

_____

g My husband goes for a walk with the baby.

_____

h I cook lunch while the baby is asleep.

_____

i On two afternoons a week I work in the supermarket at the till.

_____

_____

Answers and full transcript p. 96

5 **Im Klartext**. In other words. Just in case you want to break out of your daily grind, what do the horoscopes have to say? Read the extracts and decide which statement applies to which sign.

Widder:
Sie sind von Kopf bis Fuß auf Liebe eingestellt.

Skorpion:
Sie haben auch Appetit auf fremde Töpfe. Vorsicht! Sie könnten sich die Finger verbrennen!

Waage:
Wenn Sie fremdgehen wollen, kommen Sie nicht weit. Bleiben Sie daheim, bei Hausmannskost!

Wassermann:
Sie schwimmen in einem Meer von unerfüllten Wünschen. Kommen Sie an Land und sehen Sie die Welt mal etwas trockener!

a Your life is full of wishes and dreams. You need to be more realistic!

sign: _____

b If you want some fun on the side, you won't get very far! Better stick with what you've got.

sign: _____

c You've only got one thing on your mind!

sign: _____

d You too are looking further afield, but careful, you might burn your fingers.

sign: _____

Answers p. 96

CONVERSATION 2

An atypical routine – the journalist

Biba

Normalerweise steh' ich so um neun auf. Der Wecker klingelt schon eine halbe Stunde vorher. Dann mach' ich ein bißchen Frühgymnastik, nehm' eine Dusche, höre Radio, les' die Zeitung und mache nebenher das Frühstück.

Danach setz' ich mich an die Arbeit und schreibe einen Artikel. Oder ich gehe in die Bibliothek, wenn ich noch Literatur brauche. Mittags gehe ich dann einkaufen, mach' die Hausarbeit: aufräumen, staubsaugen, waschen – und dann koch' ich mir noch schnell was Kleines.

Nachmittags schreibe ich dann weiter oder lese etwas oder denke nach, was ich als Nächstes schreiben werde. Und wenn mir nichts mehr einfällt, geh' ich erst mal spazieren.

Abends hab' ich dann meistens Termine. Entweder ich muß ins Theater gehen, oder in eine Ausstellung, über die ich dann am nächsten Tag schreiben muß.

der Wecker   alarm clock
klingeln   to ring
vorher   before that
die Frühgymnastik   morning exercises
die Dusche   shower
hören   to hear, to listen to
nebenher   at the same time
danach setz' ich mich an die Arbeit   after that I sit (myself) down to work. **sich setzen** to sit down; more about **sich** in Grammar, this unit. **Bitte setzen Sie sich!** Please be seated! But remember: **ich sitze auf dem Stuhl** I sit on the chair (I am already seated).
schreiben   to write
der Artikel   article
die Bibliothek   library
brauchen   to need
aufräumen (sep.)   to clear up; **ich räume morgen auf** I will clear up tomorrow.
staubsaugen   to vacuum; **ich staubsauge** I vacuum; **der Staub** dust; **saugen** to suck.
weiterschreiben (sep.)   to go on writing: **sie schreibt den Brief weiter** she goes on writing the letter.
nachdenken (sep.)   to think about, to ponder: **er denkt nach** he ponders.
was ich als Nächstes schreiben werde   what I will write next

wenn mir nichts mehr einfällt   if I have no more ideas; **einfallen** (sep.) to occur to (of ideas, inspiration): **mir fiel plötzlich ein, daß ...** I suddenly thought that ... **Fällt dir nichts ein?** Can't you think of anything?
der Termin   appointment (business or doctor); engagement; booking. A very useful word: **ich habe einen Termin beim Arzt** I have a doctor's appointment.
die Ausstellung   exhibition
über die ich schreiben muß   about which I have to write

Unit 6   Routines

6 Translate into German:

a The alarm clock rings at seven.

_____

b I get up at half past seven.

_____

c I take a shower and listen to the radio.

_____

d Then I make breakfast and read the paper.

_____

e I go to the library or I go for a walk.

_____

f After that I sit down to work.

_____

g In the afternoon I have lots of appointments.

_____

h In the evening I go to the theatre or to an exhibition.

_____

Answers p. 96

7 **Der emanzipierte Mann –**
the emancipated man ….
How many men are really
prepared to share the
housework? Listen to the
radio extract on the
recording, and tick the
correct boxes below –
sometimes you can tick both boxes.

VOCABULARY	
das Haushaltsgerät	household appliance
höchstens	at most
die Gleichberechtigung	equal rights
aufhören (sep.)	to stop
abwaschen (sep.)	to wash up

a Wieviel Prozent der Männer helfen ihren Frauen bei der Hausarbeit?

12 % ☐ 20 % ☐

b Im typisch deutschen Haushalt ist es wie ...

vor 1000 Jahren. ☐ vor 100 Jahren. ☐

c Der Mann hilft höchstens mal beim ...

Kochen. ☐ Staubsaugen. ☐

d Manchmal hilft er vielleicht auch beim ...

Abwaschen. ☐ Fensterputzen. ☐

e Aber eines macht er ganz sicher nicht:

Aufräumen. ☐ Putzen. ☐

Answers and transcript p. 96

8 Desperate! Uschi has a totally different problem with her boyfriend Maxi. Study her letter to her friend Vera, then complete the dialogue below, where Vera's boyfriend Hans compares notes with Maxi. What would Maxi say?

Liebe Vera

Was soll ich machen? Mein Maxi hat sich so verändert. Früher war er ein Langschläfer, jetzt steht er schon um 6 Uhr auf und macht Yoga. Danach nimmt er ein kaltes (!) Bad und meditiert für eine ganze Stunde. Dann macht er für mich das Frühstück – das hat er früher auch nie gemacht! Er selbst ißt kein Frühstück. Erst am Mittag ißt er dann braunen Reis mit Gemüse. Dazu trinkt er nur heißes Wasser. Du weißt ja, früher hat er immer kräftig gefrühstückt und zu Mittag entweder einen Hamburger oder ein paar Würstchen gegessen und eine Flasche Bier dazu getrunken. Plötzlich hilft er auch im Haushalt – aber viel zu viel, das geht mir schon auf die Nerven! Er kocht, er wäscht ab, er putzt, er staubsaugt, er räumt auf. Ich habe praktisch keine Hausarbeit mehr. Wie findest Du das?!

Bitte schreibe bald zurück,

Deine Uschi

VOCABULARY

der Langschläfer   late riser (lit. long sleeper)
kräftig   here: heartily

Hans	Maxi
a Ich stehe erst um zehn Uhr auf.	_____
b Ich lese nach dem Aufstehen die Zeitung.	_____
c Ich nehme immer ein heißes Bad.	_____
d Meine Freundin macht das Frühstück für mich!	_____
e Ich esse immer viel zum Frühstück!	_____
f Mittags esse ich immer Steak mit Pommes und trinke ein großes Bier.	_____
g Ich helfe nie im Haushalt.	_____

Answers p. 96

9 Your turn to speak – with a difference. This time you are telling Johannes about Biba's morning. Turn to the recording where Hans will prompt you. You'll need phrases such as:

steht ... auf/macht/geht/hört/liest ...

Frühgymnastik/Dusche/Radio/Zeitung ...

Unit 6   Routines

CONVERSATION 3

Relaxing evenings ...

LISTEN FOR...

Sessel	armchair
sich entspannen	to relax
Nachbarn	neighbours

Horst

Ich komm' so gegen sechs Uhr abends nach Hause. Dann setz' ich mich erst mal in den Sessel, leg' die Beine hoch, trink' ein Bier, les' die Zeitung, will mich entspannen, so gut das eben geht, wenn man Kinder hat. Dann helf' ich meiner Frau beim Kochen – nicht immer! Manchmal helfen ihr auch schon die Kinder. Am Wochenende koch' ich auch mal selbst. Das mach' ich recht gerne, zur Abwechslung. Wir reden über alles Mögliche: die Kinder, die Nachbarn, Ärger bei der Arbeit, Ärger in der Schule.

Heide

Und nach dem Essen? Erst waschen wir mit den Kindern das Geschirr ab, und dann gibt's Fernsehen. Manchmal spielen wir auch Karten oder Halma, oder „Mensch ärgere dich nicht" – nicht so oft, weil ich mich dann immer schrecklich aufrege. Das hängt sehr vom Fernsehprogramm ab, was wir machen. Natürlich gibt's auch Streit über das Programm. Ich interessiere mich mehr für Politik, mein Mann dagegen für Sport. Und die Kinder wiederum sehen lieber Unterhaltungsfilme oder eine Musikshow.

der Sessel armchair

leg' die Beine hoch put my feet up; **das Bein** leg; **hochlegen** (sep.) to put up (lit. lay high).

sich entspannen to relax; **ich entspanne mich** I relax (**sich/mich** is not translated, see Grammar, this unit). **Bitte entspannen Sie sich!** Please relax!

dann helf' ich meiner Frau then I help my wife; **helfen** (to help) takes the dative. **ich helfe dem Mann** I help the man; **ich will der Frau helfen** I want to help the woman; **manchmal helfen ihr die Kinder** Sometimes the children help her; **ihr** (her) is the dative of **sie**. More in Grammar, Unit 8.

auch schon (lit. even already): filler words with little extra meaning.

zur Abwechslung for a change; **die Abwechslung** change

über alles Mögliche about all sorts of things

der Nachbar neighbour

der Ärger trouble; irritation; **sich ärgern** to be irritated, to get angry; **ich ärgere mich über die Schule** I am irritated with school.

mit den Kindern with the children; certain prepositions such as **mit** take the dative: **ich spiele mit dem kleinen Mädchen** I play with the little girl; **ich spiele mit ihr** I play with her. More in Grammar, this unit.

das Geschirr (singular only!) the dishes; **abwaschen** (sep.) to wash up

Karten spielen to play cards

„Mensch ärgere dich nicht" ludo (lit. don't get angry)

sich aufregen (sep.) to get upset; **ich rege mich auf** I get upset

das hängt ... ab that depends; **abhängen** (sep.) to depend; remember **abhängig** (Conversation 1)

das Fernsehprogramm TV schedule

was wir machen what we do; **machen** is often translated as 'to do'.

der Streit argument; **(sich) streiten** to argue

ich interessiere mich für ... I am interested in ...

dagegen here: on the other hand

wiederum yet again

die Unterhaltung entertainment

10

Time after work. What do Horst and his family do? Fill in the correct verbs without looking at Conversation 3.

a Horst _____ gegen sechs nach Hause.

b Er _____ sich in den Sessel.

c Er _____ die Beine hoch.

d Er _____ ein Bier.

e Er _____ die Zeitung.

f Er _____ seiner Frau beim Kochen.

g Er _____ mit den Kindern das Geschirr ab.

h Er _____ mit den Kindern Halma.

i Und dann _____ 's Fernsehen.

j Er _____ sich für Sport.

k Seine Kinder _____ lieber Unterhaltungsfilme oder eine Musikshow.

Answers p. 96

11

Word puzzles – stick them together! You should come up with at least 8 jumbo words.

HAUS BERECHTIGUNG KINDER ABLAUF SHOW MANN ENDE
GARTEN TAGES MUSIK WOCHEN FERNSEH FRÜH GLEICH
PROGRAMM GYMNASTIK UNTERHALTUNGS FILM

Suggestions p. 96 Example: **der Hausmann**

12

What happens if you do too much work? Here's an extract from a medical journal. You can listen to it on the recording too. Then work out the German for the English words below, and answer the questions, in English.

BURN OUT – AUSGEBRANNT!

DIE GROSSE KRISE ...

Machen Sie zu viele Überstunden? Arbeiten Sie immer mit voller Power? Irgendwann einmal sind Ihre Batterien leer. Sie können nicht mehr. Sie fühlen sich ausgebrannt. Sie können nicht mehr schlafen. Sie können sich nicht mehr konzentrieren, Sie haben Kopfschmerzen, Magenschmerzen, Infekte. Experten sprechen von „Burn out".

Erste Priorität: Nehmen Sie sich mehr Zeit – für sich selbst und für Ihre Familie. Machen Sie spontan ein paar Tage Urlaub, machen Sie einen Yogakurs, machen Sie Entspannungsübungen. Und dann: reden Sie mit der Familie, mit Freunden, mit ihrem Chef. Ändern Sie Ihr Leben, ändern Sie Ihren Arbeitsstil. Denken Sie daran, ein leerer Mensch kann überhaupt nichts mehr geben.

a overtime

b flat (of batteries), empty

c headache

d stomach ache

e relaxation exercises

f style of working

1 What are the symptoms of burn out?

Answers p. 96 2 How do you get burnt out? 3 What can you do about it?

13

Your turn to speak – about your own burn out. Keep your book open.

KEY WORDS AND PHRASES

Morgens

der Tagesablauf
der Hausmann/die Hausfrau
Der Wecker klingelt
Wir frühstücken gemeinsam
Ich ...
   stehe auf
   nehme eine Dusche
   lese (die) Zeitung
   höre Radio
   mache Frühgymnastik

In the morning

daily routine
house-husband/housewife
The alarm rings
We have breakfast together
I ...
   get up
   take a shower
   read the paper
   listen to the radio
   do (my) morning exercises

Mittags

Ich mache die Hausarbeit

staubsaugen
aufräumen
kochen
abwaschen
putzen

als nächstes
meistens
manchmal

At lunchtime

I do the housework

to vacuum
to clear up
to cook
to wash up
to clean

next
mostly
sometimes

Nachmittags

Ich ...
   gehe spazieren
   gehe in die Bibliothek
   habe Termine

In the afternoon

I ...
   go for a walk
   go to the library
   have appointments

Abends

gegen Abend
nach dem Abendessen
Ich ...
   lege die Beine hoch
   entspanne mich
Wir ...
   waschen ab
   spielen Karten
Es gibt ...
   Streit
   Ärger bei der Arbeit/in der Schule

In the evening

towards evening
after supper
I ...
   put my feet up
   relax
We ...
   wash up
   play cards
There are/is ...
   arguments
   trouble at work/school

Reflexive pronouns

■ These can be found in English phrases such as 'he washes himself', 'I ask myself.' In German, they crop up more often and are not always translated into English.

sich entspannen (to relax)

ich	entspanne	mich	I relax
du	entspannst	dich	you relax
er/sie/es	entspannt	sich	he/she/it relaxes
wir	entspannen	uns	we relax
ihr	entspannt	euch	you relax
sie/Sie	entspannen	sich	they/you relax

■ Position: in sentences with two verbs the reflexive pronoun remains in third position.

Ich	habe	mich	entspannt.	I have relaxed.
Du	hast	dich	entspannt.	You have relaxed.
Sie	müssen	sich	entspannen.	You have to relax.
Er	kann	sich	nicht richtig entspannen.	He can't relax properly.

■ In simple questions the reflexive pronoun remains in third position.

| Haben | Sie | sich | entspannt? | Have you relaxed? |
| Entspannen | Sie | sich? | | Are you relaxing? |

Here is a list of similar verbs:

sich waschen	to wash oneself
sich an etwas erinnern	to remember something
sich ausruhen (sep.)	to rest
sich für etwas interessieren	to be interested in something
sich aufregen (sep.)	to get annoyed
sich setzen	to sit down
sich über etwas ärgern	to be irritated about something

14 Translate into German:

a He washes (himself). _____

b We remember. _____

c She sits down. _____

d They rest. _____

e He is interested in theatre. _____

f They are irritated. _____

g Has she relaxed? _____

Answers p. 96

Prepositions

Prepositions are important little words such as **an**, **zu**, **in**, **nach**.

Hans fährt nach Ulm. Hans goes to Ulm.

Lina geht ins Kino. Lina goes to the cinema.

Certain prepositions take certain cases. It's best to learn them by heart. Before reading on, remind yourself of the cases in Grammar, Units 4 and 5.

■ Prepositions *that always take the accusative case*:

bis	(until)	**gegen**	(against, towards)
durch	(through)	**ohne**	(without)
für	(for)	**um**	(round, about)

Wir gehen durch den Wald.   We walk through the forest.

Das Geschenk ist für den alten Mann.   The present is for the old man.

Remember: The word for 'the' in the accusative is **die** with feminine singular and all plural nouns, **das** with neuter nouns singular and **den** with masculine nouns singular.

15 Complete the sentences with the correct definite articles.

a   Sie spielt gegen _____ ganze Familie.

b   Ohne _____ Adresse kann ich die Boutique nicht finden.

c   Ich interessiere mich für _____ alten Bücher.

d   Die Touristen sind durch _____ halbe Stadt gelaufen.

e   Er macht das Essen für _____ kranken Sohn.

Answers p. 96

■ Prepositions *that always take the dative case*:

aus	(from)	**gegenüber**	(opposite)
bei	(at)	**mit**	(with)
nach	(to, after)	**seit**	(since)
von	(from)	**zu**	(to, at)

Remember: The word for 'the' in the dative is **dem** for masculine and neuter nouns singular, **der** for feminine nouns singular, and **den** for all plural nouns.

zu + dem = zum: **Er geht zum Bahnhof.**   He goes to the station.

zu + der = zur: **Sie geht zur Post.**   She goes to the post office.

von + dem = vom: **Sie fahren vom Markt ab.**   They leave from the market.

bei + dem = beim: **Ich kaufe Brot beim Bäcker.**   I buy bread at the baker's.

Hana fährt mit der Freundin weg.   Hana is going away with the girl friend.

Sie singt das Lied von der Erde.   She sings the Song of the Earth.

16 Complete the sentences using definite articles (+ preposition if necessary).

a   Sie wohnt immer noch bei _____ Mutter.

b   Ich habe die Geschichte von _____ Nachbarin gehört.

c   Die Bank liegt gegenüber _____ Alten Rathaus.

d   Der Wind kommt aus _____ Süden.

Answers p. 96

■ Prepositions *that take either the accusative or the dative*:

an (at/on)	**auf** (on/at)	**hinter** (behind)
in (in/at/into)	**neben** (near)	**über** (over)
unter (under)	**vor** (in front of)	**zwischen** (between)

(Remember **in das** = **ins**, **in** + **dem** = **im**, **an** + **das** = **ans**, **an** + **dem** = **am**.)

This seems the trickiest category – however, the rule is straightforward:

■ If the preposition indicates the direction something is moving in, use the accusative:

Ich gehe in die Schule.   I go to school.
Er klettert auf den Berg.   He climbs up the mountain.

■ If the preposition shows location rather than direction, use the dative:
Ich bin in der Schule.   I am at school.
Er ist auf dem Berg.   He is on (top of) the mountain.

17   Complete the sentences with the appropriate definite articles.

a   Helga ist in _____ Schule.

b   Martin geht in _____ Schule.

c   Karin steigt auf _____ Berg.

d   Peter steht auf _____ Tisch.

e   Der Bahnhof ist neben _____ Post.

f   Der Garten ist hinter _____ Haus.

g   Das Kind läuft hinter _____ Haus.

h   Das Geschenk liegt unter _____ Weihnachtsbaum.

Answers p. 96

18   The ultimate challenge: mixed prepositions. Given the very complex rules governing their usage, this is an optional exercise perhaps best suited to those who enjoy puzzling things out. If you want to have a go we suggest you refer back to the previous Grammar pages. Complete the sentences with the appropriate definite articles.

a   Maria fährt in _____ Stadt.

b   Karl sitzt auf _____ Bank.

c   Hannes geht durch _____ Straßen.

d   Die Post liegt gegenüber _____ Bahnhof.

e   Das Hotel ist zwischen _____ Rathaus und _____ Post.

f   Der Hund sitzt unter _____ Tisch.

g   Das Geschenk ist für _____ Baby!

Answers p. 96

AND FINALLY...

19 **Ärgerlich, nicht?** Daily niggles ... According to the magazine *Brigitte*, these are the main sources of irritation in everyday life. ... Find some snappy English captions.

(a)

Viel Verpackung, wenig drin

(b)

Knöpfe an neuen Jacketts, die sofort abgehen

(c)

Slalomlaufen zwischen Hundehaufen

(d)

FAHRzeuge, die auf GEHwegen stehen

Suggestions p. 96

20 **„Ich ärgere mich über das Wetter!"** Your turn to speak up and say what annoys you. Here's a selection: **die Nachbarn**, **die Arbeit**, **die Kinder**, **die Politiker**, **die Preise**, **das Fernsehen** ... Turn to the recording, where Hans will tell you what to do.

21 Write down your daily agenda and describe it to your partner. Take it in turns to ask each other questions, such as:

Wann stehst du auf?
Was machst du nach dem Aufstehen?

EXERCISE 1

Corrected: At *nine* o'clock I take my *three*-year-old son to kindergarten. ... She is *two* years old. If the weather is *bad*, we go to the zoo or we go shopping. .... At lunchtime *I prepare a meal and eat* (*in*) ...

EXERCISE 2

(a) children's jeans   (b) 59,90 DM   (c) cash: he handed over 60 Mark and got 10 Pfennig back
(d) Frau Reuter   (e) Modehaus Sommer

EXERCISE 4

(a) Ich bin Hausfrau.   (b) Mein Mann ist Bauarbeiter.   (c) Im Moment hat er keinen Job und (d) so arbeite ich dreimal die Woche als Putzfrau. Wir haben ein kleines Baby, es ist vier Monate alt. (e) Normalerweise stehe ich zwei bis dreimal in der Nacht auf, weil das Baby weint, manchmal steht auch mein Mann auf und gibt ihm die Flasche. Wir frühstücken so um acht, oder neun, dann gehe ich zum Einkaufen, mein Mann liest die Zeitung. (f) Wenn ich zurückkomme, mach' ich die Hausarbeit,   (g) mein Mann geht mit dem Baby spazieren.   (h) Ich koche das Mittagessen, während das Baby schläft, meistens essen wir etwas Warmes zu Mittag. Am Nachmittag paßt mein Mann auf das Baby auf, und ich gehe zum Putzen. (i) An zwei Nachmittagen in der Woche arbeite ich im Supermarkt an der Kasse.

EXERCISE 5

(a) Aquarius (Wassermann)   (b) Libra (Waage)
(c) Aries (Widder)   (d) Scorpio (Skorpion)

EXERCISE 6

(a) Der Wecker klingelt um sieben.   (b) Ich stehe um halb acht auf.   (c) Ich nehme eine Dusche und höre Radio.   (d) Dann mache ich Frühstück und lese die Zeitung.   (e) Ich gehe in die Bibliothek oder ich gehe spazieren.   (f) Danach setze ich mich an die Arbeit.   (g) Nachmittags habe ich viele Termine.   (h) Abends gehe ich ins Theater oder in eine Ausstellung.

EXERCISE 7

(a) 12 %   (b) vor 100 Jahren   (c) Staubsaugen
(d) Abwaschen   (e) Putzen.

EXERCISE 8

(a) Ich stehe schon um sechs Uhr auf.   (b) Ich mache nach dem Aufstehen Yoga.   (c) Ich nehme immer ein kaltes Bad.   (d) Ich mache das Frühstück für meine Freundin.   (e) Ich esse kein

Frühstück.   (f) Mittags esse ich braunen Reis mit Gemüse und trinke nur heißes Wasser.   (g) Ich wasche ab, koche, putze, staubsauge, räume auf ...

EXERCISE 10

(a) kommt   (b) setzt   (c) legt   (d) trinkt   (e) liest
(f) hilft   (g) wäscht   (h) spielt   (i) gibt
(j) interessiert   (k) sehen.

EXERCISE 11

Suggestions: die Gleichberechtigung; der Kindergarten; das Fernsehprogramm; die Unterhaltungsshow; die Musikshow; die Frühgymnastik; der Tagesablauf; das Wochenende; der Musikfilm; der Unterhaltungsfilm, die Unterhaltungsmusik, das Tagesprogramm ...

EXERCISE 12

(a) Überstunden   (b) leer   (c) Kopfschmerzen
(d) Magenschmerzen   (e) Entspannungsübungen
(f) Arbeitsstil   1 insomnia, can't concentrate, head and stomach aches, infections   2 too much overtime, working at full throttle all the time   3 find time for yourself and your family, take a few days off spontaneously, go to yoga and relaxation classes, change life style, talk to boss, family and friends.

EXERCISE 14

(a) Er wäscht sich.   (b) Wir erinnern uns.
(c) Sie setzt sich.   (d) Sie ruhen sich aus.
(e) Er interessiert sich für Theater.
(f) Sie ärgern sich.   (g) Hat sie sich entspannt?

EXERCISE 15

(a) die   (b) die   (c) die   (d) die   (e) den

EXERCISE 16

(a) der   (b) der   (c) dem   (d) dem

EXERCISE 17

(a) der   (b) die   (c) den   (d) dem   (e) der
(f) dem   (g) das   (h) dem

EXERCISE 18

(a) die   (b) der   (c) die   (d) dem   (e) dem; der
(f) dem   (g) das

EXERCISE 19

(a) More wrapping than contents   (b) New jackets – buttons off   (c) Dog dirt slalom   (d) Cars rule supreme.

7 MEDIA

**WHAT YOU
WILL LEARN**

▶ selecting a newspaper

▶ saying what you think of radio or television

▶ choosing from your radio or TV listings

▶ you will also hear more about the newspaper scene in Germany

**POINTS TO
REMEMBER**

● routine activities: **ich stehe auf, nehme eine Dusche, lese Zeitung, höre Radio, mache Frühgymnastik** ...

● housework: **staubsaugen, aufräumen, kochen, abwaschen, putzen**

● in the evening: **ich entspanne mich, lege die Beine hoch, wir spielen Karten**

● verbs with **sich**: **sich entspannen, sich setzen, sich aufregen**: ich **entspanne mich, wir setzen uns, Setzen Sie sich! Er regt sich auf** ...

**BEFORE YOU
BEGIN**

Some words and phrases in this unit are rather long and somewhat daunting to start with. Fortunately, most of them can be split up quite easily into smaller segments of meaning which will make them a lot less difficult to recognise and remember. **Ausländische Zeitungen** sounds quite a mouthful, for example, but **ausländisch** is much more readily accessible if you realise that it means quite literally out-landish – i.e. foreign. Try and learn some phrases as whole chunks after you've analysed their meaning, then repeat them again and again until you know them by heart. There are several exercises throughout this unit specifically geared at making you lift longer and larger bits from German passages and re-use them yourself. The satisfaction of seasoning your conversation with such impressive ingredients is well worth the effort.

Getting a magazine

Ruth	Ich möchte gerne eine Frauenzeitung. Was haben Sie denn alles?
Frau Huber	*Frau im Spiegel, Neue Post, Tina* ...
Ruth	Haben Sie eine mit Mode bitte?
Frau Huber	Ja, haben wir da – *Neue Mode* oder *Burda* ...
Ruth	Was kostet die *Burda*?
Frau Huber	Vier Mark fünfzig.
Ruth	Dann nehme ich die *Burda*. Und haben Sie auch ausländische Zeitungen?
Frau Huber	Nein, leider nicht – nur das *Reader Digest*, in Englisch.
Ruth	Und wo kann ich 'ne ausländische Zeitung bekommen?
Frau Huber	In der Stadt: in der Buchhandlung oder am Hauptbahnhof.

LISTEN FOR...

Mode	fashion
ausländische Zeitungen	foreign papers

Frauenzeitung women's magazine; **die Zeitung** usually means 'newspaper'; more usual words for magazine are **die Zeitschrift**, or **die Illustrierte** or **das Magazin**

Frau im Spiegel (lit. woman in the mirror), ***Neue Post*, *Tina*** titles of women's magazines

Mode fashion; **die Modezeitschrift** fashion magazine. Other types of magazine you might look for are **die Wochenzeitschrift** or **das Wochenmagazin** weekly magazine; **das Sportmagazin** sport magazine; **das politische Magazin** political magazine; **die**

Fachzeitschrift special interest magazine. ***Der Spiegel*** is the biggest and best-known political magazine; ***Focus*** is also becoming very popular; ***Stern*** is a well-known general magazine, whilst ***Brigitte*** is a popular women's magazine.

'ne (= **eine**) **ausländische Zeitung** a foreign newspaper; **im Ausland** abroad

die Buchhandlung bookshop

1 Memory test. Try this exercise without looking at the Conversation.

a dort kann man ausländische Zeitungen kaufen

H				6	1					

b so heißt eine Modezeitschrift

		2	

c Frauenname und Frauenzeitschrift

7	3			

d dort kann man Bücher kaufen

B									4

e eine Frauenzeitschrift heißt „Frau im

S		5		8

The letters 1–8 will give you the name of a popular women's magazine in Germany.

Answers p. 112

1	2	3	4	5	6	7	8

2 Here's a text on German magazines:

uf dem deutschsprachigen Markt gibt es eine große Auswahl an Zeitschriften, von der „Autofachzeitschrift ADAC-Motorwelt" bis hin zu „Wohnen im eigenen Heim". Man findet Zeitschriften für Teenager, zum Beispiel „Bravo", dann gibt es Frauenzeitschriften wie „Brigitte" oder die deutsche Ausgabe von „Cosmopolitan"; auch Computer-, Hobby- und Sportmagazine sind sehr beliebt. Und dann kann man natürlich die Programmzeitschriften kaufen: sie informieren über Fernseh- und Radioprogramme.

Look at the following magazine titles and guess which magazine category they fall into.

Echo der Frau, Carina, Wohnidee, Super-TV, Zuhause Wohnen, Ein Herz für Tiere, Freundin, Mein schöner Garten, Kicker, baumagazin, Bravo

a teenager _____

b sport _____

c women _____

d gardening _____

e animals _____

f home _____

Answers p. 112 **g** radio and television listings _____

3 Your turn to speak and recap on some basic magazine words. Here are some phrases you'll need:

ich interessiere mich für ...
englische/ausländische Zeitung(en)
Magazin(e)

CONVERSATION 2

Henning and Silke prefer radio to television. Why?

Henning	Weil mir die Reporter besser gefallen, und weil ich die Sendungen interessanter finde.
Biba	Welche Sendungen hörst du am liebsten?
Henning	Die Single Hit Parade am Sonntag.
Biba	Und was noch?
Henning	Die Sportreportagen.
Biba	Und welche Sendungen hören Sie im Radio am liebsten?
Silke	Ich höre am liebsten Regionalsendungen und zwar für unseren Bereich Südfunk Stuttgart, weil da die Musik sehr gut ist. Die gefällt mir. Es wird auch Politik gesendet und aktuelle Beiträge.

LISTEN FOR...

Sendungen	programmes
Sportreportagen	sports reports
Musik	music

weil mir die Reporter besser gefallen
because I prefer the reporters; **gefallen** to like. Remember **es gefällt mir** (Unit 5): **die Musik gefällt mir** I like the music. **Gefällt Ihnen das Kleid?** Do you like the dress? **Gefallen Ihnen die Kleider?** Do you like the dresses?

die Sportreportage the sports report; similarly **die aktuelle Reportage** or **der aktuelle Beitrag** report on current affairs

die Regionalsendung regional programme; **die Sendung** programme, broadcast; **senden** to send, to broadcast

und zwar that is to say

der Bereich, die Region region

es wird auch Politik gesendet politics is broadcast as well; more on **wird** in Grammar, this unit.

4 Traffic news ... Listen to the radio extract on the recording and mark the trouble spots in the Stuttgart region.

VOCABULARY

die Meldung	piece of news
die Verkehrslage	traffic situation
die Richtung	direction
der Unfall	accident
der Stau	traffic jam
die Baustelle	roadworks

Answers p. 112

5 **Ein Reiseruf** – a radio message. Try and catch the details on the recording and fill them in in the transcript below.

VOCABULARY

amtliches Kennzeichen	registration number
wird gebeten	is asked

Ein Reiseruf: _____ aus

_____ , zur Zeit unterwegs in

_____ mit einem

_____ amtliches Kennzeichen

Answers p. 112

_____ wird gebeten, zu Hause anzurufen.

6 Your turn to speak, about your TV or radio preferences. Turn to the recording where Hans will prompt you. You'll need phrases such as:

weil ich ... finde

aktuelle Beiträge/Regionalsendungen/Sportreportagen

TV fans

Günter	Hm – ich finde, daß das Fernsehen oft umfassender und anschaulicher informiert als der Rundfunk.
Biba	Wieviel Stunden sehen Sie fern?
Günter	Vielleicht drei bis vier Stunden in der Woche – ich suche mir die Sendungen meist aus.
Amin	Ja, ich sehe eben gerne Filme, und im Fernsehen kann ich mir öfters Filme anschauen, die hier in der Stadt im Kino nicht laufen.
Biba	Und was sehen Sie am liebsten?
Amin	Am liebsten sehe ich diese leichten, amüsanten amerikanischen Komödien aus den dreißiger Jahren von Frank Capra, von William van Dyke ... und die Sportschau.

LISTEN FOR...

umfassender	more comprehensively
anschaulicher	more graphically
Komödien	comedies

umfassend comprehensive(ly)

anschaulich graphic(ally)

der Rundfunk officially 'broadcasting', but **Rundfunk** is often used, as here, to refer to radio

fernsehen (sep.) to watch TV; **ich sehe fern** I watch TV.

(sich) aussuchen (sep.) to choose; **ich suche (mir) das Geschenk aus** I choose the present; **er sucht (sich) das Geschenk aus** he chooses the present. With this verb, **sich** is optional. You could simply say: **ich suche das Geschenk aus.**

öfters fairly often

anschauen (sep.) to watch, to look at something; **ich schaue (mir) den Film an** I watch the film. **Schaust du (dir) den Film an?** Are you watching the film? Remember: **anschaulich** (lit. visibly) graphically.

laufen to run (films at the cinema); **Was läuft?** What's on?

leicht light

amüsant amusing

die Komödie comedy

die dreißiger Jahre the Thirties

Sportschau name of a sports programme

Nr. **17** Programme vom 27. 4. bis 3. Mai 1996 DM 2,30

TV

Hören und Sehen

JOB-BÖRSE 823 neue freie Stellen!

Angehimmelt und verteufelt

MACHOS
Eine kritisch-amüsante Betrachtung
– NICHT NUR FÜR FRAUEN

Wer macht die beste TV-Unterhaltung?
SHOW-TEST
Die Sieger und Verlierer

Wieviel Zukunft hat Ihr Kind?
So können Eltern die Talente ihres Kindes erkennen

7 TV listings

ARD

10.30	**Schiff ohne Heimat**
12.10	**Die Könige aus Jemen**
12.55	**Presseschau**
13.00	**Tagesschau**
13.15	**Videotext für alle**
	Eine Auswahl aus dem Angebot
13.40	**Vorschau**
14.00	**Tagesschau**
14.05	**Für Kinder**
	Sesamstraße
14.35	**ARD-Ratgeber: Essen und Trinken**
	Was Großmutter noch wußte über Milch und Käse
15.30	**Nonstop Nonsens**
	Von und mit Dieter Hallervorden
	Didi – ein Glückspilz?
	Regie: Heinz Liesendahl
16.15	**Neues vom Kleidermarkt**
	Antonia Hilke berichtet über die Mode im Herbst/Winter
17.00	**Blickfeld**
	Kirche und Gesellschaft
18.00	**Tagesschau**
18.05	**Sportschau**
	u.a. Fußball-Bundesliga

ZDF

11.50	**Nachbarn in Europa**
	Information und Unterhaltung für Ausländer und Deutsche
	Mit Beiträgen aus:
12.15	**Griechenland**
13.00	**Spanien**
13.45	**Italien**
	Im Studio Ekkehard Kuhn
14.30	**heute**
14.35	**Pinocchio**
	Zeichentrickserie
	Schreck in der Morgenstunde
14.55	**1, 2 oder 3**
	Ratespiel für Kinder
	Durch die Sendung führt Michael Schanze
15.35	**Schau zu – mach mit**
	Tips und Anregungen
16.00	**Black Beauty**
	Das Leben eines edlen Pferdes
16.45	**Enorm in Form**
	Tele-Aerobic für die Familie
17.05	**heute**
17.10	**Länderspiegel**
	Informationen und Meinungen aus der Bundesrepublik

VOCABULARY

das Ratespiel	guessing game	**in Form**	fit; in shape
die Anregung	suggestion	**die Meinung**	opinion
das Pferd	horse		

Both **heute** and **Tagesschau** are news programmes.

When and where would you tune in if you wanted to ...

	time	title of programme	channel
a watch football			
b find out about fashion			
c watch a religious programme			
d hear about regional domestic affairs			
e have the children entertained for exactly 40 minutes			
f watch a food programme			

Answers p. 112

8

Your turn to speak – and tell Gertrude what time certain programmes are on. You will need to look at the ARD schedule in Exercise 7 so keep your book open. Remember the 24-hour clock in spoken German? Here are some examples:

10.00 zehn Uhr; 05.00 fünf Uhr; 22.15 zweiundzwanzig Uhr fünfzehn; 19.30 neunzehn Uhr dreißig

CONVERSATION 4

Daily and weekly papers

Herr Frauenfeld

Tageszeitungen – wir haben da zwei Arten von Tageszeitungen, die regionalen und die überregionalen. Die wichtigsten der überregionalen sind etwa die *Süddeutsche Zeitung*, die eher liberal ist, die *Frankfurter Allgemeine Zeitung*, die sehr konservativ ist, und vielleicht noch die *Frankfurter Rundschau*, die linksliberal ist.

Von den regionalen Zeitungen gibt es sehr viele. Sie bringen auch Lokalnachrichten und sind sehr wichtig für die Bevölkerung. Dann gibt es natürlich noch die Boulevardpresse, diese Sensationsblätter, die eigentlich nur aus Schlagzeilen und Bildern bestehen und sehr wenig Informationen bringen.

Sonntagszeitungen gibt es beinahe keine. Dafür gibt es Wochenblätter und politische Magazine, die wöchentlich erscheinen. Von den Wochenblättern zum Beispiel *Die Zeit*, die liberal ist, und als politisches Magazin *Der Spiegel*.

LISTEN FOR...	
Tageszeitungen	dailies
Boulevardpresse	tabloid press
Schlagzeilen	headlines
Wochenblätter	weeklies

die Art the kind

die regionalen und die überregionalen the regional ones and the national ones. There are more regional and fewer national papers in Germany; even the nationals are regional in origin, as their names show: *Frankfurter Rundschau*, *Süddeutsche Zeitung* etc.

sie bringen auch Lokalnachrichten they also carry (lit. bring) local news

die Bevölkerung the people, population

die Boulevardpresse tabloid press; **das Sensationsblatt** tabloid. Note that **das Blatt** means 'leaf', 'sheet' (of paper) and 'newspaper'.

die eigentlich nur aus Schlagzeilen und Bildern bestehen that really consist only of headlines and pictures; **die Schlagzeile** headline; **das Bild** picture; **aus etwas bestehen** to consist of something: **der Ring besteht aus Gold** the ring consists of gold.

die Information information; **Informationen** pieces of information

dafür on the other hand

die wöchentlich erscheinen which appear weekly

Haben Sie Informationen für die Morgenpost?

Chemnitz	☎	6631300
Leipzig	☎	9824012
Dresden	☎	4864626

9 What did Herr Frauenfeld have to say about the German press? Listen to Conversation 4 again and fill in the grid.

Zeitungen	Tagesblatt	Wochenblatt/ -magazin	konservativ	liberal	linksliberal
Süddeutsche					
Frankfurter Allgemeine					
Frankfurter Rundschau					
Die Zeit					
Der Spiegel					

Answers p. 112

10 Media tastes. Listen to the recording, where Manfred and Flora are interviewed about their use of the media. Then decide which statements are true (**Richtig**) and which false (**Falsch**) ... You'll hear a new word – **Spielfilm**, feature film.

R F

a Flora mag das Fernsehen lieber als das Radio. ☐ ☐

b Manfred mag den Rundfunk nicht gerne. ☐ ☐

c Flora hört gerne Nachrichten im Autoradio. ☐ ☐

d Auch Musik hört Flora gerne im Autoradio. ☐ ☐

e Manfred findet Nachrichten mit Bildern besser. ☐ ☐

Answers p. 112   f Flora findet Fernsehnachrichten langweilig. ☐ ☐

11 Which papers was Herr Frauenfeld talking about? Complete the sentences.

> **die Sensationsblätter   die überregionalen Zeitungen**
> **die regionalen Zeitungen   die Sonntagszeitungen**

a Es gibt nicht viele _____ in Deutschland.

b Die _____ sind sehr wichtig für die Bevölkerung, weil sie auch Lokalnachrichten bringen.

c Die _____ bringen viele Bilder und

Answers p. 112   Schlagzeilen und zu wenig Informationen.

12 Your turn to speak and make a short summary of Conversation 4. Keep your book open so that you can find the relevant passages in the text.

13 DIE NEWS. *TV Hören und Sehen*, a popular magazine with information on TV and radio programmes, asked 300 families whether they thought young people should have their own news programme. Here is the result. Work carefully through the text before turning to the speaking exercise.

DIE NEWS

Extra
Nachrichtensendung
für Kinder

Ein klares Resultat, ein klarer Wunsch: 300 Familien haben für „TV Hören und Sehen" ein Jahr lang das Fernsehen getestet. Sie wollen, daß Kinder und Jugendliche eigene Nachrichtensendungen bekommen. Warum?

■ Auch Kinder und Jugendliche müssen wissen, was auf der Welt passiert. Aber die Sendezeiten müssen geändert werden. Die Sendungen sollten früher gesendet werden, so daß Eltern und Kinder die Sendungen zusammen sehen können.

■ Die Themen – Politik, Wirtschaft, Wissenschaft, Sport – sind auch für Kinder interessant. Die typische Nachrichtensprache ist aber für Kinder zu schwierig. Sie muß einfacher gemacht werden.

■ Nachrichtensendungen für Erwachsene haben zu wenig Erklärungen. Die Kinder müssen besser über die Hintergründe informiert werden.

■ Das Bild- und Filmmaterial der regulären Nachrichten ist zu blutrünstig. Diese Bilder sollten Kinder nicht sehen.

■ Die Moderation ist zu monoton. Die Sprecher müßten jünger und flippiger, aber dennoch auch seriös sein.

VOCABULARY

passieren	to happen
ändern	to change
die Wirtschaft	economy
die Wissenschaft	science
schwierig	difficult
die Erklärung	explanation
der Hintergrund	background
blutrünstig	bloodthirsty
die Moderation	presentation
monoton	monotonous
flippig	informal
seriös	respectable

And now, another turn to speak. Keep your book open and turn to the recording for a conversation with Gertrude on the article from *TV Hören und Sehen*. You will be able to use phrases directly from the text ...

KEY WORDS AND PHRASES

Die Presse

die Zeitung	newspaper
die Zeitschrift	magazine
das Magazin	magazine
die Mode/Frauen/Sportzeitschrift	fashion/women's/sports magazine
die Tages/Sonntags/Wochenzeitung	daily/Sunday/weekly paper
die Boulevardpresse	popular press
das Sensationsblatt	tabloid
die Schlagzeile	headline
die Nachricht, pl. **Nachrichten**	news
Die Zeitung/Zeitschrift ist ...	The paper/magazine is ...
regional	regional
überregional	national
konservativ	conservative
liberal	liberal

The press

Rundfunk und Fernsehen

der Rundfunk/das Radio	radio
das Fernsehen	television
die Sendung	programme
fernsehen (sep.)	to watch TV
Radio hören	to listen to the radio
das Programm	schedule
Ich sehe gern ...	I like watching ...
Filme	films
Komödien	comedies
die Sportschau	the sports show
aktuelle Beiträge	current affairs features
Reportagen	reports
Regionalsendungen	regional programmes

Radio and television

To understand only:

der Reiseruf	radio message
amtliches Kennzeichen	registration number
wird gebeten	is asked
anrufen (sep.)	to telephone
Meldungen zur Verkehrslage	traffic news
die Baustelle	road works
der Stau	traffic jam

The passive

- The passive is often used when you want to be impersonal about an action:
  Wie wird das gemacht? (How is it done?) instead of
  Wie mache ich das? (How do I do it?)

- A way round the passive is to use **man** (one) which you might find easier to use:
  Wie macht man das? How does one do it? How is it done?
  Das kann man kaufen. One can buy that.

However, you should be able to recognise the passive. So this is how it is formed:

- Passive present tense:
werden + past participle of the main verb:

ich	werde	gemalt	I am (being) painted
du	wirst	gemalt	you are (being) painted
er/sie/es	wird	gemalt	he/she/it is (being) painted
wir	werden	gemalt	we are (being) painted
ihr	werdet	gemalt	you are (being) painted
sie/Sie	werden	gemalt	they/you are (being) painted

Examples from this unit:

Es wird auch Politik gesendet.   Politics is broadcast as well.
Herr Trappe wird gebeten ...   Mr Trappe is asked ...

14   Translate into English:

a   Das Haus wird gebaut. _____

b   Im Gasthaus „Adler" wird getanzt. _____

c   Heute mittag wird ein Spielfilm gesendet. _____

d   Der Bundeskanzler wird offiziell begrüßt. _____

e   Das Baby wird jeden Tag gebadet. _____

Answers p. 112

Don't confuse the passive with the future tense. The future is
formed with **werden** plus the infinitive!

Ich werde malen   I shall paint
BUT:
Ich werde gemalt   I am (being) painted

Imperfect passive

- The passive imperfect is formed with **wurde** + past participle of the main verb:

ich	wurde	gemalt	I was (being) painted
du	wurdest	gemalt	you were (being) painted
er/sie/es	wurde	gemalt	he/she/it was (being) painted
wir	wurden	gemalt	we were (being) painted
ihr	wurdet	gemalt	you were (being) painted
sie/Sie	wurden	gemalt	you/they were (being) painted

15 Translate into English.

a Das Haus wurde 1948 gebaut. _____

b Was wurde im Kino gespielt? _____

c Ich weiß nicht, wie das gemacht wurde. _____

d Das wurde mir nie gesagt. _____

Answers p. 112

16 Mixed skills ... Complete the grid!   Answers p. 112

a	Ich werde bauen.	
b	_____	We will play.
c	Das wird oft gemacht.	
d	Wurde auch getanzt?	
e	_____	When was the house built?
f	_____	What was (being) cooked?

Relative clauses

- Compare these sentences:

Der Mann, der hier war, ist interessant. — The man who was here is interesting.

Der Mann, den du gestern gesehen hast, ist interessant. — The man (whom) you saw is interesting.

Der Mann, dem du das Buch gegeben hast, ist interessant. — The man to whom you gave the book is interesting.

The clauses beginning with **der**, **den** and **dem** are relative clauses: they refer to people or things which have already been mentioned in the sentences. **Der**, **den** and **dem** are called relative pronouns: they stand in for the people or things already mentioned – in this case **der Mann**.

In order to choose the right relative pronoun, you need to look at:

- the noun (here: **der Mann** ▷ masculine, singular)
- the function of the pronoun in the relative clause – in other words, the case:

Der Mann, der hier war, ...   The man who was here ...
... 'who' is the subject of the clause, so you need the nominative ▷ **der ...**
Der Mann, den du gesehen hast, ...   The man (whom) you saw ...
... 'whom' is the direct object of the clause (whilst **du** is the subject), so you need the accusative case ▷ **den**
Der Mann, dem du das Buch gegeben hast, ...   The man to whom you gave the book
... 'to whom' is the indirect object (whilst **du** is the subject and **das Buch** is the direct object), so you need the dative case ▷ **dem**

Here are some more examples for feminine and neuter nouns:
Das Kind, das hier war, ist nett.   The child that was here is nice (neuter, nominative).
Die Frau, die du gesehen hast, ist nett.   The women (whom) you saw is nice (fem., accus.).
And this is the grid to remember. Notice that all but one of the relative pronouns are like the definite article.

	Singular			Plural
	masculine	neuter	feminine	all genders
Nom.	..., der	..., das	..., die	..., die
Acc.	..., den	..., das	..., die	..., die
Dat.	..., dem	..., dem	..., der	..., denen

17   Translate into English.

a   Das Buch, das du gefunden hast, ist schön.
_____

b   Wo ist das Kleid, das du gekauft hast?
_____

c   Hier sind die Zeitungen, die du bestellt hast.
_____

d   Der Hund, dem du so viel Essen gegeben hast, ist zu dick.
_____

e   Wie heißt die Frau, die dort am Tisch sitzt?
_____

f   Ich habe viele Kleider, die aus Bali kommen.
_____

Answers p. 112

18   Fill in the missing words.

a   Hier ist das Kleid, _____ so teuer ist!
b   Wo ist die Verkäuferin, _____ so nett war?
c   Dort ist der Verkäufer, _____ du das Kleid gezeigt hast.
d   Aber wo ist das Geld, _____ du mir gegeben hast?
e   Und wo ist die Handtasche, _____ ich dorthin gelegt hatte?

Answers p. 112

19 Newsspeak – a puzzle. Remember the key words from the Conversations ...
The letters 1–7 will give you the name of a famous German news magazine.

a You can also watch it in the cinema.

b Won't keep you fit but it's about fit people.

c This will make you laugh, hopefully.

d He covers and investigates news.

e A word for programme.

f Listen and watch regularly and you will be well informed.

g Doesn't just mean 'leaf'.

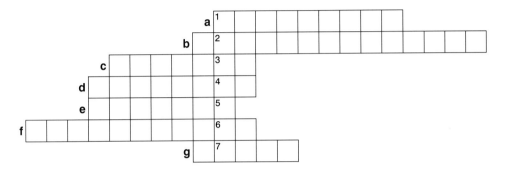

Keyword: | 1 | 2 | 3 | 4 | 5 | 6 | 7 |

Answers p. 112

20 Your turn to speak, and talk about your favourite papers and TV programmes. You will need one more essential word: **die Seifenoper** soap opera ...

21 Ask your partner questions about the TV listings from Exercise 7, for example:

Wann kann ich Nachrichten/eine Sportsendung sehen?
Gibt es auch eine Kindersendung?
Wann kommt der Film?
Wie lange dauert er? (How long does it go on?)
Wann beginnt die früheste Sendung?
Ich möchte gerne Modetips/Kochtips haben ...
Kann ich mich durch Fernsehen auch fit halten?...

EXERCISE 1

(a) Hauptbahnhof   (b) Burda   (c) Tina
(d) Buchhandlung   (e) Spiegel
Keyword: BRIGITTE

EXERCISE 2

(a) Bravo   (b) Kicker   (c) Carina; Freundin; Echo
der Frau   (d) Mein schöner Garten   (e) Ein Herz
für Tiere   (f) Wohnidee; baumagazin; Zuhause
Wohnen   (g) Super-TV

EXERCISE 4

Transcript: Radiodienst aus Baden-Baden mit
Meldungen zur Verkehrslage. A6 Mannheim
Richtung Heilbronn: Zwischen Bad Rappenau und
Heilbronn-Neckarsulm, Unfall, 5 bis 6 km Stau. A8
Stuttgart Richtung München zwischen Aichelberg
und Merklingen Baustelle, 6 bis 7 km Stau.

EXERCISE 5

Herr Friedrich Trappe; Kaiserslautern;
Süddeutschland; weißen VW Golf Diesel; KL-TR 71
Transcript: Und ein Reiseruf: Herr Friedrich Trappe.
Herr Friedrich Trappe aus Kaiserslautern, zur Zeit
unterwegs in Süddeutschland mit einem weißen VW
Golf Diesel, amtliches Kennzeichen KL-TR 71, wird
gebeten, zu Hause anzurufen.

EXERCISE 7

(a) 18.05 Sportschau ARD   (b) 16.15 Neues vom
Kleidermarkt ARD   (c) 17.00 Blickfeld ARD
(d) 17.10 Länderspiegel ZDF   (e) 14.55 1, 2 oder 3
ZDF   (f) 14.35 ARD-Ratgeber: Essen und Trinken
ARD

EXERCISE 9

Süddeutsche: Tagesblatt, liberal; Frankfurter
Allgemeine: Tagesblatt, sehr konservativ; Frankfurter
Rundschau: Tagesblatt, linksliberal; Die Zeit:
Wochenblatt, liberal; Der Spiegel: politisches
Wochenmagazin

EXERCISE 10

(a) R   (b) F   (c) F   (d) R   (e) F   (f) F

EXERCISE 11

(a) Sonntagszeitungen   (b) regionalen Zeitungen
(c) Sensationsblätter

EXERCISE 14

(a) The house is being built   (b) There's a dance at
the Adler inn.   (c) There's a feature film this
afternoon.   (d) The Chancellor is welcomed
officially. Or: There is an official welcome for the
Chancellor.   (e) The baby is bathed every day.

EXERCISE 15

(a) The house was built in 1948.   (b) What was on in
the cinema?   (c) I don't know how that was done.
(d) I was never told that, or: That was never said to
me.

EXERCISE 16

(a) I shall build.   (b) Wir werden spielen.
(c) That's often done.   (d) Was there dancing too?
(e) Wann wurde das Haus gebaut?   (f) Was wurde
gekocht?

EXERCISE 17

(a) The book you found is beautiful.   (b) Where's the
dress you bought?   (c) Here are the newspapers you
ordered.   (d) The dog you gave so much food to is
too fat.   (e) What's the name of the woman sitting
over there at the table?   (f) I have many dresses that
come from Bali.

EXERCISE 18

(a) das   (b) die   (c) dem   (d) das   (e) die.

EXERCISE 19

(a) Spielfilm   (b) Sportreportage   (c) Komödie
(d) Reporter   (e) Sendung   (f) Nachrichten
(g) Blatt; Keyword: Spiegel.

WHAT YOU WILL LEARN
- ▶ talking about your health
- ▶ describing your symptoms
- ▶ shopping at a pharmacy
- ▶ you will also be reminded of essential words to describe the body.

POINTS TO REMEMBER
- ● media words: **Tageszeitung, Wochenmagazin, Wochenblatt, Boulevardpresse, Mode/Frauen/Sportzeitschrift**; **Schlagzeile, Nachrichten**
- ● **Fernsehen, Radio, Rundfunk**; **Sendung, Programm, Reportage, aktuelle Beiträge**
- ● traffic news: **Meldungen zur Verkehrslage**; **Baustelle, Stau**
- ● the passive formed with **werden** + past participle of main verb: **das Baby wird gebadet** the baby is being bathed.
- ● the use of **man**: **Wie macht man das? Wo kann man das kaufen?**

der Arm
das Auge
der Bauch
das Bein
der Finger
der Fuß
der Hals
die Hand
das Knie
der Kopf
der Mund
die Nase
das Ohr
der Zahn
die Zehe

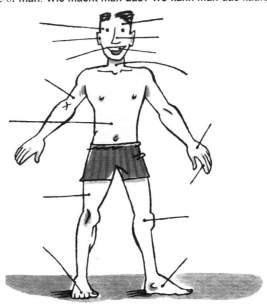

BEFORE YOU BEGIN
German is a wonderful language for combining words to produce new 'compounds'. You will come across quite a few examples in this unit. Take **Kopfschmerzen** (headache), for example: replace the first part of the compound with (almost) any other part of the body and you will have created new words and new symptoms, such as **Ohrenschmerzen** (earache), **Halsschmerzen** (sore throat) or **Bauchschmerzen** (tummy ache). All you need to do is remember and connect. To warm up, try and connect the body words to the appropriate body parts on the drawing ...

The diet

Silke	Also, morgen beginne ich mit meiner Diät.
Biba	Warum denn das?
Silke	Ach, ich fühle mich so schlaff und ungesund und unbeweglich.
Biba	Und was für eine Diät machst du denn?
Silke	Also erst mal eine Saftkur, zur Entschlackung, und dann mach' ich eine Kaloriendiät streng nach Plan: 800 Kalorien am Tag.
Biba	Was ißt du denn dann?
Silke	Ja, so fettarmes Essen, Salate, mageres Fleisch, Fisch, wenig Kohlenhydrate, ist halt sehr teuer.
Biba	Hm, und natürlich keinen Alkohol?
Silke	Ja, nee ...
Biba	Und keine Süßigkeiten?
Silke	Ja, nee ...
Biba	Das könnte ich nicht!
Silke	Ja, wieso siehst du denn so gesund aus?
Biba	Also, ich – ich mach' jeden Tag ein bißchen Gymnastik, und dann geh' ich noch zum Schwimmen, einmal in der Woche; ja, und dann achte ich darauf, daß ich genug schlafe.

LISTEN FOR...

Diät	diet
ungesund	unhealthy
Saftkur	juice diet

die Diät   diet

Warum denn das?   Why that?

ich fühle mich   I feel; similarly: **Wie fühlst du dich?** How do you feel? **er fühlt sich schlecht** he feels bad.

schlaff   limp, lacking in energy

ungesund   unhealthy; **gesund** healthy; and if somebody sneezes, you can say: **Gesundheit!** (lit. health!)

unbeweglich   immobile, heavy; the opposite is **beweglich** agile; **bewegen** to move.

Was für eine Diät?   What kind of diet? similarly: **Was für ein Buch?** What kind of book? **Was für ein Hund?** What kind of dog?

die Saftkur   juice diet; **die Kur** lit. cure, course of treatment; **die Hungerkur** fast (lit. hunger cure)

die Entschlackung   purification

die Kalorie   calorie

streng nach Plan   strictly according to plan

fettarm   low-fat; **das Fett** fat; **arm** poor; **mager** lit. meagre; here: lean.

wenig Kohle(n)hydrate   few carbohydrates

(das) ist halt sehr teuer   that's very expensive; **halt** is a filler word here, not to be confused with **halt!** stop!

die Süßigkeit   sweet

Wieso?   Why, how come?

ein bißchen Gymnastik   a bit of gymnastics (i.e. exercises)

und dann achte ich darauf, daß ...   and then I take care that ...; **Achtung!** Watch out!

genug   sufficient(ly)

schlafen   to sleep; **Schlafen Sie gut!** Sleep well!

1 Diet details. Make sure you've understood Conversation 1 really well, then complete the details about Silke's diet in the grid below – in German.

a	Wann?	ab _____
b	Warum?	sie fühlt sich _____
c	Was für eine Diät?	1 _____ 2 _____
d	Wieviel Kalorien?	pro Tag _____
e	Was darf sie essen?	_____ _____
f	Was ist verboten?	_____

Answers p. 128

2 If you wanted to go on a low-calorie diet as described by Silke, which items would you need to cross out from your list of favourite foods and drinks below?

Apfelsaft   *grüne Bohnen*   *Orangen*

Karottensalat   *Weißwein*   *Schlagsahne*

Käsekuchen   *Mineralwasser*   *Tee mit Rum*

Answers p. 128   *Steak*   *Schokoladeneis*

3

On the recording, Maria and Georg talk about how they keep fit. Listen to both of them, then read the statements below and decide who would have said what.

		Maria	Georg
a	Ich fahre im Winter immer Ski.	☐	☐
b	Ich mache keine Gymnastik.	☐	☐
c	Ich rauche nicht.	☐	☐
d	Ich mag Bier und Schnaps.	☐	☐
e	Ich trinke gerne Saft.	☐	☐
f	Ich liebe Milch und Milchprodukte.	☐	☐
g	Einmal im Monat mache ich einen Safttag.	☐	☐
h	Ich fühle mich gesund.	☐	☐
i	Ich brauche viel Energie.	☐	☐

Answers p. 128

4

Katrin has heard about Silke's diet. Here's the letter she wrote to Silke telling her why she would not like to go on a similar **Kur**. Read it, then turn to the recording and talk to Johannes from Katrin's point of view.

Liebe Silke,

Du hast ja große Pläne! Ich wünsche Dir viel Glück und Willenskraft mit Deiner Diät. Ich selbst möchte aber keine Diät machen. Wie Du weißt, liebe ich Kochen und Essen. Außerdem ist mir eine Diät viel zu teuer. Ich verstehe auch nicht, warum alle Leute schlank sein müssen. Ich bin lieber ein bißchen dick, aber glücklich. Außerdem fühle ich mich fit und gesund, ich mache ja einmal in der Woche Gymnastik und jeden Morgen 20 Minuten Yoga. Ich mag mich, wie ich bin! Dennoch: alles Gute und viel Erfolg,

Deine

Katrin

VOCABULARY

die Willenskraft	willpower
außerdem	besides
schlank	slim
dick	fat
dennoch	nonetheless
der Erfolg	success

CONVERSATION 2

At the pharmacy

LISTEN FOR...

Reiseapotheke	medical kit for travelling
beraten	to advise
das Sonnenschutzmittel	sun cream

Ruth	Guten Tag.
Herr Keidel	Guten Tag.
Ruth	Also, ich fahre in die Berge, und da möchte ich mir 'ne ganz kleine Reiseapotheke mitnehmen. Können Sie mich da beraten, können Sie mir da helfen?
Herr Keidel	Ja, gerne. Wo fahren Sie denn hin?
Ruth	Ich fahre in die Berge, nach Österreich.
Herr Keidel	Nach Österreich, ja. Da brauchen Sie ein starkes Sonnenschutzmittel, wenn Sie in die Berge fahren, weil die Sonne da sehr intensiv scheint. Dann würde ich Ihnen noch ein Verbandszeug empfehlen, für die erste Hilfe: Binden, Pflaster, vielleicht noch Desinfektionsmittel oder ein Antiseptikum für kleine Wunden. Auch den Insektenschutz sollten Sie nicht vergessen.
Ruth	Ja, und da gibt's doch auch 'n Spray, nicht?
Herr Keidel	Ja, man kann ein Spray nehmen, würd' ich Ihnen aber nicht empfehlen in den Bergen. Wenn die Sonne scheint, wird die Spraydose sehr heiß und kann explodieren. Ich würde Ihnen ein Gelee empfehlen. Das kühlt und erfrischt.

'ne (= eine) ganz kleine ...   a very small ...

die Reiseapotheke   medical kit for travelling;
   die Apotheke pharmacy

mitnehmen (sep.)   to take along

beraten   to advise

das Sonnenschutzmittel   sun cream/lotion;
   der Schutz protection; das Mittel lit.
   means, das Verkehrsmittel means of
   transport; also medication: Haben Sie ein
   Mittel gegen Kopfschmerzen? Have you
   got something for a headache?

intensiv scheinen   to shine intensely

das Verbandszeug   dressings; eine Wunde
   verbinden to dress a wound; die Binde
   bandage, das Pflaster plaster

die erste Hilfe   first aid; die Hilfe help

das Desinfektionsmittel   disinfectant; das
   Antiseptikum antiseptic

der Insektenschutz insect repellent; das Insekt
   insect

vergessen   to forget

das Spray   spray; die Spraydose lit. the spray
   can, aerosol

das Gelee (or, more usually now, das Gel)   gel

(das) würd' ich Ihnen aber nicht empfehlen
   but I would not recommend that

wenn die Sonne scheint, wird die Spraydose
   sehr heiß   if the sun shines, the aerosol
   gets very hot. More on werden in Grammar,
   this unit.

explodieren to explode; kühlen to cool;
   erfrischen to refresh

D A L L M A N N ' S

Salbei-Bonbons

mit Vitamin C

Medizinische Spezialbonbons
mit den bewährten Wirkstoffen
der Salbeipflanze (Salvia officinalis L.)

lindern sofort Heiserkeit, quälende Schluck-
beschwerden, Kratzen und Brennen in Hals
und Rachen

helfen bei hartnäckiger Verschleimung der
oberen Luftwege

fördern die Heilung schmerzhafter Entzün-
dungen der Mundhöhle und des Zahnfleisches

aktivieren die natürlichen Abwehrkräfte des
Körpers gegen Erkältungs- und Infektions-
krankheiten durch den hohen Gehalt an lebens-
wichtigem Vitamin C (15 mg in jedem Bonbon)

SCHMECKEN SÄUERLICH ERFRISCHEND

Gratisprobe

5 Translate into German, using **Sie** for 'you'.

a I'd like to take a medical kit with me.

_____

b Can you advise me?

_____

c Can you help me?

_____

d I'm going into the mountains.

_____

e I need a strong sun lotion.

_____

f I need a plaster.

Answers p. 128

_____

6 Here is a rather eccentric list for a **Reiseapotheke**. Cross out the items that the average pharmacist would find inappropriate.

Sonnenschutzmittel

Pflaster

Socken

Binden

Rotwein

Schokolade

Desinfektionsmittel

Schwarztee

Briefpapier

Insektenschutz

Bluse

Handschuhe

Answers p. 128

7 Germans are very fond of their spas. Many go there regularly every few years in order to recuperate from the stresses and strains of everyday life. If they are lucky, their health insurance will even cover some of the cost. Many spas are beautifully situated in the mountains or by the sea. On the recording, you will hear an advertisement for the Bavarian Alps. Listen and complete the transcript below.

Schau mal, die Berge!

Mit welchem _____ **(a)** Sie auch anreisen, aus

_____ , _____

_____ **(b)**, plötzlich sind sie da, die Bayerischen

Alpen. Wenn Sie hier _____ **(c)**, ist das so gut wie

die _____ **(d)**. Die höchsten Berge finden Sie

bei Berchtesgaden, Garmisch-Partenkirchen und Oberstdorf. Aber Sie

müssen nicht unbedingt _____ **(e)**. Sie können

auch einfach nur _____ **(f)**. Das gesunde Klima

ist ein Heilmittel, das jedem _____ **(g)** guttut,

besonders natürlich den Kurpatienten. Bayern ist die ideale Region für

einen _____ **(h)** : besuchen Sie Bad Aibling,

das älteste Moorbad in Bayern. Oder probieren Sie eine

_____ **(i)** in Bad Reichenhall. Doch Vorsicht!

Die Ärzte raten: Fangen Sie langsam an. Eine Liegekur ist für die ersten

Tage _____ **(j)**. Danach können Sie kurze

_____ **(k)**. Längere _____ **(l)**

sollten erst einmal warten.

Answers p. 128

VOCABULARY

das Klima	the climate
heilen	to heal; **das Heilmittel** cure
der Patient	patient
das Moorbad	spa with special mud treatments
Vorsicht!	Be careful!; **Vorsicht** care, caution

8 Your turn to speak. You are planning a trip to the mountains. First though, you need to visit the chemist. Here are some useful words:

Creme/Insektenschutz/Gel/Sonnenschutzmittel/Verbandszeug

CONVERSATION 3

 A family epidemic

Heide

Also, letzte Woche war die ganze Familie krank. Zuerst hatte Claudia die Grippe – kein Wunder bei dem Wetter! Halsweh, Schnupfen, Fieber, eben so alles, was dazu gehört ... Kopfweh ...

Dann wurde mein Mann auch noch krank. Ihm war ständig schlecht, hatte Magenschmerzen, Durchfall, keinen Appetit, und er konnte nicht schlafen. Der Arzt sagte, er hätte 'ne Darmgrippe.

Dann wurde ich schließlich auch noch krank. Ich weiß gar nicht, was (es) ist. Ich habe Muskelschmerzen, meine Augen sind ganz rot, mir wird ständig heiß und dann wieder kalt ... Wir könnten bald sowas wie 'ne Privatklinik aufmachen.

die Grippe influenza; **die Erkältung** cold

kein Wunder bei dem Wetter no wonder with this weather

das Halsweh sore throat, lit. throat ache; also **die Halsschmerzen**; similarly: **das Kopfweh** or **die Kopfschmerzen** headache; **das Magenweh** or **die Magenschmerzen** stomach ache; **die Muskelschmerzen** muscle pains; **meine Hand tut weh** my hand hurts.

der Schnupfen runny nose; **Heuschnupfen** hay fever

das Fieber fever, temperature

alles was dazu gehört everything that goes with it (lit. belongs to it)

mein Mann wurde krank my husband fell sick. More on **wurde** in Grammar, this unit.

ihm war ständig schlecht he felt constantly sick; **mir ist schlecht** I feel sick; **mir geht's schlecht** I'm not well, **mir geht's gut** I'm well

der Durchfall diarrhoea; **Verstopfung** constipation

der Appetit appetite; remember: **Guten Appetit!** Enjoy your meal!

er konnte nicht schlafen he couldn't sleep; **ich konnte nicht schlafen** I couldn't sleep; **du konntest nicht schlafen** you couldn't sleep. More on **konnte** in Grammar, this unit.

der Arzt sagte, er hätte 'ne (= **eine**) **Darmgrippe** the doctor said he had gastric flu; **der Darm** intestines

schließlich finally

das Auge eye

mir wird heiß und ... kalt I feel hot and ... cold

wir könnten bald sowas (= **so etwas**) **wie 'ne** (= **eine**) **Privatklinik aufmachen** we could soon open something like a private clinic; **aufmachen** (sep.) to open; **zumachen** (sep.) to close

9 **Was fehlt ihnen?** What's wrong with them? Study the drawings, then write down your diagnosis in German.

(a)

_____

(b)

_____

(c)

_____

(d)

_____

(e)

_____

(f)

_____

(g)

_____

(h)

_____

Answers p. 128

10 And now listen to the recording, where some more patients are complaining of various illnesses. Note down their ailments – in English.

a Frau Schuster

_____

_____

b Herr Möller

_____

_____

c Frau Professor Bremer

_____

_____

d Herr Direktor

_____

_____

e Tina

_____

Answers p. 128

_____

11 Your turn to suffer: switch on the recording and complain to Gertrude about your aches and pains. Some but not all of these words will come in handy:
Muskel/Kopf/Magen/Ohren/Hals/Augenschmerzen

KEY WORDS
AND PHRASES

Dieting and other 'cures'

Ich will eine ...
    Diät/Saftkur/Hungerkur machen

I want to go on a …
    diet/juice diet/fast

Ich esse ...
    nur 800 Kalorien pro Tag
    fettarmes Essen
    keine Süßigkeiten

I eat ...
    only 800 calories a day
    low-fat food
    no sweets

der Kurort
der Patient/die Patientin

spa
patient

Health matters

die Gesundheit
gesund/krank
die Krankheit
krank werden
Mir ist schlecht
Ich habe ...
    Grippe
    Halsschmerzen
    Kopfschmerzen
    Fieber
    eine Erkältung
    Schnupfen
    Durchfall
der Arzt/die Ärztin

health
healthy/ill
illness
to fall ill
I feel sick
I have ...
    flu
    a sore throat
    a headache
    a temperature
    a cold
    a runny nose
    diarrhoea
male/female doctor

At the pharmacy

die Apotheke
die Reiseapotheke
Ich brauche ...
    ein Sonnenschutzmittel
    Verbandszeug
    ein Pflaster
    ein Mittel gegen ...

pharmacy
medical kit for travelling
I need ...
    sun cream
    dressings
    a sticking plaster
    something for ...

Werden

In Units 3 and 7 you learned how to use **werden** to form the future and the passive.

■ **Werden** can also be used to express a process. In most cases it can be translated as 'to become' or 'to get'.

Mir wird kalt.	I'm getting cold.
Mein Mann wird krank.	My husband has been taken (lit. is becoming) ill.
Die Spraydose wird heiß.	The aerosol gets hot.
Ich will reich werden.	I want to be/become rich.

■ The imperfect tense of **werden** has already been introduced in Unit 7.

Mir wurde kalt.	I got cold.
Mein Mann wurde krank.	My husband fell ill.
Die Spraydose wurde heiß.	The aerosol became hot.

■ The past participle of **werden** is **geworden**. The perfect tense is formed by using **sein**.

ich	bin	schlank	geworden	I (have) got slim
du	bist	schlank	geworden	you (have) got slim
er/sie/es	ist	schlank	geworden	he/she/it (has) got slim
wir	sind	schlank	geworden	we (have) got slim
ihr	seid	schlank	geworden	you (have) got slim
sie/Sie	sind	schlank	geworden	they/you (have) got slim

12 Translate into English:

a Er wird bald gesund.

b Das Wetter wird schlecht.

c Wir wollen Ärzte werden.

d Meine Kinder wurden sehr krank.

e Mir wird ganz heiß.

f Er ist sehr schlank geworden.

g Der Urlaub wurde sehr teuer.

h Der Hund wird schnell aggressiv.

Answers p. 128

More on pronouns

Compare the two questions:

Können Sie mir helfen?   Can you help me?
Können Sie mich beraten?   Can you advise me?

If you refer to yourself as an object, you simply say 'me' in English; in German you say either **mir** or **mich**, depending on the case: **mich** is accusative and **mir** is dative.

■ The accusative case is used for direct objects:

Ich berate die Frau	I advise the woman	▷ **Ich berate sie**	I advise her
Ich berate den Mann	I advise the man	▷ **Ich berate ihn**	I advise him
Ich frage das Kind	I ask the child	▷ **Ich frage es**	I ask it
Ich frage die Schüler	I ask the students	▷ **Ich frage sie**	I ask them

■ The dative case is used for indirect objects:

Was können Sie mir empfehlen?   What can you recommend to me?

■ A few German verbs (such as **helfen**, to help) take a dative object rather than an accusative:

Ich helfe der Frau	I help the woman	▷ **Ich helfe ihr**	I help her
Ich helfe dem Mann	I help the man	▷ **Ich helfe ihm**	I help him

■ There are also a number of common German expressions which use the dative. The English translation often has quite a different structure:

Das Essen schmeckt den Kindern.   The children like the food. (lit. The food tastes good to the children.)

Das Essen schmeckt ihnen.   They like the food. (lit. The food tastes good to them.)

Mir ist schlecht.   I feel sick.

■ Here are the pronouns in the dative and the accusative:

Nom.	ich	du	er	sie	es	wir	ihr	sie/Sie
Acc.	mich	dich	ihn	sie	es	uns	euch	sie/Sie
Dat.	mir	dir	ihm	ihr	ihm	uns	euch	ihnen/Ihnen

13 Complete the translations.

a   How are you (formal)?   Wie geht es _____?

b   Can you help her?   Können Sie _____ helfen?

c   Can you advise us?   Können Sie _____ beraten?

d   What can you recommend her?   Was können Sie _____ empfehlen?

e   I feel constantly sick.   _____ ist ständig schlecht.

f   He feels hot and cold.   _____ ist heiß und kalt.

g   I am well, thank you.   _____ geht es gut, danke.

h   Are you (formal) enjoying your food?   Schmeckt _____ das Essen?

| Answers p. 128 |

Imperfect tense of modal verbs

To form the imperfect of a modal verb, take -**en** off the infinitive and add -**te**, -**test** or -**ten**. You also drop the umlaut.

- **können** ▷ **konnte**

Mein Mann konnte nicht schlafen.	My husband couldn't sleep.
Wir konnten nicht schlafen.	We couldn't sleep.
Konntest du schlafen?	Were you able to sleep?

- **wollen** ▷ **wollte**

Er wollte nicht kommen.	He did not want to come.
Wollten Sie zum Arzt gehen?	Did you want to go to the doctor?

- **müssen** ▷ **mußte**

Ich mußte in der Schule Englisch lernen.	I had to learn English at school.
Sie mußten viel arbeiten.	They had to work a lot.

- **dürfen** ▷ **durfte**

Durftet ihr in der Pause spielen?	Were you allowed to play during the break?
Durftest du Wein trinken?	Were you allowed to drink wine?

14 Translate into German:

a I wanted to go to the station.

_____

b He had to work.

_____

c We couldn't come.

_____

d I was allowed to see the film.

_____

e Did you (polite) want to eat?

_____

f They did not have to go.

_____

Answers p. 128

15 Do you know how to pamper yourself? Tick the boxes, count up your points according to the key below and then read the verdict ...

Was machen Sie, wenn Sie ...

1 ... plötzlich einen freien Vormittag haben?
  a Sie bleiben so lange wie möglich im Bett.
  b Sie machen einen großen Hausputz.
  c Sie gehen im Park spazieren.

2 ... von der Arbeit gestreßt sind?
  a Sie trinken eine Flasche Wein.
  b Sie essen zwei Tafeln Schokolade.
  c Sie gehen tanzen.

3 ... tausend Mark geschenkt bekommen?
  a Sie machen eine kleine Reise.
  b Sie kaufen sich einen schönen Sessel.
  c Sie tragen das Geld auf die Bank.

Punkte:

1	a	b	c
	7	2	7

2	a	b	c
	4	4	6

3	a	b	c
	7	5	2

6 – 8 Punkte: Sie müssen viel netter zu sich sein!
8 – 10 Punkte: Auch Sie müssen noch lernen, mehr für sich selbst zu tun.
10 – 16 Punkte: Sie machen meistens das Richtige!
20 Punkte: Sie sind ein Lebenskünstler – aber vielleicht gehen Sie manchmal etwas zu weit!

16 Your turn to speak about the way you pamper yourself. Turn to the recording where Hans will prompt you.

17 At the doctor's. Describe your symptoms for the various complaints below. If you are working with a partner, see if they, as the doctor, can diagnose your problem ...

Useful phrases: **Ich habe Magen/Ohren...schmerzen**
Seit wann haben Sie Schmerzen?

Here are the complaints:
a flu
b hay fever
c stomach bug
d you don't want to do a test/go to work

ANSWERS

EXERCISE 1

(a) morgen (b) schlaff, ungesund, unbeweglich
(c) 1: Saftkur (zur Entschlackung); 2 Kaloriendiät
(d) 800 Kalorien (e) fettarmes Essen: Salate,
mageres Fleisch, Fisch, wenig Kohlehydrate
(f) Alkohol und Süßigkeiten.

EXERCISE 2

Cross out: Käsekuchen; Weißwein, Schokoladeneis;
Schlagsahne; ... mit Rum

EXERCISE 3

Maria: b, c, e, g, h, Georg: a, d, f, i

EXERCISE 5

(a) Ich möchte eine Reiseapotheke mitnehmen.
(b) Können Sie mich beraten? (c) Können Sie mir
helfen? (d) Ich fahre in die Berge. (e) Ich
brauche ein starkes Sonnenschutzmittel.
(f) Ich brauche ein Pflaster.

EXERCISE 6

Cross out: Socken; Rotwein; Schokolade;
Schwarztee; Briefpapier; Bluse; Handschuhe.

EXERCISE 7

(a) Verkehrsmittel (b) Osten, Norden oder Westen
(c) Ferien machen (d) beste Kur
(e) wandern (f) ruhen (g) Besucher
(h) Kururlaub (i) Trinkkur (j) ideal
(k) Spaziergänge machen (l) Wanderungen.

EXERCISE 9

(a) Er hat Magenschmerzen! (b) Er hat Halsweh!
(c) Er hat Kopfweh (d) Sie haben Durchfall!
(e) Er hat Schnupfen! (f) Sie hat Fieber! (g) Er
hat keinen Appetit! (h) Sie haben
Muskelschmerzen!

EXERCISE 10

(a) flu and very high temperature (b) terrible
stomach pains (c) sore throat and headache, as usual
(d) too much stress, no appetite, sleeplessness; too
much alcohol, too many cigars (e) right hand hurts –
test today but cannot write

EXERCISE 12

(a) He will get better (lit. healthy) soon. (b) The
weather is getting worse. (c) We want to be doctors.
(d) My children became very ill. (e) I am getting
very hot. (f) He became very slim. (g) The
holiday became very expensive. (h) The dog quickly
gets aggressive.

EXERCISE 13

(a) Ihnen (b) ihr (c) uns (d) ihr (e) mir
(f) ihm (g) mir (h) Ihnen.

EXERCISE 14

(a) Ich wollte zum Bahnhof gehen. (b) Er mußte
arbeiten. (c) Wir konnten nicht kommen. (d) Ich
durfte den Film sehen. (e) Wollten Sie essen? (f)
Sie mußten nicht gehen.

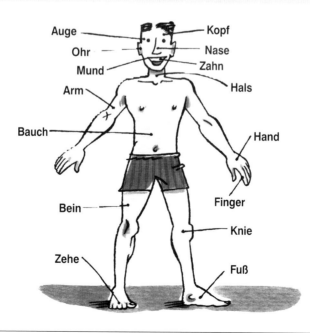

9 GOING OUT

POINTS TO REMEMBER

- at the pharmacy: **Apotheke, ich brauche ein Sonnenschutzmittel/Verbandszeug/Pflaster/ein Mittel gegen ...**
- at the doctor's: **ich bin gesund/krank; mir ist schlecht; ich habe Grippe/Halsschmerzen/Kopfschmerzen/Fieber/eine Erkältung/Schnupfen/Durchfall; ich brauche einen Arzt**
- health talk: **ich mache eine Saftkur/Diät; fettarmes Essen; Kurort**

BEFORE YOU BEGIN

Congratulations: you are already two-thirds through the course! Take some time out for revision: how about going back to an earlier unit and doing an exercise or two there? It might be especially useful to return to a previous Grammar exercise and work it out once more. This will help you consolidate your knowledge and give you a good idea of your progress.

At the box office

Biba	Guten Tag.
Kassiererin	Guten Tag, was kann ich für Sie tun?
Biba	Was spielen Sie am Donnerstag?
Kassiererin	Da haben wir eine Premiere der Oper Eugen Onegin.
Biba	Wann beginnt denn die Aufführung?
Kassiererin	Um zwanzig Uhr.
Biba	Was spielen Sie denn sonst noch in der Woche?
Kassiererin	Da haben wir einen Liederabend mit Werken von Hugo Wolf, Richard Wagner, Johannes Brahms, Otto Rino-Respighi, Richard Strauß und Gustav Mahler.
Biba	Haben Sie noch Karten?
Kassiererin	Ja, dafür haben wir noch Karten in allen Preisgruppen.
Biba	Gut, vielen Dank. Das überlege ich mir dann noch. Danke!
Kassiererin	Bitte sehr!
Biba	Wiederseh'n!
Kassiererin	Auf Wiederseh'n!

die Kassiererin or **der Kassierer** cashier, person in box office; **die Theaterkasse** box office

die Premiere premiere, first night

spielen to play (= perform); also to play cards/ball/piano etc.

die Oper opera

die Aufführung performance

was sonst what else; **sonst** otherwise

der Liederabend song recital

mit Werken with works; **das Werk** work; **Werke** (works) has an **-n** here because it is in the dative after **mit**.

die Preisgruppe price band; **die Gruppe** group

das überlege ich mir dann noch I'll think about it; **sich etwas überlegen** to think about something. This is a difficult construction which is best learnt by heart. Here is the whole pattern:

ich	überlege	mir	etwas	I think about something
du	überlegst	dir	etwas	you think about something
er/sie/es	überlegt	sich	etwas	he/she/it thinks about something
wir	überlegen	uns	etwas	we think about something
ihr	überlegt	euch	etwas	you think about something
sie/Sie	überlegen	sich	etwas	they/you think about something

1 Review the Conversation. Try to complete this exercise without referring back to the text. The letters in the squares marked 1–6 will give you the name of a famous German composer.

a Wir spielen in dieser Woche ... von Hugo Wolf und Johannes Brahms.

b Bei diesem ... hören Sie außerdem Lieder von Richard Strauß und Gustav Mahler.

c Wir haben Karten in allen ...

d Die ... beginnt um zwanzig Uhr.

e Am Samstag wird die ... Eugen Onegin gespielt.

f Auch da haben wir noch Karten. Sie können sich das ja noch...

a [1][ ][ ][ ][ ]

b [ ][ ][ ][ ][2][ ][ ][ ][ ]

c [ ][ ][ ][ ][3][ ][ ][ ][ ][ ]

d [ ][ ][ ][ ][ ][4][ ]

e [ ][5][ ]

f [ ][ ][ ][6][ ][ ][ ][ ]

Answers p. 144

Keyword: [ ][ ][ ][ ][ ][ ]

2 Buying opera tickets. You are at the box office. Complete the Conversation below by working out the questions.

a You _____?

Box Office Am Sonntag spielen wir die Oper Carmen von Bizet.

b You _____?

Box Office Nein, leider nicht mehr. Die Aufführung ist ausverkauft.

c You _____?

Box Office Am Freitag haben wir ein Konzert mit Werken von Chopin. Dafür haben wir noch Karten.

d You _____?

Box Office Sie kosten zwischen 40 und 75 Mark.

e You _____?

Answers p. 144

Box Office Die Aufführung beginnt um zwanzig Uhr.

3 An invitation. On the recording, Lena is trying to invite Frank to go out. Listen carefully, then study the summary below and correct the statements if necessary.

VOCABULARY

Lust haben   to feel like (doing something)

a   Heute abend wird Beethovens Fünfte Symphonie gespielt.
b   Frank kann nicht kommen, weil er Beethoven haßt.
c   Morgen gibt's einen Liederabend mit Werken von Händel.
d   Bei Händel bekommt Frank Kopfschmerzen.
e   Ihm gefallen Oldies aus den 50-er Jahren.
f   Am Samstag ist ein Nachmittag mit Golden Oldies.

Answers p. 144   g   Frank hat Zeit, aber keine Lust.

4 Here's a letter Ruth has written to her friend Agnes. As you will see, Ruth is a bit of an opera fan. Read the letter before you turn to the speaking exercise ...

VOCABULARY

das Lieblingsoper   favourite opera
ich freue mich darauf   I am looking forward to it; similarly: **er freut sich darauf** he's looking forward to it; **wir freuen uns darauf** we are looking forward to it.
dauert   lasts; **dauern**   to last; **die Dauer**   duration.

Liebe Agnes,

am Montag gehe ich endlich wieder ins Theater. In der Staatsoper wird eine Oper von Richard Wagner gespielt: Tristan und Isolde, du weißt ja, das ist meine Lieblingsoper. Ich habe eine sehr gute (aber teure) Karte und freue mich schon schrecklich darauf. Die Aufführung beginnt schon um sechs Uhr abends und dauert bis elf.

Alles Liebe und bis bald,

Deine

CONVERSATION 2

 Hung over

Ruth	Amin, du siehst etwas müde aus. Ist dir nicht gut?
Amin	Ach doch. Ich habe nur einen kleinen Kater.
Ruth	Hm. Zuviel gefeiert, was?
Amin	Ja, eigentlich wollten wir ja ganz früh nach Hause gehen, aber schließlich sind wir doch noch im „Hades" gelandet.
Ruth	Was, in diesem Lokal?
Amin	Ja, im „Hades". Da sollte nämlich eine gute Band spielen. Wir wollten mal wieder richtig klassisch tanzen, so wie früher in der Tanzschule: Foxtrott, Walzer, Tango ... Ja, und dann hieß es, die Band kann nicht kommen.
Ruth	Ja, gab's denn keine andere Band?
Amin	Ja, doch. Wir blieben erstmal da und warteten auf die Ersatzband. Aber die war fürchterlich: laut und langweilig. Man konnte sein eigenes Wort nicht verstehen. Und ich sag' dir, ich schlief im Stehen ein. Tanzen konnte man sowieso nicht, weil das Parkett zu voll war. Ständig trampelte mir jemand auf den Füßen 'rum, und die Luft war zum Schneiden dick. Mein Jackett war zerknittert, ich sag' dir, einfach ein völliger Reinfall. Und das Eintrittsgeld bekamen wir auch nicht mehr zurück.

LISTEN FOR...

Kater	hangover
gefeiert	celebrated
Ersatzband	replacement band

müde   tired; **der Kater** hangover, lit. male cat; **die Katze** cat.

(**Hast du**) **zuviel gefeiert?**   Have you been celebrating too much?; **feiern** to celebrate; **ich habe meinen Geburtstag gefeiert** I have been celebrating my birthday ...

gelandet   landed, here: ended up; **landen** to land.

das Lokal   pub or bar; **Speiselokal** restaurant.

da sollte eine gute Band spielen   there was supposed to be a good band playing

Nämlich is a filler word meaning 'you see'.

der Walzer   waltz

dann hieß es   then they said (lit. it was said); **hieß** is the imperfect tense of **heißen**. There are several imperfect forms in this Conversation which will be fully explained in Grammar, this unit. Three more: **wir blieben** we stayed (**bleiben** to stay); **wir warteten** we waited (**warten** to wait); **es gab** there was; (**geben: es gibt** there is).

die Ersatzband   the replacement (band)

fürchterlich   awful; **laut und langweilig** loud and boring

man konnte sein eigenes Wort nicht verstehen   you couldn't hear yourself speak (lit. one couldn't understand one's own word)

man schlief im Stehen ein   you fell asleep standing up; **einschlafen** to fall asleep.

sowieso   anyway

das Parkett   the (dance) floor

ständig trampelte mir jemand auf den Füßen 'rum   people (lit. someone) kept trampling on my feet; from **trampeln** 'to trample'.

die Luft war zum Schneiden dick   it was stuffy (lit. the air was thick enough to cut)

mein Jackett war zerknittert   my jacket was creased; **das Jackett** jacket

ein völliger Reinfall   a total washout

das Eintrittsgeld   entry fee

bekamen   imperfect form of **bekommen** to get

5 Translate into German:

a I have a hangover.

_____

b We ended up in the 'Hades'.

_____

c We wanted to dance the foxtrot.

_____

d The band could not come.

_____

e The replacement band was loud and awful.

_____

f One could not dance.

_____

g That was a washout.

Answers p. 144

_____

6 A good night out. Fill the gaps with the correct verbs from the boxes, then listen to the recording to check your answers.

VOCABULARY	gab besuchten bekamen
zufrieden content	**warteten waren schmeckte**

a Gestern _____ wir ein neues Speiselokal.

b Zuerst _____ es keinen freien Platz.

c Wir _____ eine halbe Stunde.

d Dann erst _____ wir einen Tisch.

e Das Essen _____ gut.

f Wir _____ wirklich sehr zufrieden.

7 Another hangover. Listen to the recording where Peter says why he's not feeling too well, then decide which statements are true and which false. You'll hear two new words: **deprimiert** depressed, and **geklärt** cleared up (from **klären** to clear up).

		Richtig	Falsch
a	Peter hat den ganzen Tag schwer gearbeitet.	☐	☐
b	Er wollte eigentlich schon früh in die Kneipe gehen.	☐	☐
c	Da kam Max und nahm ihn mit ins Kino.	☐	☐
d	Der Film war fürchterlich.	☐	☐
e	Max hatte das falsche Programm.	☐	☐
f	Sie gingen in die Kneipe.	☐	☐
g	Max war sehr zufrieden.	☐	☐
h	Er hatte keine Probleme mehr mit seiner Freundin.	☐	☐
i	Und so tranken sie viel Bier.	☐	☐

Answers and transcript p. 144

8 Your turn to talk about a night out ... Turn to the recording where Hans will prompt you as usual. These words will be useful:

wir wollten/tranken/sind gelandet

Kneipe/Kino/Film/Kater

wurde ... deprimiert

Ghosts and goblins

Amin

Ja, und dann kam uns plötzlich die Idee, daß wir ja auf den Fasching gehen könnten. Im „Adler" gab's einen Tanz unter dem Motto, „die weißen Nächte". Das heißt, jeder mußte sich weiß anziehen. Wir fuhren schnell nach Hause und

<table>
<tr><td></td><td></td></tr>
</table>

LISTEN FOR...

Idee	idea
Fasching	carnival
Geister	ghosts

verkleideten uns als Geister und Gespenster. Naja, nicht sehr originell, aber trotzdem. Das Auto ließen wir gleich zu Hause. Das Fest war schon in vollem Gang, wir trafen auch ein paar Freunde. Es war wirklich toll. Wir tranken viel Bier, tanzten bis zum Umfallen, und morgens um vier Uhr hatten wir einen riesigen Hunger. Und da gingen wir dann zum „Goldenen Eck" – das hat ja um die Zeit immer schon offen – und aßen ein paar Bratwürste, die fränkischen ...

dann kam uns die Idee we thought (lit. the idea came to us); **kam** from **kommen** to come.

der Fasching carnival; also: **die Fastnacht** or **der Karneval**; a big event for the Germans in the last few days before Lent

könnten might; expressing a possibility

unter dem Motto with the theme

sich anziehen to dress; **ich ziehe mich an** I dress (or: get dressed); **ich ziehe mich aus** I get undressed

wir fuhren we drove; from **fahren** to drive

wir verkleideten uns als we dressed up as; **sich verkleiden** to dress up; **ich verkleide mich als Cowboy** I dress up as a cowboy

der Geist or **das Gespenst** ghost

nicht sehr originell, aber trotzdem not very original, but never mind

wir ließen das Auto zu Hause we left the car at home; from **lassen** to let; to leave

in vollem Gang in full swing

wir trafen we met; from **treffen** to meet

toll great, fantastic

wir tranken we drank; from **trinken** to drink

wir tanzten bis zum Umfallen we danced until we dropped

wir hatten einen riesigen Hunger we were ravenous (lit. had a gigantic hunger)

wir gingen we went; from **gehen** to go

das hat um diese Zeit immer schon offen that's always already open at this time

wir aßen ein paar Bratwürste we ate a few sausages; from **essen** to eat. Note: **ein paar** a few but: **ein Paar** a pair.

die fränkischen the Franconian ones

DIE WEISSEN NÄCHTE

PRACTICE

9 Here's an account of Amin's carnival night, but six sentences are wrong. Correct them without looking at the Conversation.

a Wir gingen in den „Adler" auf den Fasching.

b Der Abend stand unter dem Motto: die schwarzen Nächte.

c Jeder mußte sich schwarz anziehen.

d Wir gingen nach Hause und verkleideten uns als Gespenster.

e Wir fuhren nicht mit unserem Auto zum „Adler".

f Das Fest hatte noch nicht angefangen.

g Wir trafen ein paar Freunde.

h Wir tranken viel Wein und tanzten bis zum Umfallen.

i Am Morgen hatten wir ein wenig Hunger.

Answers p. 144

j Wir gingen zum „Goldenen Eck" und aßen einen Salat.

10 Hidden words. Uncover them – either down or across. You should find nine altogether.

F	H	I	D	E	E	B	N	O
M	F	A	S	C	H	I	N	G
O	R	I	G	I	N	E	L	L
T	A	N	Z	E	S	R	A	I
T	H	U	N	G	E	R	N	E
O	N	K	T	O	X	L	G	D

Answers p. 144

Here are the clues:

a Ich habe eine sehr gute _____ für heute abend!

b Viele Leute verkleiden sich für den _____

c Manche Kostüme sind sehr _____

d Auch ältere Leute gehen manchmal gern zu einem

_____

e Manche Leute sitzen nur da und trinken viel _____

f Andere singen ein _____ nach dem anderen.

g Manche finden ein _____ wie zum Beispiel „schwarze Nächte" langweilig.

h Sie finden, daß solche Feste viel zu _____ dauern.

i Nach einer aktiven Nacht hat man oft einen großen

_____

11 A special offer for **Rosenmontag**, a carnival highlight in the German city of Mainz. Study this brochure from the **Deutsche Bahn**. Then listen to the recorded interview with Lukas, who went to the carnival, and answer the questions below, briefly, in English.

ROSENMONTAG IN MAINZ

Mainz, wie es singt und lacht
Bequem im InterCity nach Mainz
Reise im InterCity mit Platzbuchung

Direkt vor dem Hauptbahnhof fängt das Fest schon an. Jung und Alt ist auf den Beinen und feiert die „fünfte Jahreszeit". Freuen Sie sich über die tolle Stimmung. Feiern Sie mit! Lachen Sie über die Masken und Puppen! Werfen Sie mit Bonbons, Konfetti und Blumen! Die Garden und Musikgruppen spielen bis zum Umfallen! Singen, tanzen und schunkeln Sie mit!

Reisepreise
ab Basel Bad Bf 82,- DM
ab Freiburg 72,- DM
inklusive: Bahnfahrt, 2. Klasse mit reservierten Plätzen und IC Zuschlag,
Kinder zahlen nur den halben Fahrpreis.

VOCABULARY	
bequem	comfortable
die Platzbuchung	seat reservation
Jung und Alt ist auf den Beinen	young and old are on their feet
die Stimmung	mood; atmosphere
Masken und Puppen	masks and puppets
werfen	to throw
das Bonbon	boiled sweet
die Garde	guard, military band
schunkeln	to link arms and sway from side to side

a How did Lukas travel to Mainz?

b Where did the celebrations start?

c What did he see?

d What was the mood like?

e How did he participate?

Answers p. 144

12 Your turn to speak: this time you've been to the carnival in Mainz, too. Here are some words you'll need:
Stimmung/Rosenmontag/Umfallen/gingen/tanzten

KEY WORDS AND PHRASES

At the box office

Was spielen Sie ...	What's on ...
heute abend?	tonight?
diese Woche?	this week?
Haben Sie noch Karten?	Have you still got tickets?
Wann beginnt die Aufführung?	When does the performance start?
Das überlege ich mir noch.	I'll think about it.
das Theater	theatre
das Kino	cinema
die Theaterkasse	box office (theatre)
die Kinokasse	box office (cinema)
die Oper	opera
das Werk	work
der Liederabend	song recital
die Preisgruppe	price range
das Eintrittsgeld	the entrance fee

A night out

Ich habe einen Kater	I have a hangover
Wir sind im ... gelandet.	We ended up in ...
Das Parkett war voll.	The dance floor was full.
Die Luft war zum Schneiden dick.	It was very stuffy.
Das war ein Reinfall.	That was a washout.
Es war wirklich toll.	It was really great.
der Fasching, die Fastnacht	carnival
der Tanz	dance
unter dem Motto	with the theme
Wir verkleiden uns als Geister.	We dress up as ghosts.
sich anziehen	to dress or: get dressed
(nicht) sehr originell	(not) very original
Das Fest war in vollem Gang.	The party was in full swing.
Wir ...	We ...
trafen Freunde	ran into/met up with friends
tanzten bis zum Umfallen	danced until we dropped
ließen das Auto zu Hause	left the car at home

The imperfect tense

In Unit 5 you learned the imperfect forms of weak verbs. You were also introduced to the imperfect forms of two important strong verbs: **sein** and **haben**. Go back if you need to refresh your memory.

■ In this unit, you have met some more imperfect forms of weak verbs:

wir warteten	(from **warten**)	we waited
jemand trampelte	(from **trampeln**)	somebody trampled
wir verkleideten uns	(from **sich verkleiden**)	we dressed up

■ ... but you have also come across some imperfect forms of strong verbs. As you saw, they form their imperfect by changing their stems:

ich schlief ein	(from **schlafen**)	I fell asleep
wir bekamen	(from **bekommen**)	we got
wir aßen	(from **essen**)	we ate

■ Here are all the forms of the verb **gehen** (to go); its stem changes to **ging**. The verb endings are common to all strong verbs:

ich	**ging**	I went
du	**gingst**	you went
er/sie/es	**ging**	he/she/it went
wir	**gingen**	we went
ihr	**gingt**	you went
sie/Sie	**gingen**	they/you went

13 Write out all forms of **schlafen** (to sleep) following the example above.

a _____ I slept

b _____ you slept

c _____ he/she/it slept

d _____ we slept

e _____ you slept

f _____ they/you slept

Answers p. 144

■ Note: sometimes there is a resemblance between English and German imperfect forms which can help you recognise the verbs. For example:

kommen	kam	to come	came
trinken	trank	to drink	drank
singen	sang	to sing	sang

14 Rewrite the sentences in the present tense.
Example:

Er trank ein Bier. *Er trinkt ein Bier.*

a Ich gab ihm ein Buch. _____

b Wir sangen ein Lied. _____

c Hans trank viel zu viel. _____

d Ilse und Petra schwammen 500 Meter. _____

e Bekam ich heute keine Post? _____

| Answers p. 144 |

In most cases, you will need to learn the imperfect forms by heart. There is a list of strong verbs at the back of the book (pp. 200–1).

15 Rewrite the following sentences in the imperfect tense.

a Ich fahre schnell nach Hause.

_____

b Er läßt das Auto zu Hause.

_____

c Wir haben einen Riesenhunger.

_____

d Sie gehen alle zum Tanzen.

_____

e Ich esse ein paar Würstchen.

_____

f Wir bleiben vier Wochen in Italien.

_____

g Sie bekommt das Eintrittsgeld zurück.

_____

| Answers p. 144 |

16 Fill in the right verbs.

| freute | hatte | schlief | gab | wurde | dauerte | spielte |

a Am Sonntag _____ ich Geburtstag.

b Mein Vater _____ mir eine Karte fürs Theater.

c Ich _____ mich schon sehr.

d Aber leider _____ man an dem Abend eine Oper!

e Und nicht nur das! Die Oper _____ bis Mitternacht!

f Ich _____ furchtbar müde.

g Und zum Schluß _____ ich einfach ein!

Answers p. 144

■ Remember the word order in sentences with two verbs: the second verb is sent right to the end:

Wir gingen lange	spazieren.	We went for a long walk.
Ich ließ meine Tante zuerst	einsteigen.	I let my aunt get in first.
Mußten Sie lange	warten?	Did you have to wait for a long time?

17 Write in the correct imperfect forms of the verbs in brackets.

a Am Samstag _____ (fahren) ich nach Flensburg.

b Ich _____ (treffen) mich mit meiner Freundin.

c Es _____ (sein) ein schöner Tag.

d Wir _____ (gehen) zuerst spazieren.

e Danach _____ (trinken) wir einen Kaffee und _____
(essen) ein Stück Torte.

f Am Abend _____ (wollen) wir ins Kino gehen.

g Aber es _____ (geben) leider keine Karten mehr.

Answers p. 144

18 **Wir geben eine Party** – how to organise your party. Here are some hints from a magazine. Study the article, and answer the questions below – briefly, in English.

Wir geben eine Party!

Ein Fest zu Hause ist eine tolle Idee. Man freut sich, aber man hat auch ein wenig Angst: was wenn sich die Gäste langweilen? Dies sollte man sich überlegen ...
- Wen möchte ich einladen?
- Wo möchte ich feiern?
- Wie will ich die Gäste unterhalten?

Am besten ist es, wenn Sie nur „Wunschgäste" einladen!
- keine Muß-Einladungen – sie machen die Stimmung kaputt.

- keine Einladungen an Freunde, die große Partys nicht mögen.
- für eine gute Party brauchen Sie Gäste, die gerne aktiv sind und keine Angst haben, den ersten Schritt zu machen.

Aber auch die beste Party wird ein Flop, wenn Sie keinen Platz haben. Fragen Sie sich:
- Ist Platz zum Tanzen da?
- Ist zuviel Platz da?
- Gibt es auch intime Ecken?

... und vergessen Sie nicht: die Nachbarn informieren. Die schönste Stimmung ist kaputt, wenn ein Nachbar die Polizei holt.

VOCABULARY

der Gast	guest	**kaputt**	ruined
Angst haben	to be afraid, worry	**der Schritt**	step
einladen	to invite; **die Einladung** invitation	**die Polizei**	police
unterhalten	to entertain	**holen**	to fetch

a People look forward to celebrating – but they also worry. Why?

b What are the three main points to think about beforehand?

c Whom should you not invite?

d What do you need to think about in terms of space?

Answers p. 144

19 Your turn to speak about planning a party – leave your book open!

20 Imagine your partner is organising a party. Ask them who they want to invite, where they intend to have the party and how they want to entertain their guests. Then swop roles.

Take your questions from the article in Exercise 18:

Wen möchtest du einladen? (Ich möchte alle meine Freunde ... einladen)

Wo möchtest du feiern? (im Keller/im Garten/in einem Restaurant)

Ist das nicht zu groß/zu klein? Ist genug Platz zum Tanzen da?

Wie willst du die Gäste unterhalten?

ANSWERS

EXERCISE 1

(a) Werke (b) Liederabend (c) Preisgruppen
(d) Aufführung (e) Oper (f) überlegen
Keyword: WAGNER.

EXERCISE 2

(a) Was spielen Sie am Sonntag? (b) Haben Sie
noch Karten? (c) Und was spielen Sie am Freitag?
(d) Was kosten die Karten? (e) Wann beginnt die
Aufführung?

EXERCISE 3

(c) Morgen gibt's eine schöne Oper von Händel.
(e) Ihm gefallen Oldies aus den 60-er Jahren.
(f) Am Samstag ist ein Abend mit Golden Oldies.
(g) Frank hat Lust, aber leider keine Zeit.

EXERCISE 5

(a) Ich habe einen Kater. (b) Wir sind im „Hades"
gelandet. (c) Wir wollten Foxtrott tanzen. (d) Die
Band konnte nicht kommen. (e) Die Ersatzband
war laut und fürchterlich. (f) Man konnte nicht
tanzen. (g) Das war ein Reinfall.

EXERCISE 7

(a) R (b) F (c) R (d) F (e) R (f) R (g) F
(h) F (i) R.

Transcript: Ja, gestern arbeitete ich den ganzen Tag:
12 Stunden!! Eigentlich wollte ich dann früh ins Bett
gehen. Aber dann kam Max und sagte: komm doch
mit ins Kino, da wird ein ganz toller Film gespielt.
Also ging ich mit und dann wurde der Film gar nicht
gespielt. Max hatte das falsche Programm! Also sind
wir in der Kneipe gelandet und Max wurde plötzlich
sehr deprimiert. Er hat nämlich Probleme mit seiner
Freundin. Wir tranken ein Bier nach dem anderen
und gingen erst heim, als die Kneipe zumachte. Und
das Problem mit der Freundin haben wir immer
noch nicht geklärt ...

EXERCISE 9

(b) ... die weißen Nächte. (c) ... weiß anziehen.
(f) ... hatte schon angefangen. (h) ... tranken viel
Bier (i) ... einen riesigen Hunger. (j) ... ein paar
Bratwürste.

EXERCISE 10

(a) Idee (b) Fasching (c) originell (d) Tanz
(e) Bier (f) Lied (g) Motto (h) lang
(i) Hunger.

EXERCISE 11

(a) by train (b) directly in front of the station
(c) masks, puppets, military and music bands
(d) fantastic (e) he danced until he dropped.

EXERCISE 13

(a) ich schlief (b) du schliefst (c) er/sie/es schlief
(d) wir schliefen (e) ihr schlieft (f) Sie/sie
schliefen.

EXERCISE 14

(a) Ich gebe ihm ein Buch. (b) Wir singen ein Lied.
(c) Hans trinkt viel zu viel. (d) Ilse und Petra
schwimmen 500 Meter. (e) Bekomme ich heute
keine Post?

EXERCISE 15

(a) Ich fuhr schnell nach Hause. (b) Er ließ das
Auto zu Hause. (c) Wir hatten einen Riesenhunger.
(d) Sie gingen alle zum Tanzen. (e) Ich aß ein paar
Würstchen. (f) Wir blieben vier Wochen in Italien.
(g) Sie bekam das Eintrittsgeld zurück.

EXERCISE 16

(a) hatte (b) gab (c) freute (d) spielte
(e) dauerte (f) wurde (g) schlief.

EXERCISE 17

(a) fuhr (b) traf (c) war (d) gingen
(e) tranken; aßen (f) wollten (g) gab.

EXERCISE 18

(a) What if the guests get bored? (b) Who do I
invite? Where will the party be? How will I entertain
the guests? (c) anybody you feel obliged to invite;
friends who hate large parties; anybody who is afraid
to make the first step. (d) Is there enough space to
dance? Is there too much space? Are there also some
cosy, intimate corners?

Unit 9 Going out

WHAT YOU WILL LEARN
- ▶ discussing school and education
- ▶ comparing country and city life
- ▶ talking about learning another language
- ▶ you will also read about changing your daily routine

POINTS TO REMEMBER
- Phrases for the box office: **Was spielen Sie diese Woche? Haben Sie noch Karten? Welche Preisgruppe? Wann beginnt die Aufführung?**
- **Theater, Kino, Theaterkasse, Kinokasse, Film, Oper, Werk, Liederabend**
- A night out: **ich habe einen Kater; das war ein Reinfall; es war wirklich toll**
- Carnival: **Fasching/Fastnacht: wir verkleideten uns, trafen Freunde, tanzten bis zum Umfallen, ließen das Auto zu Hause**

BEFORE YOU BEGIN

Here's a short summary of the German school system.

German children start school at the age of six and are legally bound to stay

at school until they are eighteen. After four to six years at the **Grundschule**, the children move on to secondary school. This can be a **Gesamtschule** (comprehensive). Other options are as follows: the **Hauptschule**, followed by **Berufsschule** (part-time vocational training alongside an apprenticeship), leads to various qualifications in trade and industry. The **Realschule**, which offers a slightly more academic range of subjects than the **Hauptschule**, enables the students to go to technical colleges afterwards. The most academic option is the **Gymnasium** which leads to the **Abitur** – a qualification that opens up the full range of courses offered at university.

CONVERSATION 1

 ## School matters

Biba	Wieviel Kinder haben Sie?
Heide	Wir haben zwei Kinder – Niels und Claudia. Niels ist sieben Jahre alt. Er ist jetzt in der ersten Klasse der Grundschule. Davor war er drei Jahre im Kindergarten, und als er ganz klein war und ich noch arbeiten mußte, eine Zeitlang in der Kinderkrippe.
Biba	Und Claudia?
Heide	Claudia ist zwölf. Sie ist seit zwei Jahren auf dem Gymnasium. Sie will auf jeden Fall die Mittlere Reife machen. Also noch vier Jahre Gymnasium, und dann vielleicht auch das Abitur, das wären noch weitere drei Jahre.
Biba	Wie lange dauert eigentlich der Unterricht an der Schule?
Heide	Normal sechs Stunden. Von acht Uhr bis 13 Uhr mittags. Nachmittags ist frei, das heißt, die Kinder haben natürlich Hausaufgaben.
Biba	Ach ja – und was ist, wenn die Kinder später mal beide studieren wollen? Wird das nicht sehr teuer?
Heide	Studieren selbst kostet gar nicht so viel – aber das Leben natürlich ist teuer. Essen, Miete, Bücher ... Man kann von der Regierung ein Stipendium bekommen, das muß man aber später zum Teil zurückzahlen.

LISTEN FOR...

Grundschule	primary school
Kinderkrippe	crèche
Gymnasium	grammar school

---

die Grundschule   primary school

eine Zeitlang   for a while

die Kinderkrippe   crèche

das Gymnasium   grammar school

auf jeden Fall   in any case

die Mittlere Reife   school diploma taken at 16

das Abitur   university entrance exam

das wären   that would be

der Unterricht   the classes; **unterrichten** to teach; **er unterrichtet Deutsch** he teaches German.

Stunden here means 'school periods' (40 minutes), not 'hours'

das heißt   that is

die Hausaufgabe(n)   homework

Was ist, wenn die Kinder später mal beide studieren wollen?   What's going to happen if both children want to go to university later on? **studieren** to study, to go to university; **sie möchte studieren** she wants to go to university; **er studiert Mathematik** he is studying maths.

die Miete   rent; remember **mieten** to rent

das Stipendium   grant

zurückzahlen (sep.)   to pay back

1 Repeat extracts from the Conversation without looking at it.

a   Der Unterricht dauert normalerweise _____ Stunden.
b   Nachmittags ist _____
c   Aber die Kinder haben natürlich nachmittags _____
d   _____ kostet natürlich nicht so viel, aber das _____ ist teuer.
e   Man kann von der _____ ein _____ bekommen.

Answers p. 160

2 Pinboard. Here's a school pinboard. Listen to the recording and decide which notice the various people would be interested in.

VOCABULARY	
nach Feierabend	after work
backen	to bake
die Psychologin	psychologist
die Sprechstunde	consultation time

a   Sport nach Feierabend
Sport für Eltern und Schüler – Mittwoch abend Volleyball, Donnerstag abend Fußball, Freitag abend Gymnastik!

b   Schulpsychologin
Therapie für Jugendliche und Erwachsene.
Spieltherapie für Kinder. Sprechstunden jeden Mittwoch an der Schule!

c   *Es weihnachtet sehr ...*
Tun Sie etwas für die Schule.
Backen Sie für den Weihnachtsbazar!

d   *Es wird getanzt ... Klasse 10 geht zum Tanzkurs. Der Kurs wird von Eltern und Schülern organisiert und bezahlt.*

e   **Filmclub**
Die neuesten Filme, einmal in der Woche, jeden Mittwoch; Klassen 11-13 abends, alle anderen am Nachmittag!

f   Hilfe in allen Situationen
Praktische Tips für alle neuen Schüler und Eltern ...

Anna Lena	
Martin	
Frau Schön	
Herr Schulze	
Angelika	
Tobias	

Answers p. 160

3 An old problem. Study the article – it contains a number of unfamiliar words. See whether you can get the gist of it nonetheless. Then complete the translation below. Note that in German the present tense is used for something that will happen in the future – in English the future tense is used.

ARBEITENDE MÜTTER WOLLEN GANZTAGSSCHULEN

Michaela M. ist alleinerziehende Mutter. Sie arbeitet von neun bis sechs in einem Kaufhaus. Ihre Tochter Gabi ist fünf. Es war schwer genug, einen Platz im Kindergarten zu bekommen. Aber im nächsten Jahr wird alles noch viel schwerer: Dann kommt Gabi in die erste Klasse. Die Schule hört schon um zwölf Uhr auf – im Kindergarten konnte sie den ganzen Tag bleiben. Nun muß Gabi allein nach Hause gehen und dort auf Michaela warten. Michaela will das nicht, aber ihren Job kann sie auch nicht aufgeben, weil sie das Geld braucht.

Michaelas Fall ist typisch für viele Frauen. Mütter mit Ganztagsjobs haben es schwer – besonders im deutschen Schulsystem. Halbtagsjobs sind nicht immer möglich. Viele meinen, ihr Problem könnte durch Ganztagsschulen gelöst werden.

a _____ MOTHERS WANT ALL-DAY SCHOOLS

b Michaela M is a single _____

c She _____ from 9 to 6 in a department store.

d Her _____ Gabi is five.

e It was hard enough to get a _____ in the kindergarten.

f But _____ year everything will be much harder.

g Then Gabi will start _____

h School will finish at 12 – in the kindergarten she _____
_____

i Then Gabi will have to _____ by herself and wait for Michaela there.

j Michaela does not want this, but she cannot _____ either because she _____

k Michaela's case is _____ of many women.

l Mothers with full-time jobs have a hard time – especially in
_____

m Part-time jobs are _____

n Many think their problem might be solved by

Answers p. 160 _____

4 Your turn to speak – this time you are a working parent. Useful phrases:
arbeiten ganztags/halbtags; hört um ... auf; alleine nach Hause; können unsere Jobs nicht aufgeben; das Geld brauchen.

CONVERSATION 2

Life in the country

Silke

Ich wohne jetzt fünf Jahre auf dem Land, und es
hat mir eigentlich sehr gut gefallen, so die Nähe
zur Natur – so Berge und Wälder – mehr Kontakt
zu den Leuten zu haben, auch zum Kaufmann,
und irgendwie ist alles viel persönlicher da, kleiner und überschaubarer.
Nachteile sind die weite Entfernung zur Stadt, ich hab' kein Auto, muß immer trampen, und ich
kriege wenig Besuch, weil wenig meiner Freunde ein Auto haben. Aus dem Grunde zieh' ich
jetzt in die Stadt, um mehr Kontakt zu haben zu Freunden.

LISTEN FOR...	
auf dem Land	in the country
die Nähe zur Natur	closeness to nature
Nachteile	disadvantages

auf dem Land in the country; **das Land**
   country
die Nähe proximity
die Natur nature
der Wald forest
der Kontakt contact

der Kaufmann shopkeeper
irgendwie somehow
persönlich personal
überschaubar manageable
der Nachteil disadvantage; similarly: **der**
   Vorteil advantage
die Entfernung distance
trampen to hitchhike; **der Tramper** hitchhiker
ich kriege wenig Besuch lit. I get few visits;
   kriegen to get; **der Besuch** visit; **der**
   Besucher/die Besucherin visitor
aus dem Grund for that reason
zieh' ich jetzt in die Stadt I am now
   moving to the city; **ziehen** or **umziehen**
   to move (house): **ich ziehe um** I move
   house; not to be confused with: **ich ziehe**
   mich um I change (clothes).
um ... zu haben in order to have ... More on
   'in order to' in Grammar, this unit.

Unit 10 Life styles 149

5 Take notes – what are, according to Silke, the advantages and disadvantages of living in the country and in the town? Complete the list below, in German.

	Vorteil	Nachteil
auf dem Land	*Nähe zur Natur*	
in der Stadt		

Answers p. 160

6 Paradise Lost? Listen to Martin and decide which of the statements below are true and which false. New word: **der Lärm** noise.

		R	F
a	Martin lebte jahrelang in der Stadt.	☐	☐
b	Es hat ihm dort sehr gut gefallen.	☐	☐
c	Doch dann bekam er einen Job in einem Gasthof, auf dem Land.	☐	☐
d	Er arbeitete dort als Koch.	☐	☐
e	Zuerst wollte er nicht aufs Land.	☐	☐
f	Aber jetzt ist er sehr glücklich dort.	☐	☐

Answers p. 160

7 Not everybody's dream. Peter has just moved to the city to start his first year at university. Read the letter he wrote to Karin about his new life. Then correct the mistakes in the English summary below. All but two sentences need correcting.

> Liebe Karin,
>
> nun lebe ich also endlich in der Stadt. Ich habe ein schönes Zimmer im Stadtzentrum, und ich kann zu Fuß zur Universität. Die Uni ist OK, auch die Dozenten sind nicht schlecht, aber ich habe noch keine Freunde gefunden, und meine Komilitonen sind nicht besonders freundlich. Das Leben in der Stadt gefällt mir überhaupt nicht. Die Luft ist schlecht, die Straßen sind schmutzig, manchmal ist es so laut, daß man sein eigenes Wort nicht mehr hört! Es gibt genug Kinos und Kneipen, aber ich kenne ja niemand, und alleine habe ich keine Lust. Die Atmosphäre ist so anonym hier, ich bin gar nicht glücklich.
>
> Liebe Grüße,
>
> Dein Peter

VOCABULARY	
das Zimmer	room
der Dozent	lecturer
schmutzig	dirty
der Komilitone	fellow student

a I have a nice room in the suburbs and I can take the bus to the university.

b The university is OK, but the teachers are rotten.

c However, I have already found a friend.

d The other students are pretty silly.

e I like life in the city.

f But the air is bad, the roads are dirty and very noisy.

g There are enough cinemas and theatres but I don't know anybody and don't feel like going out on my own.

Answers p. 160

h The atmosphere is anonymous but I am happy.

8 Your turn to speak about life in the city. You will hear **der Vorort** (suburb), and you'll need **die Wohnung** (flat).

> Remember: **Ich wohne seit zwei Jahren in Ulm.** I have lived in Ulm for two years.

Evening classes

Ingrid

So abends nach der Arbeit, da geht meine Arbeit eigentlich erst richtig los. Ich besuch' nämlich seit einiger Zeit das Abendgymnasium und will in eineinhalb

Jahren Abitur machen. Es fing eigentlich damit an, daß ich früher zur Volkshochschule ging und mich schon immer für Sprachen interessiert hab' – so Englisch und Französisch. Englisch kann ich ein bißchen von der Schule her, aber nicht viel.

Was mir noch Schwierigkeiten macht, ist selber sprechen, das ist am schwierigsten. Ich versuch' so zu üben, indem ich Radio hör' in meiner Freizeit. Ich hör' da auch ausländische Sender: BBC London, oder Radio France oder Radio Luxembourg, und das macht Spaß, wenn man dann anfängt, was zu verstehen. Und so nebenbei üb' ich dann auch in der Schule, im Sprachlabor, und demnächst will ich mal in Urlaub fahren: zwei Wochen nach Frankreich und zwei Wochen nach England.

losgehen (sep.) to start. Sometimes you will hear: **'Los!'** 'Let's go!'

eigentlich erst richtig really seriously

das Abendgymnasium evening classes leading up to the university entrance exam

eineinhalb one and a half

die Volkshochschule (or **VHS**) adult education centre

was mir noch Schwierigkeiten macht ... what is still difficult for me; **die Schwierigkeit** difficulty

ich versuch' I try; **versuchen** to try

üben to practise; **ich übe** I practise; **ich habe gut geübt** I have practised well; **die Übung** exercise, practice

indem ich Radio hör' by listening to the radio

die Freizeit spare time

ausländische Sender foreign stations; **der Sender** station

das macht Spaß that's fun; **der Spaß** fun

wenn man anfängt once one begins; **anfangen** (sep.) to begin; **der Anfang** beginning

was (= **etwas**) **zu verstehen** to understand something

nebenbei on the side

das Sprachlabor language lab

demnächst in the near future

Volkshochschule Heidelberg
Poststraße 15 · Telefon 06221/21882
Berufliche Weiterbildung in der Volkshochschule – der solide Weg zur Arbeitsplatzsicherung und zum Berufserfolg

PRACTICE

9   **Richtig oder falsch?** Correct the five statements which are wrong.

                                                                                Richtig Falsch

a   Ingrid will bald das Abendgymnasium besuchen.   ☐   ☐

b   Sie hat sich schon immer für Sprachen interessiert.   ☐   ☐

c   Sie ging früher zur Volkshochschule.   ☐   ☐

d   Das Abitur will sie aber nicht machen.   ☐   ☐

e   Sie hat ein bißchen Französisch in der Schule gelernt.   ☐   ☐

f   Sie hört gerne ausländische Sender.   ☐   ☐

g   Im Sprachlabor hat sie noch nie geübt.   ☐   ☐

h   Sie war schon in Frankreich und England im Urlaub.   ☐   ☐

Corrected statements

_____

_____

_____

_____

Answers p. 160   _____

10   Take notes – in English! On the recording, Beate and Stefan talk about their education and their plans for the future.

VOCABULARY

verlassen	to leave
verdienen	to earn
Italienisch	Italian

Beate

studied what:`   _____

for how long: _____

where: _____

before that: _____

qualification: _____

at the moment: _____

wants to be: _____

Stefan

first school: _____

left school at: _____

in order to: _____

now wants to learn: _____

currently studying: _____

afterwards: _____

Answers p. 160

11 A mishap. Here's a true story from *Brigitte Young Miss*.

Bruchlandung

Vor kurzem wollte ich mit meiner Freundin ins Kino
gehen, als uns auf der Straße zwei süße Amerikaner
ansprachen. Sie hatten sich verlaufen und baten uns,
Ihnen den Weg zur Jugendherberge zu beschreiben – auf
englisch. Ich wollte sie nach ihrem Stadtplan fragen und suchte
verzweifelt nach den richtigen Vokabeln. In meiner Verzweiflung
fiel mir jedoch nur noch ein: „Take out your plane". Meine
Freundin lachte und die zwei Touristen sagten danke
und zogen weiter, ohne auf eine Antwort zu warten. ...

... and now comes the guesswork. Can you puzzle out the words or phrases for:

a crashlanding   _____
b a short while ago   _____
c two sweet Americans   _____
d they'd lost their way   _____
e youth hostel   _____
f to describe   _____
g map of the town   _____
h desperate(ly)   _____
i in (my) desperation   _____

Answers p. 160 j without waiting for an answer   _____

12 Your turn to speak about your own evening classes. Useful phrases:
**höre/übe/lerne/Volkshochschule/ausländische Sender/
Sprachlabor/einmal die Woche** (once a week)

KEY WORDS
AND PHRASES

Schule und Erziehung

die Kinderkrippe
der Kindergarten
die Grundschule
das Gymnasium
die Berufsschule
die Gesamtschule
die Universität
das Abitur
das Stipendium
die Volkshochschule (VHS)
die Abendschule

Ich bin in der ersten/achten Klasse
Ich möchte studieren
Ich übe
der Unterricht
das Sprachlabor
ausländische Sender
Das macht mir Schwierigkeiten

School and education

crèche
kindergarten
primary school
grammar school
vocational college
comprehensive school
university
university entrance exam
grant
adult education (centre)
evening classes

I am in the first/eighth form
I want to study/go to university
I practise
classes
language lab
foreign stations
I have problems with that

Lebensstil

Ich wohne ...
    auf dem Land
    in der Stadt
    in einem Vorort

Ich ziehe ...
    aufs Land
    in die Stadt

Auf dem Land hat man ...
    die Nähe zur Natur
    Kontakt zu Leuten

Auf dem Land ist alles ...
    persönlicher
    überschaubarer

Die Straßen sind schmutzig und laut

Lifestyle

I live ...
    in the country
    in town
    in a suburb

I'm moving ...
    to the country
    into town

In the country you are ...
    close to nature
    in contact with people

In the country, everything is ...
    more personal
    more manageable

The streets are dirty and noisy

GRAMMAR AND EXERCISES

The infinitive

- The infinitive is the basic form of the verb that you will find in the dictionary (for example **kommen** to come). It is used with some modal verbs, **werden** and verbs of motion:

Ich kann kommen.	I can come.
Wir werden singen.	We will sing.
Er geht morgen schwimmen.	He will go swimming tomorrow.

- The word order is the same as for other phrases with two verbs: the second verb is shunted to the end of the sentence.

13 Make sentences by using up all the words in brackets. Then translate them into English.

a   Ich (arbeiten/mußte)

b   Wir (gehen/wollen/zur Universität)

c   Anna und Philip (spazieren/gehen)

d   Sie (ihren Job/aufgeben/will)

e   Sie (fliegen/nach Amerika/müssen)

Answers p. 160

- In other cases, you will find the infinitive with **zu** (for example **zu üben** 'to practise').

Ich versuche zu üben.	I try to practise.
Man fängt an, etwas zu verstehen.	One starts to understand something.
Es war schwer, Kontakt zu bekommen.	It was difficult to make contact.

14 Rearrange the words in brackets to complete the sentences. Translate them into English.

a   Sie baten uns, (beschreiben/zu/den Weg)

b   Es war schwierig, (etwas/verstehen/zu)

c   Er versuchte, (sprechen/English/zu)

d   Ich habe keine Lust, (zu/gehen/ins Kino)

e   Es war nicht leicht, (finden/den Weg/zu)

Answers p. 160

- With separable verbs, **zu** goes between the prefix and the stem:

mitfahren   to drive/come along
▷ **Ich habe keine Lust, mitzufahren**   I don't feel like coming along
aussteigen   to get out
▷ **Ich habe vergessen, auszusteigen**   I forgot (lit: have forgotten) to get out

15
Fill in the right infinitive forms. Then translate the sentences into English.

a   Ich habe keine Lust, _____ (mich umziehen)

_____

b   Ich habe Angst, so viel Geld _____ (ausgeben)

_____

c   Ich vergesse immer wieder, die Fenster _____ (aufmachen)

_____

d   Wir haben Lust, heute abend _____ (ausgehen)

_____

| Answers p. 160 |

- The infinitive with **zu** is also used in certain phrases such as:
um ... zu   in order to
ohne ... zu   without

Ich ziehe in die Stadt, um mehr Kontakt zu haben.
  I'm moving into town in order to have more contact.
Er geht zur Abendschule, um Italienisch zu lernen.
  He's going to evening classes in order to learn Italian.
Sie gingen weiter, ohne auf uns zu warten.
  They went on without waiting for us.

16
The second half of the sentences below has been jumbled up. Rearrange the words into proper sentences.

a   Wir gehen in die Abendschule, (das Abitur/um/machen/zu)

_____

b   Sie fuhr heute zur Arbeit, (essen/zu/ohne/etwas)

_____

c   Ich mache viel Gymnastik, (um/werden/zu/fit)

_____

d   Er hat den ganzen Tag gearbeitet, (eine Pause/ohne/machen/zu)

_____

| Answers p. 160 |

Something to watch: **zu** can mean 'to' or 'too'!

Er kam zu spät.	He was too late.
Sie war viel zu müde.	She was much too tired.
Er hat vergessen, das Buch mitzubringen.	He forgot to bring the book along.

Requests and commands

The infinitive without **zu** is also used in instructions and commands:

Hier öffnen!   Open here!
Bitte einsteigen!   Please get in (into the train/tram/underground/bus)!

17 Match up the English and German signs.

a **Nicht rauchen!**

b **Bitte nicht stören!**

c **Hier schließen!**

d **Bitte warten!**

e **Nicht aussteigen!**

A **Close here**

B **Do not alight**

C **Do not disturb**

D **Please wait**

E **No smoking**

Answers p. 160

- Another way of making firm requests is the imperative, using the present tense:

Gehen Sie!   Go!
Kommen Sie!   Come!
Setzen Sie sich!   Sit down!
Ziehen Sie Ihren Mantel aus! Take your coat off!

Note: there is no personal pronoun with the familiar form:

Geh! (singular)   Go!
Geht! (plural)   Go!
Setzt euch!   Sit down!
Zieht euren Mantel aus!   Take your coats off!

VOCABULARY	
widerrechtlich	illegally
abstellen	to park
kostenpflichtig	at owner's expense
abschleppen	to tow away

Nur für Kunden
der Deutschen Bank
in der Zeit von
8 – 20 Uhr

Widerrechtlich abgestellte Fahrzeuge
werden kostenpflichtig abgeschleppt

18 **Ändern Sie Ihren Alltagstrott** – change your daily grind! That's what *Brigitte* magazine suggests by saying: **Stellen Sie einmal alles auf den Kopf** – turn everything upside down... Read the article first, then turn to the recording for some speaking practice.

Ändern Sie Ihren Alltagstrott!

Stellen Sie einmal alles auf den Kopf.

Jeder Tag ist wie der andere? Sie langweilen sich? Dann ändern Sie Ihren Alltagstrott! Hier sind ein paar Tips!
Frühstück: Butter, Brötchen, Marmelade schon seit Jahren? Probieren Sie Obst, Quark, Müsli und Schwarzbrot. Vielleicht fühlen Sie

sich besser! Und wie wär's mit klassischer Musik? Mozart macht frisch!

- Immer die gleichen Kleider? Machen Sie ein Experiment: versuchen Sie einen total anderen Stil!
- Viele Wege führen ins Büro. Entdecken Sie einen neuen Weg – auch wenn er länger ist. Das ist gut gegen den Routinetrott!
- Gehen Sie immer um 12 Uhr essen? Warum nicht einmal um 1.30 – dann sehen Sie andere Leute! ☐

VOCABULARY	
das Brötchen	breadroll
die Marmelade	jam
probieren	to try
gleich	same
führen	to lead
das Büro	office
entdecken	to discover

And now it's your turn to speak and talk to Gertrude about changing her life style. Hans will prompt you.

19 Discuss with a partner the pros and cons of country life. Here's a grid with arguments:

Stadt	Land
unpersönlich	persönlich
laut, schlechte Luft	gute Luft, gesund
hektisch	ruhig
viel zu tun: Kinos, Theater, Kneipen, Ausstellungen	langweilig: kein Kino, keine Kultur
viele verschiedene Leute	isoliert

![ANSWERS]

Exercise 1

(a) sechs (b) frei (c) Hausaufgaben
(d) Studieren; Leben (e) Regierung; Stipendium

Exercise 2

Anna Lena: (c) Martin: (d) Frau Schön: (a)
Herr Schulze: (b) Angelika: (f) Tobias: (e)

Exercise 3

(a) working (b) mother (c) works (d) daughter
(e) place (f) next (g) the first class (in primary
school) (h) could stay all day (i) go home
(j) give up her job; needs the money (k) typical
(l) the German school system (m) not always
possible (n) all-day schools.

Exercise 5

Land – Vorteil: Nähe zur Natur, mehr Kontakt zu den
Leuten, alles ist persönlicher, kleiner,
überschaubarer. Nachteil: weite Entfernung zur
Stadt, muß trampen, wenig Besuch. Stadt – Vorteil:
mehr Kontakt zu Freunden ohne Auto.

Exercise 6

(a) R (b) F (c) R (d) R (e) F (f) F.

Exercise 7

(a) I have a nice room in the city centre and can walk
to the university. (b) ... and the teachers are not bad
(c) But I haven't made any friends (d) My fellow
students are not very friendly. (e) I don't like life in
the city. (f and g are correct) (h) ... and I'm not at
all happy.

Exercise 9

(a) F (b) R (c) R (d) F (e) F (f) R (g) F
(h) F. Corrected statements: (a) Ingrid besucht seit
einiger Zeit das Abendgymnasium. (d) Sie will in
eineinhalb Jahren Abitur machen. (e) Sie hat ein
bißchen Englisch in der Schule gelernt. (g) Sie übt
nebenbei im Sprachlabor. (h) Sie will demnächst
nach Frankreich und England fahren.

Exercise 10

Beate: German, 4 years, Cologne university, girls'
grammar school, University entrance, no job,
journalist. Stefan: comprehensive, age 16, earn money,
more – especially languages, Italian, French.
Transcripts: Beate: Ich habe vier Jahre Deutsch
studiert, an der Universität Köln. Davor war ich auf
einem Mädchengymnasium. Dort habe ich auch das

Abitur gemacht. Im Moment habe ich noch keinen
Job. Ich möchte gerne Journalistin werden. Stefan:
Ich besuchte erst eine Gesamtschule, aber ich habe
die Schule mit 16 verlassen, weil ich gerne schnell
Geld verdienen wollte. Jetzt tut es mir leid. Ich
möchte gerne noch mehr lernen, vor allem
Sprachen. Im Moment mache ich einen
Italienischkurs an der Volkshochschule. Danach
möchte ich gerne einen Französischkurs machen.

Exercise 11

(a) Bruchlandung (b) vor kurzem (c) zwei süße
Amerikaner (d) sie hatten sich verlaufen
(e) Jugendherberge (f) beschreiben
(g) Stadtplan (h) verzweifelt (i) in meiner
Verzweiflung (j) ohne auf eine Antwort zu warten.

Exercise 13

(a) Ich mußte arbeiten. I had to work. (b) Wir
wollen zur Universität gehen. We want to go to
university. (c) Anna und Philip gehen spazieren.
Anna and Philip go for a walk. (d) Sie will ihren Job
aufgeben. She wants to give up her job. (e) Sie
müssen nach Amerika fliegen. They have to fly to
America.

Exercise 14

(a) ..., den Weg zu beschreiben. They asked us to
describe the way. (b) ..., etwas zu verstehen. It was
difficult to understand anything. (c) ..., Englisch zu
sprechen. He tried to speak English. (d) ..., ins Kino
zu gehen. I don't feel like going to the cinema.
(e) ..., den Weg zu finden. It was not easy to find the
way.

Exercise 15

(a) ... mich umzuziehen. I don't feel like changing.
(b) ... auszugeben. I am afraid to spend so much
money. (c) ... aufzumachen. I keep forgetting to
open the windows. (d) ... auszugehen. We feel like
going out tonight.

Exercise 16

(a) ... um das Abitur zu machen. (b) ... ohne etwas
zu essen. (c) ... um fit zu werden. (d) ... ohne
eine Pause zu machen.

Exercise 17

(a) E (b) C (c) A (d) D (e) B

11 WORK

WHAT YOU WILL LEARN

▶ discussing your day at work
▶ comparing various jobs
▶ talking about changing jobs
▶ you will also learn how to write a CV

POINTS TO REMEMBER

● various types of school: **Grundschule, Gymnasium, Gesamtschule, Berufsschule, Volkshochschule, Abendschule**
● study words: **studieren, üben, der Unterricht, Sprachlabor, Abitur**
● lifestyles: **auf dem Land, in der Stadt, in einem Vorort**
● **Vorteile, Nachteile, Nähe zur Natur, Kontakt zu Leuten, die Straßen sind schmutzig und laut**

BEFORE YOU BEGIN

Over the last few years, flexible work patterns have become a lot more common in Germany. Car manufacturers introduced three- or four-day working weeks as early as 1995, and other firms have set up **Arbeitskonten** – work accounts where the employees decide their own working patterns but must make sure they complete a certain agreed number of hours. Teleworking (**Telearbeit**) is also increasingly common, as is part-time work (**Teilzeitarbeit**). The vast majority of part-timers are still women. In the face of the growing pressures on the labour market, even long-established privileges such as an extra month's salary at Christmas (**13. Monatsgehalt**) and the Christmas bonus (**Weihnachtsgeld**) have come under threat.

A safe job

LISTEN FOR...	
Was sind Sie von Beruf?	What's your profession?
	What do you do for a living?
Buchhalter	accountant
Rente	pension

Ruth Was sind Sie von Beruf?

Herr Beck Ich bin Buchhalter in einer großen Exportfirma, und das ist für mich ein ganz sicherer Beruf mit großen Aufstiegsmöglichkeiten. Und vor allen Dingen bekomme ich eine gute Rente, wenn ich pensioniert werde.

Ruth Und wann gehen Sie in den Ruhestand?

Herr Beck Ich gehe mit 65 in den Ruhestand.

Ruth Wie sieht Ihr typischer Arbeitstag aus?

Herr Beck Mein typischer Arbeitstag beginnt um sieben Uhr und endet um 15 Uhr.

Ruth Wann haben Sie Mittagspause?

Herr Beck Ich habe Mittagspause von 12 bis ein Uhr.

Ruth Und was machen Sie da?

Herr Beck Ich gehe in die Kantine, esse da mit Kollegen zusammen.

Ruth Gibt's bei Ihnen gleitende Arbeitszeit?

Herr Beck Ja, bei uns gibt's gleitende Arbeitszeit.

Ruth Und wieviel Urlaub haben Sie im Jahr?

Herr Beck Ich habe vier Wochen Urlaub im Jahr, wobei ich aber dazu sagen muß, daß die Pfingsttage, Ostern oder Weihnachtstage nicht dazugerechnet werden.

Ruth Das ist extra?

Herr Beck Das ist extra, ja.

Was sind Sie von Beruf? What's your job?
   Beruf trade, profession
der Buchhalter accountant
die Exportfirma export firm
ein (ganz) sicherer Beruf mit großen Aufstiegsmöglichkeiten a (very) secure job with good prospects; **der Aufstieg** rise, **die Möglichkeit** possibility; other useful words: **das Gehalt** salary; **Geld verdienen** to earn money; **brutto** before tax; **netto** after tax; **das Weihnachtsgeld** Christmas bonus.
die Rente pension
wenn ich pensioniert werde when I retire; **er wird pensioniert** he retires; **wir werden pensioniert** we retire; note the passive construction based on **werden** (Grammar, Unit 7).

in (den) Ruhestand gehen to enter retirement
die Mittagspause lunch break
die Kantine canteen
der Kollege, die Kollegin colleague
gleitende Arbeitszeit or **Gleitzeit** flexitime; from **gleiten** 'to glide'.
wobei ich aber dazu sagen muß ... however I have to say to that ...
daß die Pfingsttage nicht dazugerechnet werden; die Pfingsttage werden nicht dazugerechnet the Whitsun holidays are not included; **Pfingsttage** or **Pfingsten** Whitsun. Again the passive with **werden** is used.

1 How much do you remember about Manfred Beck's job? Fill in the details.

a   Name _____

b   Beruf _____

c   arbeitet wo? _____

d   ab wann Rente? _____

e   Arbeitstag   von _____   bis _____

f   Mittagspause   von _____   bis _____

g   Gleitzeit? _____

h   Urlaub _____

Answers p. 176

i   extra Urlaub _____

2 Read through the job adverts below, then listen to Christoph and Petra on the recording. Decide which of the jobs advertised they might be suitable for. It will help to take a few notes while listening.

Stellenangebote

Berufe aktuell

Menschen im Hotel:

- Koch/Köchin
- Telefonist/in
- Verkäufer/in in der Hotelboutique

Gleitzeit, auch Nachtarbeit

Technische Universität Cottbus

In der Fakultät Elektrotechnik ab sofort
Diplom-Physiker mit guten
Englischkenntnissen für ein Jahresprojekt

BauConsult

Sekretärin mit Organisationstalent und
Flexibilität
Gute Englisch- und Spanischkenntnisse
6 Wochen Urlaub im Jahr

Max Planck Institut Berlin

Bibliothek
Mitarbeiter/in halbtags/nachmittags
Erfahrung mit MS-Word und Katalog-Arbeiten

Christoph _____

_____

Petra _____

_____

Answers p. 176

3 Puzzle. Fill in the right words to complete the sentences. The letters 1–7 will give you the keyword: it's a place to sit and eat during a work break.

a   Menschen, mit denen man zusammenarbeitet

b   Ich habe pro Jahr fünf Wochen ...

c   Normalerweise geht ein Mann mit 65 in den ...

d   Feiertage im Frühling

e   Feiertage im Spätfrühling

f   Feiertage im Winter

g   Buchhalter ist ein ganz sicherer ...

Answers p. 176

Keyword: 1 2 3 4 5 6 7

4 Your turn to speak. Look at this job profile of a computer programmer and put yourself in her shoes. Answer Johannes's questions according to the profile.

VOCABULARY

der Arbeitgeber	employer
Einzelheiten	details

Name	Cornelia Martens
Beruf	Programmiererin
Arbeitgeber	Siemens
Alter	35 Jahre
Einzelheiten	Gleitzeit
	32-Stunden-Woche
	5 Wochen Jahresurlaub
	Weihnachtsgeld
Gehalt	monatlich DM 8 000 brutto

I: Hotel-/Be.
t. (BTA/UTA).
ithagen, Tel.: (05/.

iatlich zugelassenes Fei
Fußpflege. Prospekt: CC
igen, (09071)5 85 90.

iesign-Studium. Priv. Berufsfa(
annt, Institut für Grafik Desig.
planade 30, (040) 34 53 53   unc
isenstr. 25, (0211) 37 99 00

isleiter/in Ausbildung für Kinder und
Erwachsene - Kinder/Jugendseminare. DGePE, Postfach
700 261, 63427 Hanau. TEL / FAX: (06181) 6 31 97

Mit **Abitur** zweijährige Ausbildungen: Staatlich anerkannte
Europasekretärin mit Aufbaustudium an Universitäten in
England und Frankreich. Internationale Touristik-, Direk-
tions- oder Marketingassistentin. BAFÖG, Studiendarle-
hen, Zimmerservice. Prospekt BA anfordern. Merkur Aka-
demie, Amalienstraße 81, 76133 Karlsruhe, Tel.
(0721) 2 58 71

GRAFIK-DESIGN. Professionelle Berufsausbildung BAfoG,
DTP-Computer. Prospekt: Freiburger-Grafik-Schule,
Merzhauserstr. 161, 79100 Freiburg, Tel.: (0761) 40 27 67

rb-, **Stil- und Imageberaterin** - ein Beruf mit Zukunft. Ihr
Veg in die Selbständigkeit. Gratis-Info bei **SÉLÉCTANCE**
ƆSMETICS GmbH, Postfach 32 27, 40682 Erkrath,
: (0211)2 05 61, Fax: (0211)25 26 86

Nebenberuflich zur Immobilienmaklerin. Betriebswirtin mit
Diplom. Info IBW GmbH, Telefon (07621) 79 92 50

isch an der Cote d'Azur - Antibes, seit 1985 ver-
n wir Standard- u. Intensivsprachkurse. Unter-
ıflegung in der Residenz des Institutes/Gastfa-
ıs Freizeitprogramm, Examensmöglichkeiten,
ı, Wochenpreise ab DM 640,—. Gernot
ıraße 23, 85579 Neubiberg, Tel./Fax:

Heilpraktiker/Psychotherapeutin. Verwirklichen Sie '
persönliche Neigung zum verantwortungsvollen Um·
mit Ihren Mitmenschen und seinen seelischen ur
sundheitlichen Problemen. Als Verbandsschule d
en **Verbandes Deutscher Heilpraktiker** verr
überall in Deutschland und in der Schweiz '
seriös alle Kenntnisse, die Sie zur Ausüh
praktikerberufs benötigen. Informatione·
DEUTSCHE PARACELSUS SCHULF'
fahren GmbH. Sonnenstraße19 ·
(089) 55 25 41-38

'M: Fremdsprachen + Be-
Abschluß B.A. in Euro-
' Iahr in England
· ͻͼΜΙͼ

AUSBILDUN^ ·

Working freelance

Ruth	Was sind Sie von Beruf?
Biba	Ich bin freie Journalistin.
Ruth	Haben Sie sich auch andere Berufe überlegt?
Biba	Ja, früher wollte ich mal Lehrerin werden, aber das ist heut' nicht mehr so einfach. Es gibt sehr viele arbeitslose Lehrer. Und natürlich habe ich auch an eine feste Anstellung gedacht, beim Rundfunk oder bei einer Zeitung.
Ruth	Und warum sind Sie dann freie Journalistin geworden?
Biba	Weil ich keine feste Stelle gefunden habe.
Ruth	Und sind Sie denn mit Ihrem Beruf zufrieden?
Biba	Ja und nein. Insgesamt glaube ich schon, daß ich die richtige Entscheidung getroffen habe, denn mein Beruf ist sehr abwechslungsreich. Ich komme ständig mit neuen Leuten zusammen und muß viele neue Ideen entwickeln. Aber er hat auch viele Nachteile. Zum Beispiel habe ich manchmal Geldsorgen, oder ich verdiene während des Urlaubs kein Geld. Oder wenn ich krank bin, verdiene ich kein Geld, und das sind große Unsicherheiten.

LISTEN FOR...

arbeitslos	out of work
feste Anstellung	steady job
zufrieden	content

freie Journalistin freelance journalist; other useful words: **selbständig** self-employed, independent; **ich arbeite freiberuflich** I work freelance.

arbeitslos unemployed

die feste Anstellung or **feste Stelle** steady job

gedacht (past participle) thought; from **denken** to think; **ich habe gedacht** I have thought.

der Rundfunk radio

zufrieden content, satisfied

insgesamt overall

daß ich die richtige Entscheidung getroffen habe that I made the right decision; **ich treffe eine Entscheidung** I make a decision; **er hat die Entscheidung getroffen** he made the decision

abwechslungsreich varied (lit. rich in variation); based on **wechseln** 'to change'.

entwickeln to develop

die Sorge worry

verdienen to earn

während des Urlaubs during the holidays; **während** is one of the very few prepositions that take the genitive case.

die Unsicherheit insecurity; **sicher** sure, safe

5 **Vorteil oder Nachteil?** Advantage or disadvantage? Decide whether these statements about Biba's job are an advantage (**Vorteil**) or a disadvantage (**Nachteil**) to her.

		Vorteil	Nachteil
a	Bibas Beruf ist manchmal unsicher.	☐	☐
b	Sie kommt mit vielen Leuten zusammen.	☐	☐
c	Sie muß immer neue Ideen entwickeln.	☐	☐
d	Sie verdient im Urlaub kein Geld.	☐	☐
e	In ihrem Beruf gibt es viel Abwechslung.	☐	☐
f	Wenn sie krank ist, bekommt sie kein Geld.	☐	☐

Answers p. 176

6 A brief interview. Here are the answers. Write down the appropriate questions using the polite form of address **Sie**. Then compare your dialogue with the one on the recording. Some of your questions might vary slightly.

VOCABULARY	
der Zahnarzt	dentist
die Zahntechnikerin	dental assistant
der Studienplatz	place at university

a _____?
Ich bin Zahntechnikerin.

b _____?
Ja, ich bin mit meinem Beruf zufrieden.

c _____?
Ja, früher wollte ich mal Zahnärztin werden, aber ich bekam keinen Studienplatz.

d _____?
Mein typischer Arbeitstag beginnt um acht und endet um sechzehn Uhr.

e _____?
Ich habe von dreizehn bis vierzehn Uhr Mittagspause.

f _____?
Nein, bei uns gibt's keine Gleitzeit. Wir haben feste Stunden.

g _____?
Ich habe vier Wochen Urlaub im Jahr, und dann kommen noch die Feiertage dazu.

Answers p. 176

Dr Fritz Rehm

ZAHNARZT

Sprechstunden: Mo – Fr 9-12
Di – Do 16-19
und nach Vereinbarung

7 Unemployment among young immigrants. Study the article and decide whether the statements below are true or false.

VIELE AUSLÄNDISCHE JUGENDLICHE SIND ARBEITSLOS.

Unter den ausländischen Jugendlichen gibt es besonders viele Arbeitslose. Warum? Sie sind oft schlechter auf das Berufsleben vorbereitet als die deutschen Jugendlichen. Ihr Deutsch ist nicht gut genug und ihre Allgemeinbildung ist voller Lücken, besonders, wenn sie relativ spät nach Deutschland kamen und keinen Schulabschluß haben. Sie können nur Hilfsarbeiter werden, aber Hilfsarbeiter gibt es jetzt schon zu viele. Wie kann man helfen? Das Arbeitsamt kann Sprach- und Ausbildungskurse finanzieren, um den ausländischen Jugendlichen bessere Startchancen auf dem Arbeitsmarkt zu geben.

VOCABULARY

das Berufsleben	professional life
vorbereitet	prepared
die Allgemeinbildung	general knowledge or education
die Lücke	gap
der Schulabschluß	qualification (from school)
der Hilfsarbeiter	unskilled labourer
das Arbeitsamt	job centre
der Ausbildungskurs	training course

	Richtig	Falsch
a Youth unemployment is not quite so severe among immigrants.	☐	☐
b Young immigrants are generally not as well prepared for their future careers as their German counterparts.	☐	☐
c Their job opportunities are better if they have arrived in Germany relatively late.	☐	☐
d Their German is good enough.	☐	☐
e Their general knowledge is full of gaps.	☐	☐
f They have no choice but to be unskilled labourers.	☐	☐
g The job centre can provide money for special courses.	☐	☐
h There are not enough unskilled labourers on the market.	☐	☐

Answers p. 176

8 Your turn to speak and ask Friederike about her job and career. Hans will prompt you as usual. Useful phrases:
ich bin ... zufrieden/Chefsekretärin in einer Baufirma ...
ich muß organisieren/selbständig arbeiten ...
mein Beruf ist abwechslungsreich ...   ich habe ... Jahresurlaub

CONVERSATION 3

A new life

Silke

Also, ich hab' die Schule so früh wie möglich verlassen, ich wollte nämlich ziemlich schnell Geld verdienen. Und da hab' ich 'ne Zeitlang in der Fabrik gearbeitet – am Fließband. Und da ich noch mehr Geld verdienen wollte, machte ich dann

Akkordarbeit. Aber das war ziemlich anstrengend. Wenn ich abends nach Hause kam, kam ich mir vor wie eine Maschine. Ich konnte nichts Richtiges mit mir anfangen, ich war völlig kaputt. Und dann entschloß ich mich nach einer Weile, was anderes zu machen. Es war mir egal, ob ich mehr Geld in der Tasche hatte oder nicht. Ich ging daher zum Arbeitsamt und ließ mich beraten. Und jetzt bin ich Arzthelferin. Ich komme mit Menschen zusammen. Das ist zwar auch anstrengend, aber ich hab' das Gefühl, daß ich was wirklich Wichtiges mache.

ich habe verlassen I (have) left

ich wollte nämlich ziemlich schnell Geld verdienen I wanted to earn money rather quickly, you know. Note that **schnell** can mean both 'quick' and 'quickly'.

die Fabrik factory; another useful word: **das Praktikum** work experience.

am Fließband on the production line

die Akkordarbeit piecework

anstrengend exhausting, demanding

kam ich mir vor wie eine Maschine I felt like a machine; **sich vorkommen** (sep.) to feel like; **er kommt sich vor wie ein Held** he feels like a hero.

ich konnte nichts Richtiges mit mir anfangen I didn't know what to do with myself (lit. couldn't start anything right with myself)

ich war völlig kaputt I was totally worn out; **kaputt** here is colloquial for **müde** tired

ich entschloß mich I decided; **sich entschließen** to decide; **er kann sich nicht entschließen** he can't make up his mind.

nach einer Weile after a while

etwas anderes something different; similarly: **was** (= etwas) **wirklich Wichtiges** something really important; **etwas Schönes** something beautiful; **etwas Interessantes** something interesting.

es war mir egal, ob ... I did not care whether; **es ist mir egal** I don't care; **es ist ihm egal** he doesn't care; **es ist ihr egal** she doesn't care.

Arbeitsamt job centre

ich ließ mich beraten I asked for advice (lit. I had myself advised)

die Arzthelferin doctor's assistant; this profession entails more than being a receptionist: apart from clerical duties, she would also have had some medical training and assist the doctor with the patients.

ich hab' das Gefühl I have the feeling

Dr. med. Werner Wurster
Praxis für Chinesische Medizin (TCM)
Allgemeinarzt · Kinderarzt

D 88353 Kisslegg im Allgäu · Emmeho
Telefon 07563/9225 3 Telefax 075
EMail: wuwe@w4.oe

G B

GEROLD BILEK

PRAXIS FÜR

PHYSIOTHERAPIE

Abt-Hyller Straße 5

88250 Weingarten

Telefon: (0751) 45080

9 Translate the summary below. Use as many phrases from Conversation 3 as possible.

a She wanted to earn money fast.

_____

b She worked in a factory.

_____

c She was totally worn out.

_____

d She went to the job centre.

_____

e And now she is a doctor's assistant.

_____

f She has the feeling she is doing something important.

Answers p. 176

_____

10 Cordula has just finished her final exam at school and wants some advice on her future career from her former teacher Frau Kratz. Fill in the missing words, then listen to the recording to check your answers.

Beruf   Menschen   Geld   Abitur   Idee   Berufsplänen   Computer   Arbeitsamt   abwechslungsreich

Leipzig, den 20. September

Liebe Frau Kratz,

vielen Dank für Ihr Interesse an meinen _____. *Ich*

ging gestern zum _____ *und ließ mich beraten. Sie*

wissen ja, daß mein _____ *nicht besonders gut ist.*

Leider! Nun suche ich einen _____, *der interessant*

und _____ *ist. Außerdem will ich nicht irgendwo nur*

vor einem _____ *sitzen, sondern soviel wie möglich mit*

_____ *zu tun haben. Natürlich möchte ich auch schön*

_____ *verdienen.*

Haben Sie eine gute _____ ?

Viele liebe Grüße, Ihre

Cordula

11 On the recording, Matthias and Uschi talk about their choice of jobs. Listen a few times and take notes – in English.

Matthias	Uschi
a qualification from school	qualification from school
b other qualifications/work experience	other qualifications/work experience
c interests and hobbies	interests and hobbies
d plans	plans
e what's most important in a job	what's most important in a job

Answers p. 176

12 Past tenses galore – fit them in!

hatte   ließ   konnte   kam   war   entschloß

a Ich _____ mir vor wie eine Maschine.
b Ich _____ nichts Richtiges mit mir anfangen.
c Ich _____ mich, etwas anderes zu machen.
d Ich _____ mich beim Arbeitsamt beraten.
e Ich _____ kein Geld mehr in der Tasche.
Answers p. 176 **f** Aber das _____ mir egal.

13 Your turn to speak and talk about your own plans and ambitions ... These phrases will come in useful ...

arbeitete jahrelang
wurde langweilig
arbeitslos
freie Zeit
Abendschule
Kochkurs
viel Spaß
Koch werden
in einer Kneipe

KEY WORDS AND PHRASES

Was sind Sie von Beruf?	What's your job?
Ich bin ...	I am a(n) ...
Lehrer(in)	teacher
Buchhalter(in)	accountant
Fabrikarbeiter(in)	factory worker
Journalist(in)	journalist
freie Journalistin	freelance journalist (female)
Arzthelfer(in)	doctor's assistant
Ich arbeite freiberuflich	I work freelance
Ich habe eine feste Stelle	I have a steady job
Ich arbeite ...	I work ...
in der Fabrik	in the factory
bei einer Exportfirma	in an export firm
am Fließband	on the production line
am Computer	at the computer
Mein Beruf ist ...	My job is ...
interessant	interesting
abwechslungsreich	varied
anstrengend	exhausting
langweilig	boring
Mein Beruf hat Vorteile/Nachteile	My job has advantages/disadvantages
Es gibt ...	There is/are ...
gute Aufstiegsmöglichkeiten	good career prospects
gleitende Arbeitszeit/Gleitzeit	flexitime
eine Kantine	a canteen
eine Stunde Mittagspause	a one-hour lunch break
vier Wochen Urlaub	four weeks' holiday
ein gutes Gehalt	a good salary
nette Kollegen	nice colleagues
eine Rente	a pension
Ich verdiene ...	I earn ...
ein gutes Gehalt	a good salary
brutto/netto	before/after tax
Ich gehe mit 60 in den Ruhestand	I'll take retirement at 60
Ich habe die Schule früh verlassen	I left school early
Ich will/wollte ...	I want/wanted to ...
Lehrer werden	be a teacher
viel Geld verdienen	earn a lot of money

GRAMMAR AND EXERCISES

The indefinite article

Just like the definite article **der/die/das** (the), the indefinite article **ein/eine/ein** (a) takes specific endings depending on the case it is in. Refresh your memory in Grammar, Unit 4. Here is the basic pattern.

Always remember you will be understood even if you get the endings wrong. They will come with practice. Getting bogged down by them at this stage will do more harm than good!

	masculine: **ein**		feminine: **eine**		neuter: **ein**	
Nominative	ein	Mann	eine	Fabrik	ein	Kind
Accusative	ein**en**	Mann	eine	Fabrik	ein	Kind
Dative	ein**em**	Mann	ein**er**	Fabrik	ein**em**	Kind
Genitive	ein**es**	Mann**es**	ein**er**	Fabrik	ein**es**	Kind**es**

Ich sehe einen Mann.   I see a man. (acc. masc.)
Er gab den Brief einem Mann.   He gave the letter to a man. (dat. masc.)
Sie arbeitet in einer Fabrik.   She works in a factory. (dat. fem.)
Das ist der Name einer Fabrik.   That's the name of a factory. (gen. fem.)
Die Familie hat ein Kind.   The family has a child. (acc. neut.)
Das Buch gehört einem Kind.   The book belongs to a child. (dat. neut.)

14   Fill the gaps with the correct indefinite article.

a   Haben Sie _____ Zimmer frei?
b   Ich möchte _____ Auto kaufen.
c   Ich habe _____ Tochter.
d   Ich bin in _____ Kino.
e   Er sitzt in _____ Sessel.

> **Answers p. 176**

- Avoid saying **nicht ein**. The correct word is **kein/keine/kein**. It follows the same pattern as **ein/eine/ein**. (For plural forms see next page.)
  Ich habe kein Geld.   I have no money. (acc. neut.)
  Es macht keinen Sinn.   It makes no sense. (acc. masc.)
  Er hat keine Frau.   He has no wife. (acc. fem.)

- Possessive adjectives: **mein** (my), **dein** (your), **sein** (his/its), **ihr** (her/its), **unser** (our), **euer** (your), **ihr** (their), **Ihr** (your) also follow the same pattern as **ein/eine/ein**.
  Ich habe meine Handtasche verloren.   I've lost my handbag. (acc. fem.)
  Das ist mein Geld.   That's my money. (nom. masc.)
  Er sitzt in seinem Auto.   He sits in his car. (dat. masc.)

15   Complete the translations.

a   Das ist _____ Frau.   This is my wife.
b   Er sitzt in _____ Zimmer.   He sits in his room.
c   Wo ist _____ Tante?   Where is your (informal) aunt?
d   Ich habe _____ Tochter.   I have no daughter.
e   Ich kann _____ Mann nicht sehen.   I can't see your (formal) husband.

> **Answers p. 176**

Adjective endings

You have already learnt what happens to adjectives if they are preceded by the definite article. Go back to Grammar, Unit 5 to refresh your memory.

■ If the adjectives are preceded by **ein/kein/mein** etc. they follow the patterns set out below. Don't try and learn them all at once. Concentrate on one form at a time.

■ Masculine

Nominative	ein	gut**er** Mann
Accusative	einen	gut**en** Mann
Dative	einem	gut**en** Mann
Genitive	eines	gut**en** Mannes

■ Feminine

Nominative	eine	groß**e** Fabrik
Accusative	eine	groß**e** Fabrik
Dative	einer	groß**en** Fabrik
Genitive	einer	groß**en** Fabrik

■ Neuter

Nominative	ein	klein**es** Kind
Accusative	ein	klein**es** Kind
Dative	einem	klein**en** Kind
Genitive	eines	klein**en** Kindes

■ Plural (for all three genders)

Nominative	kein**e**	klein**en** Kinder
Accusative	kein**e**	klein**en** Kinder
Dative	kein**en**	klein**en** Kindern
Genitive	kein**er**	klein**en** Kinder

16 Fill in the right masculine adjectival endings.

a   Das ist ein gut _____ Wein.

b   Hattest du einen schön _____ Tag?

c   Wir gehen zu einem lang _____ Liederabend.

d   Das ist ein groß _____ Ball.

Answers p. 176

17 Fill in the right feminine adjective endings.

a   Ich möchte eine heiß _____ Suppe.

b   Das ist meine neu _____ Wohnung.

c   Er kommt aus einer groß _____ Familie.

d   Hier ist das Zimmer meiner klein _____ Tochter.

Answers p. 176

18 Fill the gaps.

a That's an old cinema.	Das ist ein _____ _____
b I'd like to buy a small present.	Ich möchte _____ _____ kaufen.
c _____	Wo ist das Zimmer Ihres kleinen Mädchens?
d I'd like a hot drink.	Ich _____ _____ _____

Answers p. 176

The pluperfect

- Sentences such as 'I had worked' or 'They had come' are in the pluperfect tense. Their German equivalents are as follows:

Ich hatte wochenlang gearbeitet.   I had worked for weeks.
Sie waren gekommen.   They had come.

The pluperfect is often used after **nachdem** (after):

Nachdem er in der Lotterie gewonnen hatte, kaufte er sich einen dicken Mercedes.
After he had won in the lottery he bought himself a fat Mercedes Benz.

- To form the pluperfect simply translate 'had' as **hatte** + endings and add the past participle of the main verb. For verbs that take **sein** you need to use **war** + endings plus the past participle:

ich	hatte	gearbeitet	I had worked
du	hattest	gearbeitet	you had worked
er/sie/es	hatte	gearbeitet	he/she/it had worked
wir	hatten	gearbeitet	we had worked
ihr	hattet	gearbeitet	you had worked
sie/Sie	hatten	gearbeitet	they/you had worked

ich	war	gekommen	I had come
du	warst	gekommen	you had come
er/sie/es	war	gekommen	he/she/it had come
wir	waren	gekommen	we had come
ihr	wart	gekommen	you had come
sie/Sie	waren	gekommen	they/you had come

19 All the sentences should be put in the pluperfect tense. Fill in the gaps and translate them into English.

a   Ich _____ jahrelang am Fließband gearbeitet.

_____

b   Er _____ früh in der Stadt angekommen.

_____

c   Nachdem sie nach Hause gekommen _____ , setzte sie sich vor den Fernseher.

_____

d   Wir machten ein Fest, nachdem wir das Abitur gemacht _____

_____

e   Sie _____ jahrelang nicht gewußt, daß sie einen Bruder hatte.

_____

Answers p. 176

20 Curriculum vitae – **der Lebenslauf**. German CVs usually start with the past and end up with your present position. Don't forget to sign and date it! Here's a model written by the author of this coursebook. Study it and answer the questions below. Then you can write your own CV.

LEBENSLAUF

Name	Ruth Rach
Geburtsdatum	1.5.48
Geburtsort	Biberach/Deutschland
Nationalität	Deutsch

Ausbildung

1955–59	Grundschule
1959–68	Gymnasium
1966–67	Mariemont High School, Cincinnati USA
1967	American High School Diploma
1968	Abitur (Hauptfächer Deutsch, Mathematik, Französisch, Englisch)
1969–75	Studium der Philosophie, Anglistik und Germanistik an den Universitäten Berlin, München, Aberystwyth.
1975	M.A.

Berufserfahrung

1976–81	Dozentin für Deutsch an den Universitäten Sussex und Bath.
seit 1982	Journalistin beim Deutschen Dienst des BBC World Service, London und freie Autorin.

Referenzen

Prof A. Felder-Rhein, Engl. Seminar, Universität München, München, Schellingstr. 10.
M. Mangold, Head of German Service, BBC World Service, Bush House, London WC2.

Ruth Rach
London, 4. Februar 19...   *Ruth Rach*

---

a For how many years did Ruth go to primary school?

b What were her main Abitur subjects?

c What subjects did she take at university?

d What did she do at Sussex University?

Answers p. 176

21 Your turn to speak and give some details about your own curriculum vitae.

22 Interview your partner about his or her CV using similar questions to Exercise 20.

EXERCISE 1

(a) Manfred Beck (b) Buchhalter (c) in einer großen Exportfirma (d) ab 65 (e) 7 bis 3
(f) 12 bis 1 (g) ja (h) 4 Wochen (i) Pfingsten, Ostern und Weihnachten.

EXERCISE 2

Christoph: no 9–5 job; loves books and languages; Computer. Max Planck Institut Berlin. Petra: active; likes people; English, Spanish; fashion. Verkäuferin Hotelboutique. Transcript: **Christoph:** Also, ich möchte nicht jeden Tag von 9 bis 5 arbeiten. Am liebsten arbeite ich abends, oder vielleicht nachmittags. Dann kann ich am Vormittag das machen, was mich wirklich interessiert. Ich liebe Bücher und Fremdsprachen – ich habe ein Jahr in den USA studiert und spreche sehr gut Englisch – dort habe ich auch viel am Computer gearbeitet. **Petra:** Ich möchte keinen Job, wo ich den ganzen Tag sitzen muß. Ich bin gerne aktiv, ich komme gerne mit Menschen zusammen, ich spreche Englisch und etwas Spanisch, und ich interessiere mich sehr für Mode.

EXERCISE 3

(a) Kollegen (b) Urlaub (c) Ruhestand
(d) Ostern (e) Pfingsten (f) Weihnachten
(g) Beruf Keyword: Kantine

EXERCISE 5

Vorteil: (b), (c), (e) – alles andere ist ein Nachteil.

EXERCISE 6

(a) Was sind Sie von Beruf? (b) Gefällt Ihnen Ihr Beruf? or: Sind Sie mit Ihrem Beruf zufrieden?
(c) Wollten Sie früher etwas anderes werden? or: Haben Sie sich auch andere Berufe überlegt?
(d) Wie sieht Ihr typischer Arbeitstag aus? (e) Und wann haben Sie Mittagspause? (f) Gibt's bei Ihnen Gleitzeit? (g) Und wieviel Urlaub haben Sie im Jahr?

EXERCISE 7

True: (b), (e), (f), (g) – everything else is false

EXERCISE 9

(a) Sie wollte schnell Geld verdienen. (b) Sie hat in einer Fabrik gearbeitet. (c) Sie war völlig kaputt.
(d) Sie ging zum Arbeitsamt. (e) Jetzt ist sie Arzthelferin. (f) Sie hat das Gefühl, daß sie etwas Wichtiges macht.

EXERCISE 11

Matthias: (a) university entrance (b) 1 year US university; work experience on a newspaper
(c) politics and sport (d) journalist (e) must not be boring.
Uschi: (a) GCSEs (b) sales assistant in a photographic shop; Spanish (c) photography, nature, travel (d) learn Portuguese and become travel photographer (e) must involve her hobbies

EXERCISE 12

(a) kam (b) konnte (c) entschloß (d) ließ
(e) hatte (f) war

EXERCISE 14

(a) ein (b) ein (c) eine (d) einem (e) einem

EXERCISE 15

(a) meine (b) seinem (c) deine (d) keine
(e) Ihren

EXERCISE 16

(a) guter (b) schönen (c) langen (d) großer

EXERCISE 17

(a) heiße (b) neue (c) großen (d) kleinen

EXERCISE 18

(a) Das ist ein altes Kino. (b) Ich möchte ein kleines Geschenk kaufen. (c) Where is the room of your little girl? (d) Ich möchte ein heißes Getränk.

EXERCISE 19

(a) hatte; I had worked on the production line for years. (b) war; He had arrived in town early.
(c) war; After she had come home, she sat down in front of the TV. (d) hatten; We had a party after we had done the Abitur. (e) hatte; She had not known for years that she had a brother.

EXERCISE 20

(a) four years (b) German, Maths, French, English;
(c) Philosophy, English, German (d) taught German

12 DREAMS AND THE FUTURE

BEFORE YOU BEGIN

Congratulations – you have reached the final unit in this course. Take a look back at the first few units to see just how far you have come. Consolidate your knowledge by choosing some exercises from this book at random every once in a while and by attending an evening class. Some towns have German circles or German pub evenings – if yours doesn't, you might like to advertise and form your own German conversation group. Find out if your town has a German twin town and see whether you can get involved in any exchange activities. You might like to find a German penfriend in your

twin town or exchange messages through the Internet. Expand your reading with German magazine articles, comics and bilingual books – and try to tune into German TV. The language might sound rather fast to start with, especially if you listen to German news programmes, but after a while you'll get used to the speed and start recognising the language.

Dream holiday

Biba

Wie stellen Sie sich Ihren Traumurlaub vor?

Silke

Am liebsten würde ich den ganzen Tag lang nichts tun – am Strand liegen, mich von der Sonne rösten lassen, abends schön essen gehen, tanzen, vielleicht in die Disko gehen.

Amin

Ja, wissen Sie, mein Traumurlaub – das wäre, mit einem guten Freund in einem Jeep durch die Rocky Mountains zu fahren, in Amerika; abends am Lagerfeuer zu sitzen, ganz alleine, tagelang, wochenlang niemanden zu sehen. Und eine andere Möglichkeit wäre, mit der transsibirischen Eisenbahn von Moskau quer nach Peking – nicht mit dem Flugzeug, das fände ich langweilig.

Ingrid

Oh – ich würde gern einen Bildungsurlaub machen: Griechenland, Ägypten, vielleicht sogar Indien, und dort die ganzen Kunstschätze besichtigen. Vielleicht mit einem Reiseführer, der alles genau erklären kann. Also, das stelle ich mir ganz toll vor, so über die Geschichte dort etwas zu erfahren, und so über die Hintergründe, wie die Menschen dort gelebt haben.

LISTEN FOR...

Strand	beach
Lagerfeuer	campfire
Kunstschätze	art treasures

Wie stellen Sie sich ... vor? How do you imagine ...? **sich vorstellen** (sep.) to imagine; **ich stelle mir etwas vor** I imagine something; **Können Sie sich vorstellen?** Can you imagine?

der Traumurlaub dream holiday

am liebsten würde ich best of all I would; more on **würde** in Grammar, this unit.

am Strand liegen to lie on the beach; **der Strand** beach

mich von der Sonne rösten lassen to (let myself) roast in the sun.

das wäre that would be; more on **wäre** in Grammar, this unit.

am Lagerfeuer (zu) sitzen to sit by the campfire; **das Lagerfeuer** campfire.

tagelang, wochenlang for days, for weeks; similarly: **jahrelang** for years.

niemanden (zu) sehen to see nobody

mit der transsibirischen Eisenbahn von Moskau quer nach Peking on the Transsiberian Railway from Moscow right across to Peking (Beijing)

das fände ich ... that I would find ... (see Grammar, this unit for **fände**)

der Bildungsurlaub educational holiday

Griechenland, Ägypten, vielleicht sogar Indien Greece, Egypt, perhaps even India

der Kunstschatz art treasure

besichtigen to look at, visit

der Reiseführer tour guide

genau erklären to explain precisely

etwas über die Geschichte erfahren to learn something about the history; **die Geschichte** can also mean 'story'.

die Hintergründe background(s); **der Hintergrund** background; similarly **der Vordergrund** foreground

wie die Menschen dort gelebt haben how the people lived there

1 Review Conversation 1 and decide who would say what.

		Silke	Amin	Ingrid
a	Ich würde am liebsten quer durch Amerika fahren.	☐	☐	☐
b	Ich würde am liebsten am Strand liegen.	☐	☐	☐
c	Ich würde am liebsten eine Bildungsreise machen.	☐	☐	☐
d	Ich würde am liebsten mit der Eisenbahn bis Peking reisen.	☐	☐	☐
e	Ich würde gerne am Lagerfeuer sitzen.	☐	☐	☐
f	Ich würde gerne schön essen gehen.	☐	☐	☐
g	Ich möchte gerne nach Indien fliegen.	☐	☐	☐
h	Ich würde nicht gerne viel herumreisen.	☐	☐	☐
i	Ich würde oft in die Disko gehen.	☐	☐	☐

Answers p. 192

2 Word building. Stick the words together to make longer ones (so-called 'compounds'). Translate them into English. You should come up with at least 7 new words. You can use the individual words as often as you like. Remember that the new compound always has the same gender as the last word in it.

BAHN	LAGER	ZEUG	SCHATZ	HINTER	URLAUB	GRUND
EISEN	FEUER	FLUG	FÜHRER	KUNST	T̶R̶A̶U̶M̶	R̶E̶I̶S̶E̶

die Traumreise   dream journey

_____

_____

_____

Answers p. 192 _____

3 On the recording, Gisela is interviewed about her dream holiday. Listen and decide which of the statements below are true.

		R	F
a	Sie würde am liebsten nach Rio de Janeiro fliegen.	☐	☐
b	Sie würde mit dem Zug durch Südamerika fahren.	☐	☐
c	Sie würde sich ein halbes Jahr frei nehmen.	☐	☐
d	Sie würde tagelang und wochenlang nur reisen.	☐	☐
e	Sie würde auch gerne die Sprache lernen.	☐	☐
f	Sie würde aber nie irgendwo länger bleiben.	☐	☐

Answers p. 192

4 On the recording you will hear a clip about new trends in travelling. Here's the transcript. Listen carefully and answer the questions below – in English.

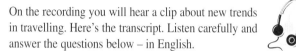

NEUER TREND
die „Reise nach innen"

Früher machte man exotische Reisen, heute faszinieren die inneren Welten. Wer nach innen reist, liegt voll im Trend: Meditation auf Las Palmas, Bauchtanz auf Korfu, Trommeln in Gambia, Energiearbeit und Tai Chi am Gardasee. Das sind nur einige Angebote aus dem Katalog von „Eso-Tours", eine Reisefirma für Individualisten und Esoteriker. Wie wär's mit einer Traumakademie in Tirol, oder einer Fastenwoche im Kloster? Sie können aber auch mit einem Elefanten durch Südindien reisen, oder per Fahrrad durch Südafrika. Sie reisen in kleinen Gruppen mit maximal sechs Personen und übernachten in Zelten oder Gästehäusern ... ∎

VOCABULARY

das Trommeln	drumming
das Angebot	offer
das Kloster	monastery
das Fahrrad	bicycle
übernachten	to stay overnight
das Zelt	tent

a Where would you go if you wanted to meditate?

b What's the name of the travel firm for esoteric journeys?

c Where could you work on your energy fields?

d Where can you do an in-depth study of your dreams?

e What unusual means of transport could you choose?

f How big would the groups be?

g And where would you spend the nights?

Answers p. 192

5 Your turn to dream up your own ideal holiday ...

CONVERSATION 2

Dream gifts

Biba Was würden Sie machen, wenn Sie zehntausend Mark geschenkt bekämen?

Amin Ja, zuerst einmal gehe ich davon aus, daß man mit zehntausend Mark wenig machen kann. Angenommen, ich hätte hunderttausend Mark. Da würde ich mir eine Insel kaufen, im Atlantik, und mal versuchen, ganz einfach zu leben – ohne Elektrizität, Waschmaschine, Radio, Fernseher, elektrischen Herd, Telefon, und was es da so alles gibt ...

Biba Würden Sie nichts vermissen?

Amin Ja, ich würde mir von den hunderttausend Mark trotz alledem noch so viel übrig lassen, um gelegentlich mal nach Berlin zu fliegen, oder nach New York, um zu sehen, wie die Welt sich inzwischen weiterentwickelt hat. Wissen Sie, ganz zurückziehen will ich mich trotzdem nicht, aber ausprobieren, das wär' schon gut.

LISTEN FOR...

Insel	island
vermissen	to miss
zurückziehen	to withdraw

wenn Sie ... geschenkt bekämen if you were given ...; see Grammar, this unit for **bekämen.**

zuerst einmal gehe ich davon aus first of all I assume; **davon ... ausgehen** to assume; **ich gehe davon aus, daß ...** I assume that. Similarly: **Davon kann man nicht ausgehen!** One cannot assume that!

angenommen assuming (lit. assumed); **angenommen ich hätte ...** assuming I had ... Amin's statements are all rather hypothetical – he probably would not get an island for that sum of money. More on hypothetical phrases in Grammar, this unit.

eine Insel im Atlantik an island in the Atlantic; **der Atlantik** Atlantic Ocean.

die Elektrizität electricity; **die Waschmaschine** washing machine; **der Herd** cooker.

Würden Sie nichts vermissen? Wouldn't you miss anything? **ich vermisse dich** I miss you.

ich würde mir noch so viel übrig lassen I would leave (myself) sufficient (funds) (lit. so much over)

trotz alledem in spite of everything; **trotzdem** nonetheless

gelegentlich occasionally

die Welt world

inzwischen meanwhile

sich weiterentwickeln (sep.) to move on, to develop further; **er entwickelte sich weiter** he developed; **ich entwickle mich weiter** I develop.

ganz zurückziehen will ich mich trotzdem nicht I don't want to withdraw completely after all; **sich zurückziehen** (sep.) to withdraw.

ausprobieren (sep.) to try out; **ich probiere das aus!** I'll try that! **er hat das ausprobiert** he has tried that out.

6 Here's a summary of Conversation 2. Some sentences are correct, others have one or more mistakes in them. Spot the mistakes and correct them!

a Wenn Amin zehntausend Mark geschenkt bekäme, würde er sich ein Haus auf einer Insel im Pazifik kaufen.

b Er würde versuchen, einfach zu leben.

c Er würde keine Waschmaschine, keinen Fernseher und keinen Elektroherd haben.

d Aber er würde sich nicht ganz von der Welt zurückziehen.

Answers p. 192   **e** Gelegentlich würde er nach Rom oder New York fliegen.

7 Martin wants to change his life. Read this passage from a letter about his plans. (You can also listen to it on the recording.) Then find the German equivalents to the English phrases.

> **Meine Kollegen sagten: du bist total verrückt! Als Lehrer hast du einen Job auf Lebenszeit, du hast eine sichere Rente – was willst du denn mehr? Doch ich will etwas anderes. Ich will keine soziale Sicherheit bis ans Lebensende. Ich mag keine Routine mehr. Ich möchte viel reisen, am liebsten rund um die Welt – bis ich das Land finde, wo ich mich wirklich wohl fühle – irgendwo im Süden. Wenn ich mehr Geld hätte, würde ich mir ein Segelschiff kaufen und um die Welt segeln.**

a you are totally mad

_____

b job for life

_____

c what more do you want

_____

d security until the end of (one's) life

_____

e preferably round the world

_____

f somewhere in the South

_____

g if I had more money

_____

h sail around the world

Answers p. 192   _____

8 On the recording Katrin talks about her life dream. Listen carefully and complete the transcript below ...

Wenn ich eine Million Mark geschenkt _____ (a),
_____ (b) ich eine große Villa in Südeuropa
_____ (c), irgendwo am Meer, und alle meine Freunde
_____ (d). Ich würde aber auch gerne Workshops
_____ (e), Bauchtanz, Trommeln, Meditation, Yoga.
Vielleicht _____ (f) meine Villa auch ein Zentrum für
Reisen nach innen _____ (g), und später dann eine
Art privates Altenheim.

Answers p. 192

9 Woulds ... Write out the answers – in German. Remember that the second verb goes to the end of the phrase.

Was würden Sie machen, wenn ich Sie in die Oper einladen würde?
(I would say yes)

a   _____

Was würden Sie machen, wenn ich Ihnen ein Auto schenken würde?
(I would drive to Italy)

b   _____

Was würden Sie machen, wenn ich Ihnen eine Million Mark geben würde?
(I would buy a small island)

c   _____

Was würden Sie machen, wenn ich keinen Pfennig Geld hätte?
(I would invite you!)

Answers p. 192

d   _____

10 Your turn to practise phrases with 'would'. Exercise 9 will have prepared you for this. Hans will prompt you as usual.

Talking about the future

Silke Ich finde, wir haben schon viel zu viel technische Neuerungen. Wir sind viel zu weit und können das gar nicht mehr richtig gebrauchen.

Ingrid Da kann ich nicht so ganz zustimmen. Auf manchen Gebieten, finde ich, könnten wir schon technische Neuerungen gebrauchen, zum Beispiel, was die Energiegewinnung angeht. Wir müßten sparsamer und sinnvoller mit unserer Energiegewinnung umgehen, zum Beispiel Sonnenenergie und so Gebiete weiter erforschen.

Silke Ja, Sonnenenergie ist – da stimme ich dir zu – das ist ein guter Punkt. Aber das ist wieder so eine Spezialistenangelegenheit.

Günter Also, ich hab' mir schon oft Gedanken darüber gemacht, daß besonders unser Transportwesen umstrukturiert werden sollte. Das heißt, daß man mehr Nachdruck auf den öffentlichen Verkehr legen sollte und weniger auf den Verkehr mit Individualfahrzeugen.

LISTEN FOR...	
Neuerungen	innovations
gebrauchen	to use
Energiegewinnung	production of energy

technische Neuerungen technical innovations

wir sind viel zu weit we've gone much too far

gebrauchen to use

da kann ich nicht so ganz zustimmen I can't agree altogether with that; **zustimmen** (sep.) to agree; **ich stimme (dir/Ihnen) zu** I agree (with you).

auf manchen Gebieten in some areas; **das Gebiet** area; and further down in the Conversation: **und so** (= **solche**) **Gebiete** and such areas.

was die Energiegewinnung angeht as far as energy production is concerned. Similarly: **was mich angeht** as far as I'm concerned.

wir müßten we should. More on **müßten** in Grammar, this unit.

sparsam economical(ly)

sinnvoll sensible, sensibly

mit ... umgehen to deal ... with

die Sonnenenergie solar energy

weiter erforschen to explore further

der Punkt point

die Spezialistenangelegenheit specialist matter

ich hab' mir Gedanken darüber gemacht I have thought about; **sich Gedanken über etwas machen** to think about something; **Machen Sie sich keine Gedanken darüber!** Don't worry about it!

das Transportwesen transport system

umstrukturieren to restructure

daß man mehr Nachdruck auf den öffentlichen Verkehr legen sollte that one should put more emphasis on public transport; **öffentlich** public; **der Verkehr** traffic, transport

das Individualfahrzeug private (lit. individual) vehicle.

Source: Zeitbild-Verlag

PRACTICE

11 Go over Conversation 3 again. Then study the statements below and decide who would have said what. Sometimes you may mark more than one name.

		Ingrid	Silke	Günter
a	Wir sollten mehr Energie sparen.	☐	☐	☐
b	Wir müssen die öffentlichen Verkehrsmittel weiter ausbauen.	☐	☐	☐
c	Ich möchte gerne noch mehr technische Neuerungen.	☐	☐	☐
d	Ich möchte keine technischen Neuerungen mehr.	☐	☐	☐
e	Wir sollten unser Transportsystem ändern.	☐	☐	☐
f	Ich bin für Sonnenenergie.	☐	☐	☐
g	Wir brauchen weniger Privatautos.	☐	☐	☐

Answers p. 192

12 Innovation with a difference. Listen carefully to the news item on the recording and fill in the gaps in **a**–**d**. Then answer questions **1**–**4**, in English.

VOCABULARY

der Schadstoff	pollutant
der Motor	engine
der Wasserstoff	hydrogen
der Sauerstoff	oxygen
der Ottomotor	4-stroke engine, invented by Otto
die Geschwindigkeit	speed

a Daimler-Benz hat am Dienstag in Berlin ein _____ vorgestellt, das keinen Schadstoff produzieren soll.

b Das _____ hat keinen Motor. Es produziert seine _____ aus der Reaktion von Wasserstoff- und Sauerstoffgas.

c Wie die _____ erklärt, könnte das Auto in zehn bis zwölf Jahren eine Alternative zu Fahrzeugen mit Otto- oder Dieselmotor werden.

d Der Wagen kann 6 Personen _____ und hat eine Höchstgeschwindigkeit von 100 Stundenkilometern.

1 What's the advantage of the new car?

_____

2 Why is it different from traditional cars?

_____

3 How long might it take to develop?

_____

4 Any other technical details?

Answers p. 192 _____

Unit 12   Dreams and the future

13

müßte? sollte? wäre? würde? könnte? Franz and Inge are discussing personal transport issues. What would they have said in German? Unravel the wordworms into single words and re-organise their sequence into proper German sentences. You'll find the answers on your recording.

a I think we should sell our car.
FINDEICHWIRUNSERAUTOSOLLTENVERKAUFEN

b But how would I get to work?
ZURARBEITABERKOMMENWIEICHWÜRDE

c You could take the bus!
BUSDENNEHMENDUKÖNNTEST

d But then I would have to change three times!
DANNABERDREIMALMÜSSTEUMSTEIGENICH

e How about the bicycle?
FAHRRADWÄREWIEESDEMMIT

f Good idea, but that would be too dangerous.
GUTEABERGEFÄHRLICHZUIDEEWÄREDAS

Answers p. 192

14

Long words – they are all from Conversation 4. Stick the pieces together again and provide a translation.

GEWINNUNG SPEZIALISTEN FAHRZEUGE ENERGIE WESEN
TRANSPORT INDIVIDUAL ENERGIE ANGELEGENHEIT SONNEN

Answers p. 192

15

Your turn to speak and discuss transport issues. Hans will prompt you. Useful phrases: **Wie würde ich ... kommen? Das wäre ... gefährlich. Dann müßte ich ... . Wir sollten ... verkaufen.**

Was würden Sie machen, wenn ...?

Ich würde ...	
mir eine Insel kaufen	
das einfache Leben ausprobieren	

ohne Elektrizität/Telefon/
Waschmaschine/Elektroherd

Angenommen, ich hätte ...

Das wäre gut/besser

Würden Sie nichts vermissen?

Wir ...
könnten
sollten
müßten

Technologie

technische Neuerungen
die Energiegewinnung
der Schadstoff
der Motor
die Sonnenenergie
produzieren
Wir sind viel zu weit

Pro und contra

Ich finde ...
Das finde ich auch
Da kann ich nicht zustimmen
Da stimme ich dir zu
Das ist ein guter Punkt

What would you do if ...

I would ...
buy myself an island
try out the simple life

without electricity/telephone/
washing machine/electric cooker

Let's assume I had ...

That would be good/better

Would you not miss anything?

We ...
could
should
ought to

Technology

technical innovations
production of energy
pollutant
engine
solar energy
to produce
We have gone much too far

For and against

I think ...
I think so too
I can't agree with that
I agree with you there
That's a good point

Talking about possibilities – the subjunctive

■ If you want to give a sentence a hypothetical character and to express what would or could happen if ... , you use the subjunctive. The subjunctive is most often used after **wenn** (if), to express something which has not happened but might happen. It's also used when you'd use 'could/would/ought' in English:

■ For German strong verbs, the subjunctive is nearly the same as the imperfect form except that you add an umlaut to **a**, **o**, or **u** and you also add an **-e** to the **ich** and **er/sie/es** forms. For example, the imperfect forms of **bekommen** (to get) are **ich bekam** (I got), **du bekamst** (you got), etc. The subjunctive forms follow the pattern below.

wenn	ich	bekäme	if	I were to get
	du	bekämst		you were to get
	er/sie/es	bekäme		he/she/it were to get
	wir	bekämen		we were to get
	ihr	bekämt		you were to get
	sie/Sie	bekämen		they/you were to get

Ich wäre froh, wenn wir Geld bekämen.   I would be happy if we were to get money.
Es wäre furchtbar, wenn ich die Grippe bekäme.   It would be awful if I got the flu.

16 Following the example of **bekommen**, write out the subjunctive forms of **finden** (to find) with their translations.

wenn   ich fände

_____

_____

_____

_____

_____

Answers p. 192

The most important subjunctive forms (and the ones you are most likely to use) are those of **sein** and **haben**.

■ **sein** (to be)

wenn	ich	wäre	if	I were
	du	wärst		you were
	er/sie/es	wäre		he/she/it were
	wir	wären		we were
	ihr	wärt		you were
	sie/Sie	wären		they/you were

Wenn ich reich wäre.   If I were rich.
Das wäre besser.   That would be better.

■ **haben** (to have)

wenn	ich	hätte	if	I had
	du	hättest		you had
	er/sie/es	hätte		he/she/it had
	wir	hätten		we had
	ihr	hättet		you had
	sie/Sie	hätten		they/you had

Wenn ich ein Auto hätte ... If I had a car ...
Wenn ich Hunger hätte ... If I were hungry ...

17 Translate into German:

a If I had a bicycle ... _____
b If you were older (use **Sie**) ... _____
c If we had a big garden ... _____
d If they were in Paris ... _____
e If the restaurant were cheaper ... _____
f If Hans had a better car ... _____
g If you had more books ... _____

Answers p. 192

Other verbs commonly used in the subjunctive are:

■ **können** (to be able to)

wenn	ich	könnte	I could
	du	könntest	you could
	er/sie/es	könnte	he/she/it could
	wir	könnten	we could
	ihr	könntet	you could
	sie/Sie	könnten	they/you could

Wir könnten morgen kommen. We could come tomorrow.
Könnte ich das noch ändern? Could I still change that?
Es wäre schön, wenn Sie kommen könnten. It would be nice if you could come.

■ **müssen** (to have to)

wenn	ich	müßte	I had to
	du	müßtest	you had to
	er/sie/es	müßte	he/she/it had to
	wir	müßten	we had to
	ihr	müßtet	you had to
	sie/Sie	müßten	they/you had to

Ich müßte dringend nach Prag. I would have to (or ought to) go to Prague urgently.
Müßtest du nicht nach Hause? Wouldn't you have to go home?
Wir müßten sparsamer damit umgehen. We ought to handle it more economically.

- To make a tentative statement you can use **würde** + infinitive. This construction is very common in German and is usually translated with 'would'.

Ich würde nicht soviel erklären.	I would not explain so much.
Ich würde nicht soviel arbeiten.	I would not work so much.
Am liebsten würde ich jetzt heimgehen.	I would prefer to go home now.

- Here are all the forms:

ich	würde	I would
du	würdest	you would
er/sie/es	würde	he/she/it would
wir	würden	we would
ihr	würdet	you would
sie/Sie	würden	they/you would

18 Translate into German:

a   I would drive to Paris.

___

b   We would travel to India.

___

c   She would read more books – if she had the time.

___

d   I would go now.

___

e   They would come if they had the money.

___

Answers p. 192

- You can also use **würde** or another subjunctive if you want to be especially polite:

Ich hätte gerne ...   I would like (to have) ...
Würden Sie bitte kommen?   Would you please come?
Wären Sie bitte so freundlich und ...?   Would you be so kind as to ...?
(or: **Würden Sie bitte so freundlich sein...?**)

19 Translate into German:

a   Could I try this out? ___

b   Would you explain this please? ___

c   That would be nice! ___

d   I'd like a cup of coffee please! ___

Answers p. 192

20 Daydreams. What would they do if they won a million Marks in the lottery? Match the statements to the people.

1   der Tierliebhaber

2   der Menschenfreund

3   der Genießer

4   der Filmfanatiker

5   der Autofan

a   Ich würde mir den schönsten Rolls Royce kaufen.

b   Ich ginge jeden Tag ins Kino.

c   Ich würde nach Afrika fahren und alle Safariparks besuchen.

d   Ich würde mir einen großen Keller bauen und mit den besten Weinen füllen.

e   Ich würde das Geld verschenken.

Answers p. 192

21 Your turn to speak and daydream. Turn to the tape where Hans will prompt you... Some, but not all of these words will be useful. Some might come in handy for Exercise 22...

Ich würde ... arbeiten/kaufen/einladen/feiern/schwimmen/einladen/reisen/heiraten/fliegen/ mich entspannen/Urlaub machen

22 You win 10 million Marks in the lottery. Discuss with a partner or work out for yourself – in German – what you would do with it. Try and come up with ten statements. You could use phrases from Exercises 20 and 21 as your model.

EXERCISE 1

Amin (a), (d), (e); Silke (b), (f), (h), (i); Ingrid (c), (g).

EXERCISE 2

der Reiseführer, tour guide; das Flugzeug, aircraft; der Kunstschatz, art treasure; der Traumurlaub, dream holiday; der Hintergrund, background; das Lagerfeuer, campfire; die Eisenbahn, railway; you could also have: der Kunstführer, art guide; die Flugbahn, trajectory ...

EXERCISE 3

(a) R; (b) F; (c) F; (d) R; (e) R; (g) F
Transcript: Ich würde am liebsten nach Rio de Janeiro fliegen und dann mit dem Bus durch Südamerika fahren. Da würde ich mir ein ganzes Jahr frei nehmen, und dann tagelang, wochenlang nur reisen. Fremde Menschen kennenlernen, fremde Städte und Dörfer, die Sprache lernen, und dann vielleicht auch irgendwo länger bleiben und ein ganz einfaches Leben führen.

EXERCISE 4

(a) Las Palmas (b) Eso-Tours (c) Lake Garda (d) the Tyrol (e) elephant (f) small – max. 6 people (g) tents or guesthouses

EXERCISE 6

(a) Er würde eine Insel im Atlantik kaufen.
(e) Manchmal würde er nach Berlin oder New York fliegen.

EXERCISE 7

(a) du bist total verrückt (b) Job auf Lebenszeit (c) was willst du denn mehr
(d) Sicherheit bis ans Lebensende (e) am liebsten rund um die Welt (f) irgendwo im Süden (h) wenn ich mehr Geld hätte (i) um die Welt segeln.

EXERCISE 8

(a) bekäme (b) würde (c) kaufen (d) einladen (e) organisieren (f) würde (g) werden.

EXERCISE 9

(a) Ich würde ja sagen. (b) Ich würde nach Italien fahren. (c) Ich würde eine kleine Insel kaufen. (d) Ich würde Sie einladen!

EXERCISE 11

Ingrid (a), (c), (f); Silke (a), (d), (f); Günter (b), (e), (g).

EXERCISE 12

(a) Auto (b) Fahrzeug; Energie (c) Firma
(d) transportieren 1 it produces no pollutants.
2 it has no engine; it generates energy through a reaction between hydrogen and oxygen. 3 10 to 12 years 4 carries up to 6 passengers; top speed 100 kilometres per hour.

EXERCISE 13

(a) Ich finde, wir sollten unser Auto verkaufen.
(b) Aber wie würde ich zur Arbeit kommen?
(c) Du könntest den Bus nehmen.
(d) Aber dann müßte ich dreimal umsteigen.
(e) Wie wäre es mit dem Fahrrad?
(f) Gute Idee, aber das wäre zu gefährlich.

EXERCISE 14

Energiegewinnung production of energy; Spezialistenangelegenheit matter for specialists; Individualfahrzeuge private vehicles; Sonnenenergie solar energy; Transportwesen transport (system).

EXERCISE 16

du fändest, er/sie/es fände, wir fänden, ihr fändet, sie/Sie fänden

EXERCISE 17

(a) Wenn ich ein Fahrrad hätte (b) Wenn Sie älter wären (c) Wenn wir einen großen Garten hätten (d) Wenn sie in Paris wären (e) Wenn das Restaurant billiger wäre (f) Wenn Hans ein besseres Auto hätte (g) Wenn du mehr Bücher hättest.

EXERCISE 18

(a) Ich würde nach Paris fahren. (b) Wir würden nach Indien reisen. (c) Sie würde mehr Bücher lesen, wenn sie die Zeit hätte. (d) Ich würde jetzt gehen. (e) Sie würden kommen, wenn sie das Geld hätten.

EXERCISE 19

(a) Könnte ich das (aus)probieren? (b) Würden Sie das bitte erklären? (c) Das wäre nett (or schön). (d) Ich hätte gerne eine Tasse Kaffee.

EXERCISE 20

(a) 5 (b) 4 (c) 1 (d) 3 (e) 2

GRAMMAR SUMMARY

Below you will find a short summary of what we think are the most important grammar points occurring in this course. Some useful grammar terms will also be explained.

Verbs

infinitive A verb is a word denoting action or being, e.g. 'I *am*', 'he *goes*', 'she *loves* him'. The simplest form of the verb is called *infinitive*. In English this form is preceded by 'to': 'to love', 'to go', 'to be', etc. In German all verbs in the infinitive end in **-en** or **-n**, e.g. **geh<u>en</u>** (to go), **tu<u>n</u>** (to do).

stem If you remove the **-en** or **-n** from the infinitive, you have the *stem*. In general you add other endings onto this to make *tenses* of the verb.

tenses A tense says *when* you are doing something, e.g. now (in the *present*), some time ago (in the *past*) or at some point sooner or later (in the *future*).

no continuous and no 'do' While in English there are two ways of expressing an action, e.g. 'I eat' and 'I am eating', in German there is only one: **ich esse**. This applies to all tenses. In German questions and negatives there is no equivalent to the English 'do': **Singen Sie? Ich singe nicht.** 'Do you sing? I don't sing.'

present tense The present-tense endings of the verb change according to the subject of the verb, i.e. who or what acts: **ich geh<u>e</u>** (I go), **du geh<u>st</u>** (you go), **er/sie/es geh<u>t</u>** (he/she/it goes), **wir geh<u>en</u>** (we go), **ihr geh<u>t</u>** (you go), **sie/Sie geh<u>en</u>** (they/you go). These endings are the same for most verbs, but sometimes the vowel in the stem, or main part of the verb, changes in the **du**, **er**, **sie** and **es** forms, e.g. **sprechen** (to speak), **du spr<u>i</u>chst**, **er/sie/es spr<u>i</u>cht**; **fahren** (to go, to drive), **du f<u>ä</u>hrst**, **er/sie/es f<u>ä</u>hrt**. (See *strong verbs* below.)

perfect There are three ways of talking about the past in German: the *perfect* tense, the *imperfect* tense and the *pluperfect*. The perfect tense is explained in Units 1 and 3. It is more widely used than the imperfect, so it is more important for you to learn. It is often translated by the simple past tense in English:

Gestern habe ich bis elf Uhr geschlafen. Yesterday *I slept* till eleven o'clock.

The perfect is formed with the present of **haben** or **sein** plus the past participle, e.g. **ich habe gewohnt, ich bin gereist** (I have lived, I have travelled).

Gereist and **gewohnt** are the past participles of the verbs **reisen** and **wohnen**. As explained in Unit 1, past participles are formed by adding **ge-** before the stem and **-t** (for weak verbs) or **-en** (for strong verbs) after the stem: **g̲e̲reist, g̲e̲komm̲e̲n**. Strong verbs may also change the stem (see below). Exceptions are verbs with prefixes. Separable verbs (see below) insert the **ge** between the prefix and the stem: **ang̲e̲fangen**; inseparable verbs, e.g. **unterrichten** (to teach), do not add **ge** at all: **unterrichtet**. (See Unit 3.)

imperfect
The imperfect is explained in Units 5, 7, 8 and 9. It is used to describe actions which took some place some time ago, e.g. **vor zehn Jahren wohnte er in Ulm** (ten years ago he lived in Ulm). Again it is formed slightly differently for weak and strong verbs – see below.

weak verbs
Weak verbs, such as **wohnen** (to live), do not have vowel changes in the stem. The imperfect is formed by adding endings after the stem: **ich wohn̲te̲, du wohn̲test̲, er/sie/es wohn̲te̲, wir wohn̲ten̲, ihr wohn̲tet̲, sie/Sie wohn̲ten̲**. Verbs which are weak in English (play, play̲ed̲) are often weak in German (**spielen, spiel̲te̲**).

strong verbs
These are verbs such as **fahren** which change the stem in some forms. For instance, the imperfect of **fahren** (to go, to drive) is formed by changing the stem to **fuhr** and adding endings as follows: **ich fuhr, du fuhr̲st̲, er/sie/es fuhr, wir fuhr̲en̲, ihr fuhr̲t̲, sie/Sie fuhr̲en̲**. These endings are the same for all strong verbs. (See Unit 9.) There is a list of the strong verbs used in this course, showing the stem changes, on pp. 200–1.

Note that stem changes are often the same as in closely related English verbs:

singen	**sang**	**gesungen**	(sing, sang, sung)
trinken	**trank**	**getrunken**	(drink, drank, drunk)

pluperfect
The pluperfect is explained in Unit 11. It is often used after **nachdem** (after): **nachdem er in der Lotterie gewonnen hatte, kaufte er sich einen dicken Mercedes** (after he had won in the lottery he bought himself a fat Mercedes Benz). To form the pluperfect translate 'had' as **hatte** + endings and add the past participle of the main verb: **ich hatte gearbeitet** (I had worked). For verbs that take **sein** in the perfect you need to use **war** + endings plus the past participle: **ich war gereist** (I had travelled).

future
The future is formed in German with the present of **werden** and the infinitive of the verb, e.g. **ich werde gehen, du wirst gehen, er/sie/es wird gehen, wir werden gehen, ihr werdet gehen, sie/Sie werden gehen** (I'll go, you'll go, etc.) (see Unit 3). As in English you can often use the present tense to state future intentions:

Morgen fahre ich nach Hause. Tomorrow I'm going home.

passive
The passive is often used when you want to be impersonal about an action: **Wie wird das gemacht?** (How is that done?). It is formed by using **werden** + past participle of the main verb: **ich werde gefahren** (I am driven); **du wirst gefahren** (you are driven). (See Unit 7.) (See *future* for other forms of **werden**.)

Grammar summary

subjunctive and conditional	If you want to give a sentence a hypothetical character and want to express what would or could happen if ... you can use the imperfect subjunctive. For weak verbs, the imperfect subjunctive is the same as the imperfect form, so it is rarely used. For strong verbs, the imperfect subjunctive is nearly the same as their imperfect form except that you add an umlaut when there is an **a**, **o**, or **u** and you also add an **-e** to the **ich** and **er/sie/es** forms. For example, the imperfect form of **bekommen** (to get) is **ich bekam** – the subjunctive form is: **ich bekäme**. Most commonly used subjunctives are for **haben** (**ich hätte**) and **sein** (**ich wäre**). Another common way of expressing possibilities is to use the conditional: **würde**. (See Unit 12.)	

Ich würde kommen, wenn ich Geld hätte. I would come if I had money.

modal verbs These are verbs such as **müssen** (must), **können** (can), **dürfen** (may), **wollen** (to want to), **sollen** (shall, is to). They are explained in Units 2 and 8.

separable verbs These are verbs such as **anfangen** (to begin), **zumachen** (to shut), **aufhören** (to stop), etc. They consist of two parts, a short prefix (such as **an**, **auf**, **zu**, etc.) and then a verb. In the infinitive these two parts appear together, but otherwise they are split up: **ich fange an** (I begin), **wir machen zu** (we shut). In longer sentences the prefix goes right to the end:

Wir fangen um neun Uhr an. We start at nine.
Wir hören um 12 Uhr auf. We stop at 12.

If there is also a modal verb or **werden**, the separable verb is joined up again, e.g. **ich möchte aufhören** (I would like to stop), **wir wollen jetzt anfangen** (we want to start now), **ich werde aufhören** (I shall stop). Where the infinitive is used with **zu**, the **zu** comes between the prefix and the stem: **um mitzufahren** (in order to come along). See Unit 10. In the past participle the **ge** comes between the prefix and the stem: **angefangen** (started). See Unit 3.

Nouns

A noun is the name of a person or thing, e.g. 'James', 'dog', 'book', 'fun'. In German all nouns have a capital initial letter: **da ist ein Mann** (there is a man); **Siehst du die Frau?** (Do you see the woman?).

genders All German nouns are either masculine, feminine or neuter, i.e. they have a gender. You can tell the gender of a noun when it is used with the words for 'the' (**der/die/das**) and 'a' (**ein/eine/ein**).

articles The words for 'the' and 'a' are called articles:

masculine:	**der/ein**	**Mann**	the/a man
feminine:	**die/eine**	**Frau**	the/a woman
neuter:	**das/ein**	**Kind**	the/a child

subject/object In German the article often undergoes a change according to the function a noun has in a sentence. It can, for example, be the subject or the object. A subject is a person or thing that acts, e.g. '*the woman* is reading'. The object is the person or thing on the receiving end, e.g. 'the woman reads *the paper'*. Whereas in English 'the' or 'a' is used regardless of whether a noun is a subject or an object, in German the articles often change when a noun becomes an object, i.e. when its function or case is changed (see Unit 4). This can also be affected by prepositions (see below).

cases   There are four cases altogether (see Unit 4):
the *nominative*, e.g. **Der Mann ist hier.** The man is here.
the *accusative*, e.g. **Ich sehe den Mann.** I see the man.
the *genitive*, e.g. **das Foto des Mannes** the man's photo/the photo of the man.
the *dative*, e.g. **Ich gebe dem Mann das Buch.** I give the man the book/I give the book to the man.

Here are the nominative, accusative, genitive and dative forms for **der/die/das**:

	singular			**plural**
	masculine	feminine	neuter	all genders
n.	der Mann	die Frau	das Kind	die Männer/Frauen/Kinder
a.	den Mann	die Frau	das Kind	die Männer/Frauen/Kinder
g.	des Mannes	der Frau	des Kindes	der Männer/Frauen/Kinder
d.	dem Mann	der Frau	dem Kind	den Männern/Frauen/Kindern

Here are the forms for **ein/eine/ein**, as well as their negative: **kein/keine/kein** (no, none), and the possessives: **mein/dein** (my, your) etc.:

	singular			**plural**
	masculine	feminine	neuter	all genders
n.	ein Mann	eine Frau	ein Kind	keine Männer/Frauen/Kinder
a.	einen Mann	eine Frau	ein Kind	keine Männer/Frauen/Kinder
g.	eines Mannes	einer Frau	eines Kindes	keiner Männer/Frauen/Kinder
d.	einem Mann	einer Frau	einem Kind	keinen Männern/Frauen/Kindern

Pronouns

Pronouns stand for a noun, e.g. 'Mary loves Fred - *she* loves *him*'. See Unit 8. Here are the nominative, accusative and dative pronouns:

nominative		accusative		dative	
ich	I	**mich**	me	**mir**	(to) me
du	you	**dich**	you	**dir**	(to) you
er	he/it	**ihn**	him/it	**ihm**	(to) him/it
sie	she/it	**sie**	her/it	**ihr**	(to) her/it
es	it	**es**	it	**ihm**	(to) it
wir	we	**uns**	us	**uns**	(to) us
ihr	you	**euch**	you	**euch**	(to) you
Sie	you	**Sie**	you	**Ihnen**	(to) you
sie	they	**sie**	them	**ihnen**	(to) them

Note that the dative is often translated by 'to' + pronoun in English, e.g.

Er gab es mir. He gave it *to me.*
Wir sagten es ihm. We said it *to him.*

Often you will find the dative form of pronouns in phrases such as **es gefällt mir, es schmeckt Ihnen, Wie geht es dir?** etc. (See Unit 8.)

Reflexive pronouns ('myself', 'yourself' etc. in English) are the same as the accusative pronouns except that you use **sich** instead of **ihn, sie, Sie,** and **es**. See Unit 6.

Here are the possessive pronouns. Remember they take endings like those on **ein/eine/ein** according to the case they are in and the gender of the noun (see above).

mein	my	**unser**	our
dein	your	**euer**	your
sein	his/its	**Ihr**	your
ihr	her/its	**ihr**	their
sein	its		

Relative pronouns are found in relative clauses, such as 'the boy *who* is eating the bread', 'the man (*whom*) I saw in the garden'. In German they are the same as the forms of **der/die/das**, according to the noun they represent, except that the dative plural is **denen**. See Unit 7.

Prepositions

Prepositions are words such as 'near', 'by', 'in', 'to', 'through', 'over', etc. (see Unit 6). In German certain prepositions take certain cases, e.g. **aus** (out of, from) takes the dative:

Er kommt aus dem Norden. He comes from the north.

And **durch** (through) takes the accusative:

Wir gehen durch den Garten. We go through the garden.

Prepositions which take only the dative:

aus	out of, from	**nach**	after, to
außer	except	**seit**	since, for
bei	at	**von**	from, of
gegenüber	opposite	**zu**	to, at
mit	with		

Prepositions which take only the accusative:

durch	through	**ohne**	without
entlang	along	**um**	around, at
für	for		
gegen	against, towards		

With some prepositions the accusative is used if the preposition shows the direction of movement, e.g.

Er ging in den Garten. He went into the garden.

The dative is used if the preposition shows location rather than direction, e.g.

Er stand im (= **in dem**) **Garten**. He was standing in the garden.

an	on, to, at	**über**	over, across
auf	on, onto	**unter**	under, below
hinter	behind	**vor**	in front of, ago
in	in, into	**zwischen**	between
neben	next to		

Adjectives

Adjectives are words such as 'good', 'bad', 'red', 'pretty', etc. You use adjectives if you want to describe things. To compare things you add **-er** to the adjective for the comparative and **am ...-sten** for the superlative. You often add an umlaut as well. See Unit 1.

Das Kind ist groß. The child is tall.
Die Frau ist größer. The woman is taller.
Der Mann ist am größten. The man is tallest.

If they are in front of the noun, adjectives, like articles, change depending on the case they are in, as shown in the tables below. After **kein** and possessives such as **mein/dein**, adjectives follow the same pattern as after **ein** in the singular, and **die** in the plural. See also Units 5 and 11.

singular							
	masculine			feminine		neuter	
n.	der	kleine	Mann	die kleine Frau	das	kleine	Kind
a.	den	kleinen	Mann	die kleine Frau	das	kleine	Kind
g.	des	kleinen	Mannes	der kleinen Frau	des	kleinen	Kindes
d.	dem	kleinen	Mann	der kleinen Frau	dem	kleinen	Kind
n.	ein	kleiner	Mann	eine kleine Frau	ein	kleines	Kind
a.	einen	kleinen	Mann	eine kleine Frau	ein	kleines	Kind
g.	eines	kleinen	Mannes	einer kleinen Frau	eines	kleinen	Kindes
d.	einem	kleinen	Mann	einer kleinen Frau	einem	kleinen	Kind

plural - all genders			
n.	die kleinen Männer/Frauen/Kinder	kleine	Männer/Frauen/Kinder
a.	die kleinen Männer/Frauen/Kinder	kleine	Männer/Frauen/Kinder
g.	der kleinen Männer/Frauen/Kinder	kleiner	Männer/Frauen/Kinder
d.	den kleinen Männern/Frauen/Kindern	kleinen	Männern/Frauen/Kindern

Word order

simple sentences with one verb In simple sentences (i.e. sentences which contain only one verb), the most important rule is that the main verb always goes in second position, e.g.

Ich	**fahre** nach London.	I travel to London.
Mein Haus	**ist** **groß.**	My house is big.

This rule also applies when the sentence begins with an expression of time, place or even the object. See Unit 4.

Im September	**fahre**	**ich nach London.**	I'm going to London in September.
Nach London	**fahre**	**ich im September.**	
Das Auto	**nehme**	**ich.**	I take that car.

In questions without a question word, the verb comes first. See Unit 2.

Fahren Sie nach London? Are you going to London?

Sentences with two verbs In sentences with two verbs the second verb is sent to the end.

Ich möchte nach London	**gehen.**	I would like to go to London.
Ich habe das Auto	**gekauft.**	I have bought the car.

Sentences with two clauses In clauses beginning with e.g. **wenn, daß, weil** (subordinate clauses), the verb goes to the end.

Ich fahre nach London, wenn das Wetter gut ist. I'm going to London if the weather is good.

If the subordinate clause comes at the beginning of the sentence, the main verb in the main clause comes immediately after it, in second place in the sentence as usual. (See Unit 4.)

Wenn das Wetter gut ist, fahre ich nach London. If the weather is good I'm going to London.

Numbers

1	**eins**	11	**elf**	21	**einundzwanzig**
2	**zwei**	12	**zwölf**	22	**zweiundzwanzig**
3	**drei**	13	**dreizehn**	30	**dreißig**
4	**vier**	14	**vierzehn**	40	**vierzig**
5	**fünf**	15	**fünfzehn**	50	**fünfzig**
6	**sechs**	16	**sechzehn**	60	**sechzig**
7	**sieben**	17	**siebzehn**	70	**siebzig**
8	**acht**	18	**achtzehn**	80	**achtzig**
9	**neun**	19	**neunzehn**	90	**neunzig**
10	**zehn**	20	**zwanzig**	100	**hundert**

Strong verbs

Compound verbs, such as **ankommen** and **bekommen**, follow the same pattern as their stem, in this case **kommen**:

ankommen	to arrive	kommt an	kam an	angekommen
bekommen	to receive	bekommt	bekam	bekommen

Infinitive	English	Present	Imperfect	Perfect
abhängen	to depend	hängt ab	hing ab	hat abgehangen
anbieten	to offer	bietet an	bot an	hat angeboten
anfangen	to begin	fängt an	fing an	hat angefangen
anrufen	to telephone	ruft an	rief an	hat angerufen
beginnen	to begin	beginnt	begann	hat begonnen
beißen	to bite	beißt	biß	hat gebissen
bitten	to request	bittet	bat	hat gebeten
bleiben	to stay	bleibt	blieb	ist geblieben
braten	to fry	brät	briet	hat gebraten
brennen	to burn	brennt	brannte	hat gebrannt
bringen	to bring	bringt	brachte	hat gebracht
denken	to think	denkt	dachte	hat gedacht
dürfen	to be allowed	darf	durfte	hat gedurft
einfallen	to occur to	fällt ein	fiel ein	ist eingefallen
einladen	to invite	lädt ein	lud ein	hat eingeladen
empfehlen	to recommend	empfiehlt	empfahl	hat empfohlen
essen	to eat	ißt	aß	hat gegessen
fahren	to go (vehicle)	fährt	fuhr	ist gefahren
finden	to find	findet	fand	hat gefunden
fliegen	to fly	fliegt	flog	ist geflogen
geben	to give	gibt	gab	hat gegeben
gefallen	to please	gefällt	gefiel	hat gefallen
gehen	to go	geht	ging	ist gegangen
gewinnen	to win	gewinnt	gewann	hat gewonnen
haben	to have	hat	hatte	hat gehabt
halten	to hold, keep	hält	hielt	hat gehalten
heißen	to be called	heißt	hieß	hat geheißen
helfen	to help	hilft	half	hat geholfen
kennen	to know	kennt	kannte	hat gekannt
klingen	to sound	klingt	klang	hat geklungen
kommen	to come	kommt	kam	ist gekommen
können	to be able to	kann	konnte	hat gekonnt
lassen	to leave	läßt	ließ	hat gelassen
laufen	to walk, run	läuft	lief	ist gelaufen
lesen	to read	liest	las	hat gelesen
liegen	to lie	liegt	lag	hat gelegen
mögen	to like	mag	mochte	hat gemocht
müssen	to have to	muß	mußte	hat gemußt
nehmen	to take	nimmt	nahm	hat genommen
raten	to advise	rät	riet	hat geraten
reiten	to ride	reitet	ritt	hat/ist geritten

Infinitive	English	Present	Imperfect	Perfect
scheinen	to shine	scheint	schien	hat geschienen
schlafen	to sleep	schläft	schlief	hat geschlafen
schließen	to close	schließt	schloß	hat geschlossen
schneiden	to cut	schneidet	schnitt	hat geschnitten
schreiben	to write	schreibt	schrieb	hat geschrieben
schwimmen	to swim	schwimmt	schwamm	ist geschwommen
sehen	to see	sieht	sah	hat gesehen
sein	to be	ist	war	ist gewesen
singen	to sing	singt	sang	hat gesungen
sitzen	to sit	sitzt	saß	hat gesessen
sollen	to be supposed to	soll	sollte	hat gesollt
sprechen	to speak	spricht	sprach	hat gesprochen
stehen	to stand	steht	stand	hat gestanden
steigen	to climb	steigt	stieg	ist gestiegen
tragen	to carry	trägt	trug	hat getragen
treffen	to meet	trifft	traf	hat getroffen
treiben	to do (sport)	treibt	trieb	hat getrieben
trinken	to drink	trinkt	trank	hat getrunken
tun	to do	tut	tat	hat getan
umfallen	to fall over	fällt um	fiel um	ist umgefallen
verbinden	to dress (wound)	verbindet	verband	hat verbunden
waschen	to wash	wäscht	wusch	hat gewaschen
werden	to become	wird	wurde	ist geworden
werfen	to throw	wirft	warf	hat geworfen
wissen	to know	weiß	wußte	hat gewußt
wollen	to want	will	wollte	hat gewollt
ziehen	to move (house)	zieht	zog	ist gezogen

VOCABULARY

The gender of nouns is given after the brackets: *m* means masculine, *f* feminine and *n* neuter

The plural of nouns is given in brackets, for example:
Zimmer (-) room ▷ no change in plural: **Zimmer**
Mutter (¨) mother ▷ no ending but an umlaut in stem vowel: **Mütter**
Wurst (¨e) sausage ▷ add **e** and stem vowel takes an umlaut: **Würste**
Abend (e) evening ▷ add **e**: **Abende**
Bank (en) bank ▷ add **en**: **Banken**
and so on.

If nothing is given in brackets, there is no plural for that particular word or it is hardly ever used. For example: **Wasser** water

If (*pl*) appears in brackets, the word is only used in the plural with the meaning given. For example: **Leute** (*pl*) people

* next to a verb indicates that it, or its stem form, is in the list on pp. 200–1.

A

ab   off; from
Abend (e) *m*   evening
Abendessen (-) *n*   evening meal
Abendgymnasium (-gymnasien) *n*   evening school
Abendschule (n) *f*   evening classes
aber   but
*abfahren   to leave
Abfahrt (en) *f*   departure
*abgehen   to come off
*abhängen   to depend
abhängig   dependent
Abitur (e) *n*   university entrance exam (A-levels)
*abwaschen   to wash up
Abwechslung (en) *f*   change, variety
abwechslungsreich   diversified, varied
ach   oh, well
achten   to take care, pay attention
Adresse (n) *f*   address
aggressiv   aggressive
Ägypten *n*   Egypt
Akkordarbeit *f*   piecework
aktiv   active
aktuell   topical
Alkohol *m*   alcohol
alkoholfrei   non-alcohol
alkoholisch   alcoholic
alle   all

allein   alone
alleinerziehende Mutter *f*   single mother
allerdings   though, but
alles   everything
alles andere   everything else
alles Gute   all the best
Allgemeinbildung *f*   general knowledge, education
Alltagstrott *m*   daily grind
allzu   (all) too
als   as; when
also   so, that is to say
alt   old
Altenheim (e) *n*   old people's home
Alter *n*   age
Altstadt (¨e) *f*   old part of town
am besten   best of all
Amerika *n*   America
Amerikaner (-) *m*   American *m*
amerikanisch   American
am liebsten   best of all
amtlich   official
amüsant   amusing
*anbehalten   to keep on (clothes)
*anbieten   to offer
andere   different, other
ändern   to change
*anfangen   to start
Angebot (e) *n*   offer
*angehen   to concern
Angelegenheit (en) *f*   matter, affair

angenommen assuming
Anglistik English (language and literature)
Angst (¨e) *f* fear
***Angst haben** to be afraid, worried
***ankommen** to arrive
Ankunft (¨e) *f* arrival
anonym anonymous
Anregung (en) *f* suggestion, inspiration
anreisen to arrive, get there
***anrufen** to telephone
anschauen to watch
anschaulich clear, graphic
***ansprechen** to speak to
Anstellung (en) *f* job, position
anstrengend exhausting
Antiseptikum (Antiseptika) *n* antiseptic
Antwort (en) *f* answer
***(sich) anziehen** to get dressed, put on
anzünden to light
Apfel (¨) *m* apple
Apfelsaft *m* apple juice
Apotheke (n) *f* pharmacy
Apotheker (-) *m* pharmacist *m*
Appetit *m* appetite
April *m* April
Arbeit (en) *f* work
arbeiten to work
Arbeiter (-) *m* worker *m*
Arbeitgeber (-) *m* employer *m*
Arbeitsamt (¨er) *n* job centre
arbeitslos unemployed
Arbeitsmarkt (¨e) *m* labour market
Arbeitsstil (e) *m* style of working
Arbeitstag (e) *m* working day
Ärger *m* trouble
ärgerlich irritating
(sich) ärgern to get angry
Arm (e) *m* arm
Art (en) *f* sort
Artikel (-) *m* article
Arzt (¨e) *m* **Ärztin (nen)** *f* doctor
Arzthelferin (nen) *f* doctor's assistant *f*
Atlantik *m* Atlantic Ocean
Atmosphäre (n) *f* atmosphere
auch also
Aufführung (en) *f* performance
Aufgabe (n) *f* task
***aufgeben** to give up
aufhören to stop
aufmachen to open
aufpassen to take care of
aufräumen to tidy up
(sich) aufregen to get worked up
***aufstehen** to get up
Aufstieg (e) *m* rise
Aufstiegsmöglichkeit (en) *f* promotion prospect
Auge (n) *n* eye
August *m* August
aus out (of), from
ausbauen to extend, build up
Ausbildung (en) *f* training, education
Ausbildungskurs (e) *m* training course
Ausflug (¨e) *m* excursion, trip
Ausgabe (n) *f* edition
***ausgeben** to spend

***ausgehen** to go out
  (davon) ausgehen to assume
ausgezeichnet excellent
Ausgleich (e) *m* balance
Ausländer (-) *m* foreigner *m*
ausländisch foreign
ausprobieren to try out
ausruhen to rest
***aussehen** to look, appear
außer except
außerdem besides
***aussteigen** to get out, off
Ausstellung (en) *f* exhibition
aussuchen to select
Australien *n* Australia
ausverkauft sold out
Auswahl (en) *f* selection
Auto (s) *n* car
Automatik *f* automatic (transmission)
Autorin (nen) *f* author *f*
Autovermietung (en) *f* car hire

B

Baby (s) *n* baby
babysitten to babysit
Bad (¨er) *n* bath
baden to bathe
Badewanne (n) *f* bathtub
Bahn (en) *f* (rail)track
Bahnfahrt (en) *f* rail journey
Bahnhof (¨e) *m* railway station
bald soon
Ball (¨e) *m* ball
Banane (n) *f* banana
Band (s) *f* band, group
Bank (¨e) *f* bench
Bank (en) *f* bank
bar cash
Bar (s) *f* bar
Batterie (n) *f* battery
Bau (ten) *m* construction
Bauarbeiter (-) *m* building worker *m*
Bauch (¨e) *m* belly
Bauchtanz (¨e) *m* belly dance
bauen to build
Bauernhof (¨e) *m* farm
Baustelle (n) *f* building site, roadworks
Bayern *n* Bavaria
Bayrischer Wald Bavarian Forest
beachten to consider
Beamte (n) *m* **Beamtin (nen)** *f* official
bedeckt overcast
Bedeutung (en) *f* meaning, significance
bedienen to serve
Beere (n) *f* berry
***beginnen** to begin
begrüßen to welcome, greet
Begrüßung (en) *f* welcome
beide both
***beißen** to bite
Bein (e) *n* leg
beinahe nearly
Beispiel (e) *n* example
Beitrag (¨e) *m* contribution

Bekanntgabe (n) *f*   announcement
*bekommen   to get, receive
beliebt   popular
bequem   comfortable
*beraten   to advise
Bereich (e) *m*   region, sector
bereits   already
Berg (e) *m*   mountain
Beruf (e) *m*   job, profession
Berufsleben (-) *n*   professional life
Berufsplan (¨e) *m*   career plan
Berufsschule (n) *f*   vocational college
*beschreiben   to describe
besichtigen   to view
besonders   especially
besser   better
*bestehen   to consist
bestellen   to book, order
bestimmt   certainly
Besuch (e) *m*   visit
besuchen   to visit
Besucher (-) *m* **Besucherin (nen)** *f*   visitor
Bett (en) *n*   bed
Bevölkerung (en) *f*   population, people
beweglich   supple, fit
bewölkt   cloudy
Bewölkung (en) *f*   cloud cover
bezahlen   to pay
Bibliothek (en) *f*   library
Bier (e) *n*   beer
Bild (er) *n*   picture
bilden   to form
Bildschirm (e) *m*   computer or TV screen
Bildungsurlaub (e) *m*   educational holiday
billig   cheap
Binde (n) *f*   bandage
bis   to, till
bißchen *n*   bit
bitte   please; you're welcome
*bitten   to ask for
bitter   bitter
Blatt (¨er) *n*   leaf; sheet; newspaper
blau   blue
*bleiben   to stay
Blume (n) *f*   flower
Bluse (n) *f*   blouse
blutig   rare, bloody
blutrünstig   full of blood
Bohne (n) *f*   bean
Bohnenstange (n) *f*   beanpole
Bonbon (s) *n*   sweet
Bootfahren *n*   boating
Boulevardpresse *f*   popular press
Boutique (n) *f*   boutique
*braten   to fry
Bratwurst (¨e) *m*   fried/grilled sausage
brauchen   to need
braun   brown
*brennen   to burn
Brief (e) *m*   letter
*bringen   to bring
Brot (e) *n*   bread
Brötchen (-) *n*   bread roll
Bruchlandung (-) *f*   crashlanding
Bruder (¨) *m*   brother

brutto   gross (before tax)
Buch (¨er) *n*   book
buchen   to book
Bücherregal (e) *n*   bookshelf
Buchhalter (-) *m*   accountant *m*
Buchhandlung (en) *f*   bookshop
Bundeskanzler (-) *m*   Federal Chancellor
Bundesrepublik Deutschland *f*   Federal Republic
   of Germany
Bundestag *m*   Federal Parliament
Büro (s) *n*   office
Bus (se) *m*   bus
Butter *f*   butter
Butterbrot (e) *n*   sandwich

C

Café (s) *n*   café
CDU = Christlich-Demokratische Union *f*
   Christian Democrats
Chalet (s) *n*   chalet
Chance (n) *f*   chance
chaotisch   chaotic
Chef (s) *m* **Chefin (nen)** *f*   boss
China *n*   China
Cola (s) *n*   cola drink
Computer (-) *m*   computer
CSU = Christlich-Soziale Union *f*   Bavarian
   Christian Democrats

D

dagegen   on the other hand
daheim   at home
daher   so
Dame (n) *f*   lady
danach   afterwards
danke   thank you
dann   then
daran   at it, to it
*darauf achten   to take care, watch
Darmgrippe *f*   gastric flu
dauern   to last
davor   before that
dazu   with it, to it
dazurechnen   to include
demnächst   in the near future
*denken   to think
denn   then; for
dennoch   however, though
deprimiert   depressed
Desinfektionsmittel (-) *n*   disinfectant
deswegen   therefore
Deutsch *n*   German (language)
deutschsprachig   German-speaking
Dezember *m*   December
Diät (en) *f*   diet
dick   fat, thick
Dienst (e) *m*   service
diese(r/s)   this
Diesel *m*   diesel
Diplom-   qualified
direkt   direct(ly)
Distanz (en) *f*   distance

doch though, but
Dom (e) *m* cathedral
dort there
Dozent (en) *m* **Dozentin (nen)** *f* lecturer
dringend urgent(ly)
dünn thin
durch through; well done
Durchfall *m* diarrhoea
*dürfen to be allowed to
Dusche (n) *f* shower

E

eben just, simply; exactly
Ecke (n) *f* corner
egal the same
eher rather
Ei (er) *n* egg
eigen own
eigentlich really, actually
eineinhalb one and a half
einfach easy, simple; single
*einfallen to occur to
eingelegt pickled
einige some, several
einkaufen to shop
einkehren to drop in at a pub/inn
*einladen to invite
Einladung (en) *f* invitation
einmal once
    auf einmal at once
*einschlafen to fall asleep
*einsteigen to get on
einstellen to employ
Eintrittsgeld (er) *n* entrance fee
Einzelheit (en) *f* detail
Eis (-) *n* ice cream; ice
Eisen *n* iron
Eisenbahn (en) *f* railway
Eissalat (e) *m* iceberg lettuce
Elefant (en) *m* elephant
elektrisch electric
Elektrizität *f* electricity
Elektrotechnik *f* electrical engineering
Eltern *(pl)* parents
emanzipiert emancipated
*empfehlen to recommend
Ende (n) *n* end
enden to end
endlich at last
Energie (n) *f* energy
Energiegewinnung *f* production of energy
englisch English
Enkelkind (er) *n* grandchild
entdecken to discover
Entfernung (en) *f* distance
Entscheidung (en) *f* decision
entschieden decidedly
Entschlackung (en) *f* purification
*entschließen to decide
Entschuldigung! Excuse me!
(sich) entspannen to relax
Entspannungsübung (en) *f* relaxation exercise
entweder – oder either – or
entwickeln to develop

Erdbeere (n) *f* strawberry
Erde *f* earth
*erfahren to find out
Erfahrung (en) *f* experience
Erfolg (e) *m* success
erforschen to research
erfrischen to refresh
(sich) erinnern to remember
Erkältung (en) *f* cold
erklären to explain
Erklärung (en) *f* explanation
Ermäßigung (en) *f* reduction
Ersatzband (s) *f* replacement band
erst first; not until
Erwachsene (n) *m/f* adult
Erziehung *f* upbringing, education
es gibt there is, there are
esoterisch esoteric
*essen to eat
Essen *n* food
es tut mir leid I'm sorry
etwa roughly
etwas something; some
Europa *n* Europe
existieren to exist
Experiment (e) *n* experiment
Experte (n) *m* **Expertin (nen)** *f* expert
explodieren to explode
Exportfirma (-firmen) *f* export firm
exotisch exotic
extra in addition

F

Fabrik (en) *f* factory
Fachzeitschrift (en) *f* special-interest magazine
*fahren to drive, go, travel
Fahrpreis (e) *m* fare
Fahrrad (¨er) *n* bicycle
Fahrzeug (e) *n* vehicle
Fall (¨e) *m* case
    auf jeden Fall in any case
falsch wrong
Familie (n) *f* family
Familienfest (e) *n* family occasion
Fasching *m* carnival
Fassade (n) *f* façade
fast almost, nearly
fasten to fast
faszinieren fascinating
faul lazy
FDP = Freie Demokratische Partei *f* Liberal Party
Februar *m* February
Feierabend (e) *m* end of work; evening
feiern to celebrate
Feiertag (e) *m* public holiday
fein nice, delicate, fine
Fenster (-) *n* window
Ferien *(pl)* holidays
Ferienhaus (¨er) *n* holiday house
*fernsehen to watch television
Fernsehen *n* television
Fernseher (-) *m* TV set
fest steady, fixed

Fest (e) *n*   party, festival
fettarm   low-fat
Feuer (-) *n*   fire
Fieber (-) *n*   fever, temperature
Figur (en) *f*   figure
Film (e) *m*   film
finanzieren   to finance
***finden**   to find
Finger (-) *m*   finger
Firma (Firmen) *f*   firm, company
Fisch (e) *m*   fish
fischen   to fish
fit   fit
Flasche (n) *f*   bottle
Fleisch *n*   meat
Flexibilität *f*   flexibility
***fliegen** to fly
Fließband ("er) *n*   production line
flippig   informal
Flug ("e) *m*   flight
Flugzeug (e) *n*   aeroplane
Form (en) *f*   shape
    in Form   fit
Fotogeschäft (e) *n*   photographic shop
fotografieren   to photograph
Frage (n) *f*   question
fragen   to ask
Frankenwein (e) *m*   wine from Franconia
fränkisch   Franconian
Frankreich *n*   France
Französisch *n*   French (language)
Frau (en) *f*   wife; woman
Frauenzeitschrift (en) *f*   women's magazine
frei   free; freelance
freiberuflich   freelance
Freizeit *f*   leisure
fremd   foreign, other people's
Fremdsprache (n) *f*   foreign language
freuen   to please
    (sich) freuen auf   to look forward to
    (sich) freuen über   to be pleased about
Freund (e) *m* **Freundin (nen)** *f*   friend
freundlich   friendly, kind
frisch   fresh
froh   glad, happy
Frost ("e) *m*   frost
früh   early
früher   at one time; earlier
Frühgymnastik *f*   morning exercise
Frühling *m*   spring
Frühstück (e) *n*   breakfast
frühstücken   to have breakfast
(sich) fühlen   to feel
führen   to lead
Führer (-) *m*   leader, guide
füllen   to fill
Funktion (en) *f*   function
furchtbar   terrible, terribly
fürchterlich   terrible, terribly
Fuß ("e) *m*   foot
    zu Fuß   on foot
Fußball *m*   football, soccer
Fußballplatz ("e) *m*   football pitch

G

gähnen   to yawn
Gang ("e) *m*   course; corridor
    im Gang   in progress
ganz   whole; quite
ganztags   full-time, all-day
Garde (n) *f*   Guards, military band
Garten (") *m*   garden
Gasse (n) *f*   alleyway
Gast ("e) *m*   guest
Gästehaus ("er) *n*   guesthouse
Gastgeber (-) *m*   host
Gastgeberin (nen) *f*   hostess
Gasthof ("e) *m*   inn, pub
***geben**   to give
    es gibt   there is, there are
gebraten   fried
gebrauchen   to use
Geburtstag (e) *m*   birthday
Gedanke (n) *m*   thought
gefährlich   dangerous
***gefallen**   to please
    es gefällt mir   I like it
gefroren   frozen
Gefühl (e) *n*   feeling
gegen   towards; against
Gegend (en) *f*   area
gegenüber   opposite
Gehalt ("er) *n*   salary
***gehen**   to go
gehören   to belong
Gehweg (e) *m*   pavement
Geist (er) *m*   ghost; wit
Geld (er) *n*   money
Geldsorgen *(pl)*   financial worries
Gel(e) *n*, **Gelee (s)** *n*   gel, jelly
gelegentlich   occasional
Gemälde (-) *n*   painting
gemeinsam   together
Gemüse *n*   vegetable(s)
gemütlich   cosy
genau   exact
Genießer (-) *m*   bon viveur
genug   enough
gerade   just
geradeaus   straight ahead
Gerät (e) *n*   appliance
Germanistik *f*   German (language and literature)
gern/gerne   with pleasure
Gesamtschule (n) *f*   comprehensive school
Geschäft (e) *n*   shop
Geschenk (e) *n*   present
Geschichte (n) *f*   history, story
Geschirr *n*   dishes, crockery
Geschwindigkeit (en) *f*   speed
Gesellschaft (en) *f*   society, party
Gespenst (er) *n*   phantom, ghost
gestern   yesterday
gesund   healthy
Gesundheit *f*   health
Getränk (e) *n*   drink
***gewinnen**   to win
Gewitter (-) *n*   thunderstorm
Glas ("er) *n*   glass

Glatteis *n*   black ice
glauben   to think, believe
gleich   straight away; same
Gleichberechtigung *f*   equality
Gleis (e) *n*   platform, track
gleitende Arbeitszeit/Gleitzeit *f*   flexitime
Glück *n*   luck; happiness
glücklich   happy, lucky
Glückspilz (e) *m*   lucky devil
Grad (e) *m*   degree
gratulieren   to congratulate
Griechenland *n*   Greece
Grillbraten (-) *m*   grilled meat
Grillparty (s) *f*   barbecue (party)
Grippe *f*   flu
groß   big
Gruppe (n) *f*   group
grün   green
Grund ("e) *m*   reason, ground
Grundschule (n) *f*   primary school
Grünen (*pl*)   the Green Party
Gruß ("e) *m*   greeting
grüßen   to greet
gültig   valid
günstig   reasonable, good-value
gut   good, well
    was Gutes   something good (i.e. special)
Gymnasium (Gymnasien) *n*   grammar school, high school
Gymnastik *f*   gymnastics, exercises

H

*haben   to have
halb   half
halbtags   part-time
Hals ("e) *m*   neck, throat
Halsweh (e) *n*   sore throat
*halten   to stop, keep
    *(sich) halten   to keep
Haltestelle (n) *f*   stop
Hamburger (-) *m*   hamburger
Hand ("e) *f*   hand
Handballplatz ("e) *m*   handball pitch
Handschuh (e) *m*   glove
Handtasche (n) *f*   handbag
Handy (s) *n*   mobile phone
hart   hard
hassen   to hate
Hauptbahnhof ("e) *m*   main station
Hauptfach ("er) *n*   main subject
Hauptstadt ("e) *f*   capital city
Haus ("er) *n*   house
    *nach Hause gehen   to go home
    zu Hause   at home
Hausarbeit (en) *f*   housework
Hausaufgabe (n) *f*   homework
Hausfrau (en) *f*   housewife
Haushalt (e) *m*   household
Hausmann ("er) *m*   house-husband
Hausmannskost *f*   plain food
Hausputz *m*   house-cleaning
Hecke (n) *f*   hedge
Heiliger Abend *m*   Christmas Eve
Heilmittel (-) *n*   remedy

heiraten   to marry
heiß   hot
*heißen   to mean; be called
Hektik *f*   hectic rush
hektisch   hectic
Held (en) *m*   hero
*helfen   to help
Hemd (e) *n*   shirt
*herausfinden   to find out
herb   dry (of wine)
Herbst (e) *m*   autumn
Herd (e) *m*   stove, cooker
Hering (e) *m*   herring
herumreisen   to travel around
Herz (en) *n*   heart
herzlichen Glückwünsch   congratulations
heute   today
hier   here
Hilfe (n) *f*   help
Hilfsarbeiter (-) *m*   unskilled labourer *m*
Himmel (-) *m*   sky
*hinkommen   to get there
hinschauen   to look at
hinter   behind
Hintergrund ("e) *m*   background
hin und zurück   return
historisch   historic
Hobby (s) *n*   hobby
*hochgehen   to go up
hochlegen   to put up
höchstens   at most
Höchstgeschwindigkeit (en) *f*   top speed
Höchsttemperatur (en) *f*   maximum temperature
Hochzeit (en) *f*   wedding
holen   to fetch
hören   to hear, listen to
Hosentasche (n) *f*   trouser pocket
Hotel (s) *n*   hotel
Hund (e) *m*   dog
Hundehaufen (-) *m*   dog's mess
Hunger *m*   hunger
Hungerkur (en) *f*   fast
Hut ("e) *m*   hat

I

ideal   ideal
Idee (n) *f*   idea
Idiotenhügel (-) *m*   nursery slope
idyllisch   idyllic
immer   always
indem   by
Indien *n*   India
Individualfahrzeug (e) *n*   private vehicle
Individualist (en) *m*   individualist
Industriezentrum (-zentren) *n*   centre of industry
Infekt (e) *m*   infection
Information (en) *f*   information
informieren   to inform
inklusive   including
innen   inside
inner   inner
in Ordnung   all right
Insektenschutz *m*   insect repellent
Insel (n) *f*   island

insgesamt   all together
intensiv   intensiv
interessant   interesting
(sich) interessieren für   to be interested in
intim   intimate
inzwischen   meanwhile
irgend (et)was   something
irgendwann   some time
irgendwelche   some sort of
irgendwie   somehow
irgendwo   somewhere
isoliert   isolated
Italien *n*   Italy
italienisch   Italian

J

Jackett (s) *n*   jacket
Jägerschnitzel (-) *n*   veal or pork escalope with
   spicy mushroom sauce
Jahr (e) *n*   year
jahrelang   for years
Jahresurlaub (e) *m*   annual holiday
Jahreszeit (en) *f*   time of year, season
Jahrhundert (e) *n*   century
-jährig   -year-old
Januar *m*   January
Japan *n*   Japan
jede(r/s)   each
jedoch   however
jemand   somebody
je nachdem   depending
jetzt   now
Job (s) *m*   job
Journalist (en) *m*   journalist
Jugend *f*   youth
Jugendherberge (n) *f*   youth hostel
Jugendliche (n) *f/m*   young person, teenager
Juli *m*   July
Juni *m*   June
jung   young
Junge (n) *m*   boy

K

Kabinett (e) *n*   cabinet
Kaffee (s) *m*   coffee
Kaffeekränzchen (-) *n*   coffee circle
Kalbsleber *f*   calf's liver
Kalorie (n) *f*   calorie
kalt   cold
Kanada *n*   Canada
Kandiszucker *m*   rock candy
Kantine (n) *f*   canteen
Kanu (s) *n*   canoe
kaputt   exhausted; broken
Karottensalat (e) *m*   carrot salad
Karte (n) *f*   card; ticket; menu
Karten spielen   to play cards
Kartoffel (n) *f*   potato
Käse (-) *m*   cheese
Käsekuchen (-) *m*   cheesecake
Kasse (n) *f*   cashdesk, box office
Kassiererin (nen) *f*   woman in box office

Katalog (e) *m*   catalogue
Kater (-) *m*   hangover; tomcat
kauen   to chew
kaufen   to buy
Kaufhaus ("er) *n*   department store
Kaufmann (Kaufleute) *m*   shopkeeper,
   commercial manager
Kaugummi (s) *n*   chewing gum
Kegelbahn (en) *f*   bowling alley
kegeln   to play skittles
kein   no, none
Keller (-) *m*   cellar
*kennen   to know, be familiar with
Kenntnis (se) *f*   knowledge
Kennzeichen (-) *n*   registration number
Kerze (n) *f*   candle
Kilo (s) *n*   kilogram
Kilometergeld (er) *n*   rate per kilometre
Kind (er) *n*   child
Kindergarten (") *m*   kindergarten
Kinderkrippe (n) *f*   crèche
Kino (s) *n*   cinema
Kirche (n) *f*   church
Kirsche (n) *f*   cherry
klar   clear
Klasse (n) *f*   class
klassisch   classical
Kleid (er) *n*   dress
Kleidermarkt ("e) *m*   clothes market
klein   small
klettern   to climb
Klima (ta) *n*   climate
*klingen   to sound
klingeln   to tinkle, chime
Kloster (") *n*   monastery
Kneipe (n) *f*   pub
Knie (-) *n*   knee
Knoblauch *m*   garlic
Knödel (-) *m*   dumpling
Knopf ("e) *m*   button
knuddelig   cuddly
Koalitionspartner (-) *m*   coalition partner
Koch ("e) *m* Köchin (nen) *f*   cook
kochen   to cook
Kohle(n)hydrat (e) *n*   carbohydrate
Kollege (n) *m* Kollegin (nen) *f*   colleague
komisch   funny, strange
*kommen   to come
kommerzialisieren   to commercialize
Kommilitone (n) *m* Kommilitonin (nen) *f*   fellow
   student
Komödie (n) *f*   comedy
Konfetti *n*   confetti
König (e) *m*   king
*können   can, to be able to
konservativ   conservative
Kontakt (e) *m*   contact
(sich) konzentrieren   to concentrate
Konzert (e) *n*   concert
Kopf ("e) *m*   head
Kopfhörer (-) *m*   headphones
Kopfschmerzen (*pl*)   headache
Kopfweh (e) *n*   headache
Korfu *n*   Corfu
körperlich   physical

kosten to cost
kräftig vigorously
krank sick, ill
Krankenhaus (¨er) *n* hospital
Krankheit (en) *f* illness
kreativ creative
Kreditkarte (n) *f* credit card
kriegen to get, receive
Krise (n) *f* crisis
Küche (n) *f* kitchen
Kuchen (-) *m* cake
kühlen to cool
Kühlschrank (¨e) *m* fridge
Kultur (en) *f* culture
Kunst (¨e) *f* art
Kunstschatz (¨e) *m* art treasure
Kur (en) *f* cure, treatment
Kuriosität (en) *f* curiosity
Kurs (e) *m* course
kurz short
Küste (n) *f* coast

Liebe (n) *f* love
lieben to love
lieber rather
Liebhaber (-) *m* lover
Lieblings- favourite
Lied (er) *n* song
Liederabend (e) *m* song recital
*liegen to lie
links left
linksliberal liberal to left-wing
Literatur (en) *f* literature
LKW = Lastkraftwagen (-) *m* lorry
Lokal (e) *n* bar, pub
Lokalnachrichten (*pl*) local news
lösen to solve
*losgehen to start
Lücke (n) *f* gap
Luft (¨e) *f* air
*Lust haben auf to feel like
lustig funny, jolly
Luxushotel (s) *n* luxury hotel

L

lachen to laugh
Lager (-) *n* camp
Lagerfeuer (-) *n* campfire
Land *n* countryside
Land (¨er) *n* country, state
landen to land
Landschaft (en) *f* landscape
lang long
lange for a long time
länger longer
langsam slow
Längschläfer (-) *m* lie-abed
(sich) langweilen to be bored
langweilig boring
Lärm *m* noise
*lassen to leave
*laufen to walk, run, be on (film)
laut loud; noisy
leben to live
Leben (-) *n* life
Lebensende *n* end of one's life
Lebenskünstler (-) *m* someone who makes the
   best of life
Lebenslauf (¨e) *m* curriculum vitae
Lebensmittel (*pl*) groceries
Lebenszeit *f* lifetime
leer empty, flat (battery)
legen to lay, put
Lehrer (-) *m* Lehrerin (nen) *f* teacher
leicht light, easy
Leichtathletik *f* athletics
leider unfortunately
*leid tun to make one feel sorry
   es tut mir leid I'm sorry
lernen to learn
*lesen to read
letzte(r/s) last
Leute (*pl*) people
liberal liberal
Liberalen (*pl*) Liberals

M

machen to do, make
Mädchen (-) *n* girl
Magazin (e) *n* magazine
Magenschmerzen (*pl*) stomach ache
mager lean
mähen to mow
Mai *m* May
Mal (e) *n* time (s)
   fünfmal five times
malen to paint
malerisch picturesque
manche some
manchmal sometimes
Mango (s) *f* mango
Manieren (*pl*) manners
Mann (¨er) *m* man; husband
Markt (¨e) *m* market
Marktplatz (¨e) *m* marketplace
Marmelade (n) *f* jam
März *m* March
Maschine (n) *f* machine
Maske (n) *f* mask
Masse (n) *f* mass
Mathematik *f* mathematics
matschig mushy
maximal at most
meditieren to meditate
Meer (e) *n* sea
mehr more
meinen to think
Meinung (en) *f* opinion
meist in most cases
meistens mostly
Meldung (en) *f* bulletin
Mensch (en) *m* person
Mensch ärgere dich nicht ludo
Metzger (-) *m* butcher *m*
Miete (n) *f* rent
mieten to rent, hire
Milch *f* milk

Mineralwasser (") *n*   mineral water
Minute (n) *f*   minute
Mitarbeiter (-) *m*   staff member
miteinander   with each other
***mitfahren**   to go too
***mitnehmen**   to take along
Mittag (e) *m*   noon, midday
Mittagessen (-) *n*   lunch
mittags   at lunchtime
Mittagspause (n) *f*   lunch break
Mitte (n) *f*   middle
Mittel (-) *n*   means, remedy
Mitternacht *f*   midnight
Mittlere Reife *f*   school-leaving certificate (GCSEs)
Mode (n) *f*   fashion
Moderation *f*   TV presentation
***mögen**   to like
möglich   possible
Möglichkeit (en) *f*   possibility
Moment (e) *m*   moment
Monat (e) *m*   month
monatlich   monthly
monoton   monotonous, dull
Moorbad ("er) *n*   mud bath
morgen   tomorrow
Morgen (-) *m*   morning
morgens   in the morning
Morgenstunde (n) *f*   morning hour
Motor (en) *m*   motor, engine
Motto (s) *n*   theme, motto
müde   tired
München   Munich
Mund ("er) *m*   mouth
Musik *f*   music
Muskelschmerzen *(pl)*   sore muscles
Müsli (s) *n*   muesli
***müssen**   to have to, must
Mutter (") *f*   mother

N

Nachbar (n) *m*   neighbour
nachdem   after
***nachdenken**   to think, consider
Nachdruck *m*   emphasis
Nachmittag (e) *m*   afternoon
nachmittags   in the afternoon
Nachricht (en) *f*   news
nächste(r/s)   next, nearest
Nacht ("e) *f*   night
Nachteil (e) *m*   disadvantage
Nachtisch (e) *m*   dessert, pudding
nah   near, nearby
Nähe *f*   proximity
Name (n) *m*   name
nämlich   actually, namely, you see, you know
Nase (n) *f*   nose
naß   wet
Natur (en) *f*   nature
natürlich   of course
Nebel (-) *m*   fog
neben   next to, beside
nebenbei   as well
nebenher   at the same time

neblig   foggy
***nehmen**   to take
Nerv (en) *m*   nerve
nett   nice
netto   after tax
neu   new
Neuerung (en) *f*   innovation
nichts   nothing
nie   never
Niederschlag (" e) *m*   rainfall, precipitation
niemals   never
niemand   nobody
noch   still, also
noch nicht   not yet
Norddeutschland *n*   North Germany
Norden *m*   North
Nordost *m*   North-East
Nordsee *f*   North Sea
normal   normal, ordinary
normalerweise   normally
November *m*   November
nur   only
Null *f*   zero

O

Ober (-) *m*   waiter
Obst *n*   fruit
offen   open
öffentlich   public
öffnen   to open
oft   often
öfters   fairly often
ohne   without
Ohr (en) *n*   ear
Oktober *m*   October
Oma (s) *f*   granny, grandma
Oper (n) *f*   opera
Orange (n) *f*   orange
Ordnung (en) *f*   order
   in Ordnung   all right
organisieren   to organise
originell   ingenious, original
Osten *m*   East
Ostern *n*   Easter
Österreich *n*   Austria
Ostfriesentee *m*   East Frisian tea
Ostsee *f*   Baltic Sea

P

Paar (e) *n*   pair
Papier (e) *n*   document, paper
parken   to park
Parkett (e) *n*   dance floor
Partei (en) *f*   (political party)
passieren   to happen
passiv   passive
Pastete (n) *f*   pâté, pie
Patient (en) *m*   patient
Pause (n) *f*   break, interval
Pazifik *m*   Pacific
***pensioniert werden**   to retire
Perle (n) *f*   pearl

Person (en) *f* person
persönlich personal
Pferd (e) *n* horse
Pfingsten *n* Whitsun
Pflaster (-) *n* sticking plaster
Pfund (e) *n* pound, 500 grams
Philosophie (n) *f* philosophy
Physiker (-) *m* physicist
Pilz (e) *m* mushroom
PKW = Personenkraftwagen (-) *m* car
Plan (¨e) *m* plan
Platte (n) *f* platter (of food)
Platz (¨e) *m* space
plaudern to chat
plötzlich suddenly
Politik *f* politics
politisch political
Polizei *f* police
Pommes frites (*pl*) chips
portugiesisch Portuguese
Post (Postämter) *f* post office
Prag Prague
Praktikum *n* work experience
praktisch practical
Präsident (en) *m* president
Preis (e) *m* cost, price; prize
Preisgruppe (n) *f* price-band
preisgünstig reasonably priced
preiswert reasonably priced
Premiere (n) *f* première
Presse *f* press
Priorität (en) *f* priority
Privatauto (s) *n* private car
Privatklinik (en) *f* private clinic
pro per
probieren to taste, try
Problem (e) *n* problem
Produkt (e) *n* product
produzieren to produce
Programm (e) *n* schedule, programme
Programmiererin (nen) *f* programmer *f*
Prozent (e) *n* per cent
Psychologin (nen) *f* psychologist *f*
Punkt (e) *m* point
Puppe (n) *f* puppet, doll
putzen to clean
Putzfrau (en) *f* cleaning woman

Q

Quark *m* curd cheese
quer durch right across
quer nach right across to

R

Radio (s) *n* radio
Radiodienst (e) *m* radio service
Rasen (-) *m* lawn
*raten to advise; guess
Ratespiel (e) *n* guessing game
Rathaus (¨er) *n* town hall
rauchen to smoke
Raum (¨e) *m* room

rechts right
rechtzeitig in time
reden to talk
Regen *m* rain
Regie *f* directing
Regierung (en) *f* government
regional regional
Regionalsendung (en) *f* regional programme
regnen to rain
regulär regular
Rehrücken (-) *m* saddle of venison
reich rich
Reinfall (¨e) *m* flop, fiasco
Reis *m* rice
Reise (n) *f* journey
Reiseapotheke (n) *f* medical kit for travelling
Reiseführer (-) *m* guide *m*
reisen to travel
Reiseruf (e) *m* radio message
*reiten to ride
relativ relatively
Rente (n) *f* pension
Reportage (n) *f* report
Reporter (-) *m* reporter *m*
repräsentativ representative
Restaurant (s) *n* restaurant
Resultat (e) *n* result
Rezept (e) *n* recipe
richtig right, proper
Richtung (en) *f* (in the) direction (of)
Riese (n) *m* giant
riesig gigantic
Ring (e) *m* ring
riskant risky
Rolle (n) *f* role
romantisch romantic
rösten to roast
rot red
Routine (n) *f* routine
Ruhestand *m* retirement
ruhen to rest
ruhig quiet
Ruine (n) *f* ruin
Rum *m* rum
Rumpsteak (s) *n* rumpsteak
rund round; about
Rundfunk *m* radio
Rundreise (n) *f* round trip

S

Sache (n) *f* matter, thing
Saft (¨e) *m* juice
Saftkur (en) *f* fruit-juice diet
sagen to say
Sahne *f* cream
salzig salty
sauer sour
Sauerstoff *m* oxygen
Sauna (s) *f* sauna
Schadstoff (e) *m* pollutant
scharf spicy, hot; sharp

Schatz (¨e) *m* treasure
Schauer (-) *m* shower
*scheinen to shine
schenken to give away
Schiff (e) *n* ship
*schlafen to sleep
schlaff listless; limp
Schlagsahne *f* whipped cream
Schlagzeile (n) *f* headline
Schlange (n) *f* queue; snake
schlank slim
schlecht bad
*schließen to close
schließlich finally
schlimm bad
Schloß (Schlösser) *n* castle
Schluß (Schlüsse) *m* end
    zum Schluß in the end
schmecken to taste
Schmerz (en) *m* pain
schmutzig dirty
Schnaps (¨e) *m* schnapps
Schnee *m* snow
*schneiden to cut
schneien to snow
schnell fast, quick
Schnupfen (-) *m* runny nose
Schokolade *f* chocolate
Schokoladeneis *n* chocolate ice-cream
Scholle (n) *f* plaice
schon already
schön beautiful, nice
schrecklich awful
*schreiben to write
Schritt (e) m step, move
Schulabschluß (-schlüsse) *m* final school
    examination
Schule (n) *f* school
schunkeln to link arms and sway to and fro
Schutz *m* protection
schützen to protect
schwach light, weak
schwarz black
Schwarzbrot (e) *n* black (rye) bread
Schwarzwald *m* Black Forest
Schwarzwälder Kirschtorte (n) *f* Black Forest
    gateau
Schweiz *f* Switzerland
schwer difficult, hard, heavy
schwierig difficult
Schwierigkeit (en) *f* difficulty
Schwimmbad (¨er) *n* swimming pool
*schwimmen to swim
See (n) *m* lake
segeln to sail
Segelschiff (e) *n* sailing ship
*sehen to see
sehr very
Seifenoper (n) *f* soap opera
*sein to be
seit since
Sekretärin (nen) *f* secretary *f*
selber myself, yourself etc.
selbst even; self
selbständig self-employed

selbstgemacht home-made
senden to broadcast
Sender (-) *m* broadcaster, station
Sendezeit (en) *f* time of broadcast
Sendung (en) *f* programme, broadcast
Sensationsblatt (¨er) *m* tabloid
September *m* September
seriös serious, trustworthy
servieren to serve (food and drink)
Sessel (-) *m* armchair
(sich) setzen to sit down
sicher safe, secure, certain
*singen to sing
Sinn (e) *m* sense, meaning
sinnvoll sensible, meaningful
Situation (en) *f* situation
*sitzen to sit
*Ski fahren to ski
Skigymnastik *f* pre-ski exercises
Skikurs (e) *m* skiing lessons
Skiurlaub (e) *m* skiing holiday
Skorpion *m* Scorpio
Socke (n) *f* sock
sofort at once
sogar even
Sohn (¨e) *m* son
solche such
*sollen to be supposed to
Sommer (-) *m* summer
Sommerferien (*pl*) summer holiday
sondern but
Sonne (n) *f* sun
Sonnenenergie *f* solar energy
Sonnenschein *m* sunshine
Sonnenschutzmittel (-) *n* sun cream
sonnig sunny
Sonntagszeitung (en) *f* Sunday paper
sonst otherwise, else
Sorge (n) *f* worry, care
sowieso anyway
sozial social
Sozialpolitik *f* social policy
Spanien *n* Spain
Spanisch *n* Spanish (language)
spannend exciting
sparen to save, economise
sparsam economical
Spaß (¨e) *m* fun; joke
spät late
später later
*spazierengehen to go for a walk
Spaziergang (¨e) *m* walk
Spazierweg (e) *m* footpath
SPD = Sozialdemokratische Partei
    Deutschlands *f* Social Democrats
Speiselokal (e) *m* restaurant
Spezialist (en) *m* specialist, expert
Spezialistenangelegenheit (en) *f* matter for the
    experts
Spiegel (-) *m* mirror
spielen to play
Spielfilm (e) *m* feature film
Spitze (n) *f* top, summit
spontan spontaneous
Sport *m* sport

Sportart (en) *f*   kind of sport
Sportschau (en) *f*   sports programme
*Sport treiben   to do sport
Sprache (n) *f*   language
Sprachlabor (e) *n*   language laboratory
Spray (s) *n*   spray, aerosol
Spraydose (n) *f*   aerosol can
*sprechen   to speak
Sprecher (-) *m*   speaker
Sprechstunde (n) *f*   consulting hours
Stadt (¨e) *f*   town
Stadtplan (¨e) *m*   town plan
Stadtzentrum (-zentren) *n*   town centre
Stand (¨e) *m*   stall
ständig   constantly
stark   strong, heavy
Stau (e) *m*   (traffic) jam
staubsaugen   to vacuum, hoover
Staubsauger (-) *m*   vacuum cleaner
Steak (s) *n*   steak
*stehen   to stand
*steigen   to climb
Stelle (n) *f*   job, situation, vacancy
Stil (e) *m*   style
Stimmung (en) *f*   atmosphere, mood
stinklangweilig   deadly boring
Stipendium (Stipendien) *n*   grant, scholarship
stören   to disturb
Strand (¨e) *m*   beach
Straße (n) *f*   street
Streit (e) *m*   quarrel
streng   strict
Streß (Stresse) *m*   stress
Stück (e) *n*   piece
Student (en) *m*   student *m*
Studie (n) *f*   study
Studienplatz (¨e) *m*   university/college place
studieren   to study
Stunde (n) *f*   hour, school period
suchen   to seek, look for
süddeutsch   South German
Süddeutschland *n*   South Germany
Süden *m*   South
Supermarkt (¨e) *m*   supermarket
Suppe (n) *f*   soup
Surfen *n*   (wind)surfing
süß   sweet
Süßigkeit (en) *f*   sweet

T

Tafel (n) *f*   bar (chocolate, soap)
Tag (e) *m*   day
       *an den Tag bringen   to bring to light
tagelang   for days
Tagesablauf (¨e) *m*   daily routine
Tageskarte (n) *f*   menu of the day
Tageszeitung (en) *f*   daily paper
Tal (¨er) *n*   valley
Talkshow (s) *f*   chat show
Tante (n) *f*   aunt
Tanz (¨e) *m*   dance
tanzen   to dance
Tanzschule (n) *f*   dance school
Tanzveranstaltung (en) *f*   dance

Tasche (n) *f*   pocket, bag
Taxi (s) *n*   taxi
technisch   technical
Tee (s) *m*   tea
Telefon (e) *n*   telephone
telefonieren   to telephone
Telefonist (en) *m* Telefonistin (nen) *f*   telephonist
Tennis spielen   to play tennis
Termin (e) *m*   appointment, engagement
testen   to test
teuer   expensive
Theater (-) *n*   theatre
Theaterkasse (n) *f*   theatre box office
Thema (Themen) *n*   theme, topic
Therapie (n) *f*   therapy
Tier (e) *n*   animal
Tirol *n*   the Tyrol
Tisch (e) *m*   table
Tochter (¨) *f*   daughter
toll   super, great, exciting
Topf (¨e) *m*   pot
Tour (en) *f*   trip
Tourist (en) *m*   tourist *m*
*tragen   to carry, wear
trampeln   to trample
trampen   to hitchhike
Transportwesen *n*   transport system
transsibirisch   Trans-Siberian
Traum (¨e) *m*   dream
Traumurlaub (e) *m*   dream holiday
*treffen   to meet
*treiben   to do (sport)
Treppe (n) *f*   staircase, stairs
*trinken   to drink
Trinkgeld (er) *n*   tip
trocken   dry
Trommeln *n*   drumming
trotz   despite
trotzdem   all the same
*tun   to do
Typ (en) *m*   type
typisch   typical

U

U-Bahn (en) *f*   underground (railway)
üben   to practise
über   over
überall   everywhere
überhaupt   at all
überlegen   to think, consider
übernachten   to stay the night
überregional   national
überschaubar   manageable
Überstunden (*pl*)   overtime
überwiegend   mainly
üblich   customary
übrig   remaining, left over
Übung (en) *f*   exercise
um   round
*umfallen   to fall over
umfassend   comprehensive
Umgebung *f*   surroundings
*umgehen (mit)   to deal (with)
*umsteigen   to change (trains, etc.)

umstrukturieren   to restructure
Umwelt *f*   environment
Umweltschutz *m*   environmental protection
*umziehen   to change (clothes); move house
unbedingt   necessarily
unbeweglich   immobile
unerfüllt   unfulfilled
Unfall (¨e) *m*   accident
ungefähr   approximately
ungesund   unhealthy
Universität (en) *f*   university
unpersönlich   impersonal
Unsicherheit (en) *f*   insecurity
unter   among, under
unwichtig   unimportant

V

Vater (¨) *m*   father
Vegetarier (-) *m* **Vegetarierin (nen)** *f*   vegetarian
veränderlich   changeable
(sich) verändern   to change
Verbandszeug *n*   dressings
*verbinden   to dress (wound)
*verbrennen   to burn
verdienen   to earn
*vergessen   to forget
verkaufen   to sell
Verkäufer (-) *m* **Verkäuferin (nen)** *f*
   shop-assistant
Verkehr *m*   traffic
Verkehrslage (n) *f*   traffic conditions
Verkehrsmittel (-) *n*   means of transport
(sich) verkleiden   to dress up (as)
verlängert   extended
*verlassen   to leave
*(sich) verlaufen   to get lost
vermissen   to miss
Verpackung (en) *f*   wrapping
verrückt   crazy
verschenken   to give away
verschieden   different, diverse
*verstehen   to understand
versuchen   to try
verzweifelt   desperate
Verzweiflung *f*   desperation
viel   much, many
vielleicht   perhaps
Villa (Villen) *f*   villa
Vokabel (n) *f*   item of vocabulary
Volkshochschule (n) *f*   adult education centre
voll   full
voller   full of
völlig   completely
von   from, of, by
vor   before, in front of, ago
vor allem, vor allen Dingen   above all
Vordergrund (¨e) *m*   foreground
vorher   before
*(sich) vorkommen   to feel like
vor kurzem   recently
Vormittag (e) *m*   late morning
Vorort (e) *m*   suburb
Vorschau (en) *f*   preview
Vorsicht *f*   care, attention

vorstellen   to introduce
(sich) vorstellen   to imagine
Vorteil (e) *m*   advantage

W

Waage *f*   Libra
wackelig   wobbly
Wagen (¨) *m*   car, carriage
wählen   to elect, vote
während   during
Wald (¨er) *m*   wood, forest
Walzer (-) *m*   waltz
Wand (¨e) *f*   wall
wandern   to hike
Wanderung (en) *f*   hike
wann   when
warm   warm
warten   to wait
warum   why
was   what
Wäsche *f*   washing, laundry
*waschen   to wash
Waschmaschine (n) *f*   washing machine
was für   what kind of
Wasser *n*   water
Wassermann *m*   Aquarius
Wasserstoff *m*   hydrogen
wechseln   to change, exchange
Wecker (-) *m*   alarm-clock
weg   away
Weg (e) *m*   way
*wegfahren   to go away
Weihnachten *n*   Christmas
Weihnachtsbaum (¨e) *m*   Christmas tree
Weihnachtsbazar (e) *m*   Christmas bazaar
Weihnachtsgeld (er) *n*   Christmas bonus
Weihnachtslied (er) *n*   Christmas carol
Weihnachtstage (*pl*)   Christmas and Boxing
   Day
weil   because
Weile (n) *f*   while
Wein (e) *m*   wine
weinen   to cry
weiß   white
weit   far
weiter   further
*weiterziehen   to move on
welche(r/s)   which
Welt (en) *f*   world
wenig   little
wenn   when; if
wer/wem/wen   who(m)
*werden   to become
*werfen   to throw
Werk (e) *n*   work
Wertkarte (n) *f*   phone card
Westen *m*   West
westlich   west
Wetter *n*   weather
Wetterbericht (e) *m*   weather report
Widder *m*   Aries
wie   how, like, as
wieder, wiederum   again
Wiese (n) *f*   meadow
